Framing the Word:
Gender and Genre
in Caribbean Women's Writing

Framing the Word:

Gender and Genre in Caribbean Women's Writing

edited by

Joan Anim-Addo

Whiting and Birch Ltd

MCMXCVI

Published by Whiting & Birch Ltd,
PO Box 872, London SE23 3HL, England.
USA: Paul & Co, Publishers' Consortium Inc,
PO Box 442, Concord, MA 01742.

British Library Cataloguing in Publication Data.
A CIP catalogue record is available from the British Library

ISBN 1 871177 96 0 (cased)
ISBN 1 871177 91 X (limp)

Printed in England by Ipswich Book Company

This book is dedicated to the memory of my grandmother

Juliana "Lily" Joseph

(née Mulzac)

1886-1969

who, through her storytelling,

truly taught me the power of words

Acknowledgements

I am indebted to Alan Durant who generously allowed this process to begin.

All the contributors in this collection are thanked for their interest in and patience with the making of this book.

Thanks are due also to Diana Birch for her unwavering enthusiasm from the very beginning.

I would like to thank, too, Mary Boley, Sharon Joseph, Jean Radford and Pam Taylor for their support and invaluable comments which altogether has made this a better book.

Finally, a special thanks to An'Yaa, Kofi and Kwesi, the support team at home.

Contents

Introduction

Joan Anim-Addo

The turn of the twentieth century marks an historic moment for Caribbean women's literature. This body of work, more and more inclusive, increasingly representative of all Caribbean women, continues to expand, the range and vitality of the writing constantly attracting new readers. Not only have individual texts penetrated the ivory towers of universities as far afield as Britain, Australia, the USA, Italy and the Caribbean, but courses, specifically focused on Caribbean women's writing, are gradually being made available in higher education institutions world wide.

Women writers of the Caribbean are black and white[1] and shades between, they write in Creoles as well as the dominant languages of Europe. They write, too, in language which privileges both Caribbean Creole and European language forms simultaneously. It is this language, the continuum from Creole to European language, to which Nourbese Philip refers as 'my language, the Caribbean demotic'.[2] From Belize in the west of the region, to Trinidad and Tobago in the eastern section of the chain of islands forming the Caribbean archipelago, as greater numbers of women writers are published, literary interpreters move towards a keener awareness and appreciation of the works available. Yet, much of the appreciation still represents isolated pockets of literary activity. An alternative scenario, and this remains a feature reflecting the current status of the writing, is publication greeted with a familiar silence.

Interpreters of texts created from the complex social, historical and linguistic web which comprises the Caribbean context may be as steeped in 'hierarchies of privilege' as other critics.[3] Readings of Caribbean women's literature reflect, to a greater or lesser degree, such groundings. In the process, influential theories based on cultures and traditions intimately experienced and understood by critics are extended to accommodate the lesser known literatures. Critical attention deriving from this, whilst given a mixed reception, is nonetheless invaluable to the stimulating of further debate and interest in the literature.

Some resistance to critical readings by Caribbean women writers has been documented.[4] Dominance and resistance, however, are central themes of the history of the region and its literature and this is no less the case for literature produced by women of the region. Furthermore, as the writing becomes more accessible, questions concerning interpreters and interpretations become more insistent: who will interpret or frame the words of Caribbean women writers, on what terms - privileging which references - and with what consequences?

Key sites of the overall debate have been the periodic conferences held variously in the Caribbean, the USA and finally in London, in 1994. Out of each has come information and new resolve impacting upon readers, writers, critics and education institutions alike. Equally importantly, publications made available following the conferences have been invaluable to the disseminating of the substance of the most recent debate. *Framing The Word* follows in that tradition and is a direct result of the conference organised by the Caribbean Centre at Goldsmiths College out of which has come the London based Caribbean Women Writers' Alliance and its publication, *Mango Season*.[5]

Two earlier critical texts, one edited by Carole Boyce Davies and Elaine Savory Fido,[6] the other by Selwyn Cudjoe,[7] both published in 1990, separately heralded literary recognition of the body of work upon which *Framing The Word* focuses. Since that date, students, teachers and interested readers have charted the difficulties of access to critical material, despite the increasing availability of the literature.[8] Questions of access gave rise to the London conference[9] out of which came this collection.

With the emergence of Caribbean women's writing in the field of new literature, principally during the final three decades of the twentieth century, the debate intensified. Who are Caribbean women writers? Out of what kind of tradition or traditions are they writing? What is the significance of the literature? These are just some of the questions addressed in *Framing The Word*.

It is already known about this body of writing that there has been an explosion in works made available. Anthologies as well as critical volumes have documented as much.[10] It is equally well known that the writing includes groups which, prior to the late twentieth century were largely excluded from publication. Amongst these are to be found African and Indo-Caribbean women. It is gradually being appreciated, too, that poetry, novels, short stories and drama, as well as other works 'between genres', feature in the growing literature of the region.

To indicate, other than minimally, the multiple marginalised position of Caribbean women's literature in Britain,[11] whether in classrooms, within higher education, or, in mainstream bookshops would require more than the scope allowed in this introduction. In contradiction to the marginalisation, there are, apart from the writers themselves, those within publishing and 'academia' well aware of the literature. However, whilst it is important that an albeit small but privileged group of academics, writers, and others hold knowledge of output, availability and so on, of contemporary Caribbean women's writing, *it is not enough*. Access, then is an urgent, practical question which this book addresses firstly, by beginning to redress the balance in terms of publication and secondly, by incorporating papers which assume, not only an academic, but also a wider readership.

Lorna Goodison's *We Are The Women* speaks of 'women with thread bags anchored deep in our bosoms containing blood agreements'.[12] Are these the women of the Caribbean? Amerindian, European, African and Asian women have shaped the nations of the Caribbean, the last three groups arriving in the region, roughly, in that order, from the sixteenth to the nineteenth century.[13] In the latter part of the twentieth century, however, by an interesting reversal of socio-historical events, increased voluntary migration, markedly so, has been matched by a signal increase in literary production. Noticeably, amongst the published women are those of the 'blood agreements'; black women.

Black women, however defined, are increasingly represented in the writing. The voices of black women represent a key part of the literary whole within the region. In a socio-political context premised upon hierarchical racial divisions riddled with issues of oppression, dominance and resistance, in the first instance, black women's writing is a vital sign of re-empowerment within the emergent literature. The umbrella term, 'Caribbean literature', however, is, by intention, antithetical to the pointing up of societal divisions. It flags a concern with recognising cultural influences held in common which inform and shape the literature. Yet differences cannot be ignored. The influential Grenadian-American poet, Audre Lorde warns of the inherent dangers of ignoring rather than recognising and exploring difference.[14] Differences of language, culture, ethnicity and so on contribute powerfully to creative tensions within the women's literature of the region.

Literary production by all women of the region, published locally or world wide, in the 'Caribbean diaspora,' is referred to as Caribbean women's literature. Expansion of the literature can be seen in the steady proliferation of published writing from Caribbean women whether located in the region or in the wider diaspora. That diaspora includes not only the UK and highly profiled USA but also Canada as well as areas such as Holland and West Africa, not always readily associated with Caribbean women's writing.[15] Included, too, are worlds of Francophone, Hispanophone and Dutch speakers and writers forming a whole multi-lingual Caribbean. The West Indies and the Anglophone territories remain only a part of this whole.

Caribbean women's literature is characterised tantalisingly by literary forms indicating, in comparison to other literatures, both similarity and diversity. Whether the literature is read through critical frames that privilege post-colonialism, cultural nationalism, feminism, formalism or any other theoretical stance, it is undeniably and overwhelmingly a literature shaped by experiences of gender in interaction with the socio-cultural historical period of the latter twentieth century. In similar ways, absence of writing, particularly from black women was consequential upon earlier historical moments.

We move now to what is less well known about the growing literature. The variety of writing, whether across languages that have traditionally divided the Caribbean; its richness, and experimentation in output is only just being written about. How gender has shaped the literary production of the region is one of the larger questions to which critical debate returns despite resistance to 'appropriating and totalising tendencies'.[16] The question of gender and genre, the special relationship between Caribbean women and the literary forms of cultural production issuing from the region is central to the literature.

Finally, from experience of teaching the literature to classes of students many of whom claim little knowledge of the socio-cultural context of the Caribbean, there is evident need of bridges to understanding of the literature. At this juncture it is useful to be aware of the part played by interested, responsive teaching of the texts.

It is the quest for understanding of new works which has motivated the constant search for material treating the literature. This, in turn, stimulates dialogue which promotes further writing and publication of critical material offering fresh insight, fresh interpretation. The classroom as a site of critical reception is not to be underestimated.

Those of us with a special interest in the literature look forward to further development of a range of critical frames allowing analysis and discussion in a variety of stimulating ways. Caribbean women's literature available on bookshelves today marks significant beginnings. In part, the development of the literature lies in the impact it makes upon its readers. The papers gathered between these covers are intended to play a key part in both signalling and shaping this critical reception.

The book is divided into four sections, each with its own introduction.

Notes

1. See discussion below which expands upon this point.
2. M. Nourbese Philip, *She Tries Her Tongue, Her Silence Softly Breaks*, Women's Press, 1993, p.89.
3. Patricia Hill Collins, *Black Feminist Thought*, Routledge, 1990, p.xii.
4. See for example, Carole Boyce Davies and Elaine Savory Fido, *Out of the Kumbla*, Africa World Press, 1990.
5. *Mango Season* is published termly through the Caribbean Women Writers'

Alliance. Writer delegates at the first Caribbean Women Writers' conference held in London from 1-2 July 1994 at Goldsmiths College were instrumental in setting up the Alliance.

6. Carole Boyce Davies & Elaine Savory Fido, 1990, op. cit.
7. Selwyn Cudjoe, *Caribbean Women Writers*, Callaloux, Mass, 1990.
8. Both critical texts cited earlier are USA publications and consequently not readily available on the UK market.
9. See also *New Encounters*, in Part Two of this volume, which reflects upon the problems of availability of critical works but also creative texts many of which, to date, need to be imported.
10. Examples are the critical selections, already cited, as well as, for example, Betty Wilson and Pamela Mordecai's 'Introduction' to *Her True - True Name,* Heinemann, 1989.
11. I refer to this in an earlier paper, 'No Longer Singing to Herself,' given at the Society for Caribbean Studies Conference, Oxford 1993.
12. Lorna Goodison, *I Am Becoming My Mother*, New Beacon, London, 1986.
13. For a general history, see for example, Eric Williams, *From Colombo to Castro*, André Deutsch, 1970.
14. See Audre Lorde's essay 'Age, Race, Class and Sex: Women Redefining Difference' in *Sister Outsider*, The Crossing Press, 1984, p.115.
15. See, for example, Karen King-Aribisala *Our Wife and Other Stories*, Malthouse Press Ltd., Lagos, 1990 (published in Nigeria where she resides).
16. Carolyn Cooper refers to this in a paper 'Loosely Talking Theory: Oral/Sexual Discourse in Jamaican Popular Culture' given at the Society for Caribbean Studies Conference, Oxford, 1993.

ISMS AND SCHISMS IN THE CRITICAL FRAME

'Isms and Schisms in the Critical Frame', presents essays offering a diversity of interpretations or framings of the words of Caribbean women writers. The section indicates this volume's interest in a variety of readings rather than theoretical uniformity or similarity of perspective. Furthermore, the collection itself speaks to a resistance to 'neat pigeon-holing of the writing' and this is reflected in the choice of the four papers in part one.

Merle Collins's 'Framing the Word: Caribbean Women's Writing' was delivered originally as the keynote address to the first London conference of Caribbean women's writing.[1] It is apt, therefore, that Merle Collins offers a historical frame which indicates the fashioning of earlier frames allowing access to the publication of silence-breaking works by African-Caribbean women. The legacy of this remains and the 'brief' history given of the period sets the scene before moving to address issues of voicing and re-voicing of the Caribbean woman's story.

The central question explored is that of the 'main concerns' of Caribbean women's writing. The parts played by the historical shaping of Caribbean societies and consequent 'formation of the individual' are highlighted. Merle Collins also addresses current concerns about 'reclaiming and revoicing', 'female sexuality' and the role of relationships which inform the writing by women of the region. A role for the critic is urged which moves beyond concerns of 'artistic analysis' and 'theoretical abstractions' and into a focus privileging the 'developing (of) an understanding of the society' which shapes the literary product of Caribbean women.

The significance of spatial relations is explored in the poetry of the writers in Elaine Savory's 'Engendering Spaces: The Poetry of Marlene Nourbese Philip and Pamela Mordecai'. A paradoxical space is examined, one which acknowledges a complex relationship between regional, Caribbean experience and individual, personal and gendered experience differentiated by race. The textual space which evolves is shown to be encoded in verbal constructions of self involving race, ethnicity, nationality and class, as well as the consciousness of being a woman.

Ways in which each writer contributes to and is energised by a 'tidalectic' process 'reminiscent of the ebb and flow of ideas rooted in a Caribbean consciousness' are explored.[2] Nourbese Philip's i-mage and Pamela Mordecai's 'prismatic vision' are highlighted, examples of the 'complexities of vision' offered by the two writers located by Elaine Savory in the tradition of 'poet-intellectuals' of the region who 'theorise the world in poetry'. In addition, Elaine Savory indicates ways in which the writers are simultaneously reworking the notion of poet. She explores how each poet draws on contradictory strands of Caribbean heritage in reconciling contradictions of language, space and gender, influences upon the impulse to create literary space which escapes confinement whilst confirming a complex identity.

In 'Writing for Resistance: Nationalism and Narratives of Liberation', Alison Donnell focuses on a particular 'creative resistance' of Caribbean women's writing. The essay moves across a 'historical and cultural spectrum' of writers and foregrounds ways in which Caribbean women writers from Albinia Catherine Hutton to Jamaica Kincaid 'unfix dominant discursive boundaries' whilst offering grounds which allow a 'reclaiming of subjectivity'. Colonial and post-colonial female subjects, the essay suggests, have positioned themselves outside of discourses of nationalism whilst addressing 'cultural belonging'.

Through close readings of the selected texts, Alison Donnell highlights 'unstable signifiers' of nationalism encoded in the writing and, therefore, its resistance to 'confident articulation' of a fixed cultural position. In her discussion of nationalism (colonial and post-colonial), Alison Donnell opens up the debate not only about nationalism and women's writing generally, but specifically about the situation for Caribbean women who articulate complex positions within and against particular discourses.

It is the complexities of Jamaica Kincaid's writing which concerns Giovanna Covi. In 'Jamaica Kincaid's Prismatic Self and the Decolonisation of Language and Thought' Giovanna Covi foregrounds Kincaid's concern with 'the articulation of the effects of colonialism on subjectivity' and particularly female subjectivity. The essay calls attention to the interrelationship between 'discourses and colonialism' and, by implication, race, class and the 'discourse of patriarchy'. Kincaid's 'art of writing' is analysed and her 'double voice' highlighted. Giovanna Covi also points to the difficulties which lie in subsuming much of the debate about writing in the region under 'post colonial discourse'.

The essay focuses on readings of *A Small Place* and *Lucy* as critiques of colonialism and patriarchy whilst drawing upon works such as *At the Bottom of the River*. The autobiographical frame applied to Kincaid's writing opens up discussion of the 'quilted autobiographical narratives' representative of her works. Giovanna Covi indicates, also, ways in which

Kincaid 'corrodes Columbian discourse' through her textual 'voyages of recovery' which negotiate passage 'back and forth between empires and colonies', past and present. Giovanna Covi's essay demonstrates how the 'untelling of the stories of marginality' in Kincaid's works allow her complex interpretation of the world to be revealed to the reader.

The remaining parts of this book, 'Views From Within and Betwixt Genres', 'Beyond the Divide of Language', and 'Out of a Diverse Caribbean Womanhood' are separately introduced.

Notes

1. The first London Caribbean Women's Writing Conference was organised by the Caribbean Studies Centre at Goldsmith's College, University of London, 1st-2nd July, 1994.
2. See Elaine Savory's reference p.16 of this volume to Kamau Brathwaite's image.

Framing The Word: Caribbean Women's Writing

Merle Collins

The choice of theme was facilitated by two main factors: firstly, the organisers of the conference[1] chose as an over-arching title 'Framing the Word' and presented a framework for discussion and secondly I read a text entitled: *Subject To Others. British Women Writers And Colonial Slavery, 1670-1834*, written by Moira Ferguson.[2]

I will begin by explaining what bearing I believe Moira Ferguson's text, *Subject To Others*, has on Caribbean women's writing and move on to look at the main concern - the framing of the word.

One of the issues with which *Subject To Others* engages is Ferguson's perception of how to some extent the word was shaped for Caribbean people generally and for writers specifically. It traces how British women writers intervened in the anti-slavery debate from the seventeenth to the nineteenth centuries and assesses how, by agitating with authority against the white male ethos of colonial domination, white British women writers contributed to their own empowerment at home and started the development of a feminist movement shaped by attention to their concerns. The point of relevance to the theme upon which we are focused is the fact that in the process white women were voicing the experiences of African people in the Caribbean and paying specific attention to Black, enslaved Caribbean women. Working in the interests of African-Caribbean people at the time, given the historical moment, but different in race, class and culture, they were framing the word for the enslaved women and men of the Caribbean at a time when colonial law dictated that no enslaved Caribbean person had the legal right to voice their experience. And so began a very contradictory relationship, representation of the victimised which contributed not only to the empowerment of those doing the representation but also to the perception of a right to frame the word for those legally condemned to silence. And then, inevitably, when the silenced began to frame the word for themselves, their shaping of the word was guided by their benefactors. What Caribbean writers subsequently had to do, and what Caribbean women writers are today engaged in, is a framing which is distinctively Caribbean, shaped by the Caribbean experience.

Let me make this a little clearer. Moira Ferguson's text moves through the seventeenth and eighteenth century speaking for and by white women largely of the middle classes, from a base in Britain, to focus on the first known narrative by an enslaved Caribbean woman.[3] *The History Of Mary Prince* was dictated by the enslaved Antiguan Mary Prince, brought by her erstwhile owners to London, to a Quaker woman, Susanna Strickland, from whose pen we receive the word voiced by Mary Prince. And so we have the Caribbean woman's experience presented by herself for the first time in writing, as far as the research tells us to date. This is how it began: Mary Prince's words penned by Susanna Strickland. The shape the word took was influenced by the type of frame fashioned by white women writers from Aphra Behn in the seventeenth century onwards, by the expectations of the Quaker women missionaries, and by white British women's ideas on femininity. It is within this framework that the Caribbean woman first began to publish her story, concerned for her own survival and freedom, and about how it would be received by the British public. These are some of the issues that Moira Ferguson's work engages with - the word - and what circumscribes pronunciation of the word.

In the beginning was the word, and the word was powerful but the really powerful word voiced every day when women in particular argued on the estates was not heard on the streets of England. The important Caribbean word to England and the anti-slavery agitators of the time was the word first captured on paper by white women speaking for the legally voiceless. The word by the representative Mary Prince, when it appeared on paper, clear and moving as it was, not only echoed but inevitably, given the context of its appearance, watered down the vibrant voices - whether these were the songs of loss and despair of the Atlantic crossing, or the protesting women's voices of the estate records.[4] The representative voice, by the time it reached Britain, was mediated by the environment, by expectation, by attitude of the host community, by the medium of expression, the page. This is not meant so much as a critique of Mary Prince's valuable work as a statement of the historical and literary importance of the oral traditions of the region and of the fact that location and environment affect presentation of the word.

These are some of the issues that Moira Ferguson's text brings to mind and perhaps now you can understand why I thought it would be relevant to mention it in the discussions here. Now that we have come to the matter of framing the word, let us look more closely at this question of voicing. Mary Prince's text is written in English. That is quite possibly Mary Prince's actual speech, but also it is conceivably a translation from Creole speech, because then even more than now Creole speech was considered simplistic and a sign of inferior intelligence. One might, therefore, assume that any self-respecting enslaved person, seeking to be recognised as free on the English-speaking streets of London, would want to be presented in a language which would not discredit the intelligence. This is a very pertinent issue, for example, in relation to 'the subject of the Oral Tradition and Caribbean Women's Writing'.

Writing by Caribbean women has come a long way since the days of Mary Prince's framing of the word as she knew it. The concept of Caribbean literature has come into being and is constantly changing. Today there is even talk of a Caribbean diaspora and inevitably there are differences between writing which comes directly from the region and writing coming from the region's diaspora.

Perhaps it is amazing that following Caribbean women's writing in the nineteenth century and the 1831 work of Mary Prince, the first conference of women writers from the Caribbean took place in 1988: one hundred and fifty seven years later. This was the first time that women writers from the region came together as a group to discuss their framing of the word. So what happened in those intervening years? Mary Prince's work contained the words 'To be free is very sweet'. A woman speaking out against slavery and pointing towards the experiences of her compatriots.

Much later, according to the researchers, came the work of Mary Seacole and the nineteenth century and early twentieth century writing of poetry by Cuban women poets.[5] While few went into print, the voices of the majority were not silent. Story-telling, if not story-writing, by Caribbean women was continuing, as people shaped and reshaped old stories, and told with tears and laughter the stories they were living through. That voice, of course, was very different to that captured on the page. Increasingly, and perhaps most tellingly since Samuel Selvon's publication of *The Lonely Londoners*,[6] those story-telling forms are feeding into form and technique in Caribbean writing.

Shortly after the publication of Mary Prince's work, legislation had decreed freedom for the enslaved in that part of the Caribbean generally referred to as 'English-speaking'. But freedom is more than legislation. The freedom of expression which came with legislation was circumscribed by the political and socio-economic circumstances of the colonial condition. For some time words would continue to have the syntactic, cultural and colour/class imprint of those (white women and men) who fashioned the frame. And as the benefits of freedom were increasingly allowed to trickle down, written literary expression and possibility of publication were there first for those who had access to formal education, by being white and/or middle class or those who by some fortune were allowed the possibility of formal education. Post-war migration, to England or the United States, was also, for both women and men, not an insignificant factor in affording the opportunity for publication of the word.[7]

Another significant work, later in the story of the region's writing, was from a woman in the English-speaking Caribbean, that of Jean Rhys, described by Cudjoe as a 'white Creole and great-granddaughter of a slave owner'.[8] In the early part of the twentieth century, too, with a first publication *Tropic Reveries* there was Una Marson, described by Lloyd Brown as 'the earliest female poet of significance to emerge in West Indian literature'.[9] Both Rhys and Marson had travelled to England in the early parts of the twentieth century. Also publishing in the 1930s was Louise Bennett, mistress of the voice, who presented succeeding generations with a lot to think about and emulate because of that dynamic interaction between performance and publication. Bennett published her work in the *Daily Gleaner* during the thirties and is still a popular figure today.[10] We move to 1953 and Phyllis Shand Allfrey's *Orchid House.*[11] Gradually, from the 1970s to the present, work by women is increasingly appearing in print.

The 1974 edition of Kenneth Ramchand's seminal critical work, *The West Indian Novel and Its Background,*[12] listed 60 names (165 works) in its author bibliography. Six of these were women. It appears, then, that there had been a movement from what Moira Ferguson assessed to be expatriate white women largely framing the word for the region to men of the region, first white men, then Black men, framing the word. But by the 1990s, there is Brenda Berrian's bio-bibliographical index[13] of Caribbean women writers throughout the region. Selwyn Cudjoe's *Caribbean Women Writers*, in a composite list of 'prose works by English-speaking women writers of the West Indies', listed seventy women.

What becomes clear from this brief history is that early Caribbean writing, reflecting the patriarchal, class and colour dimensions in the society being shaped, was very male-centred and very white-centred. Without declaring itself a collection of work by Caribbean men writers, a collection could easily be that. Ann Walmsley's 1968 publication *The Sun's Eye*, an important formative influence for many young people of the period, contained among its 30 contributors, one woman.[14] G.R. Coulthard's publication, *Race and Colour in Caribbean Literature*,[15] focuses almost exclusively on the male of the species. That was the tenor of the times. The comment is not meant to reflect negatively on the very important work of the men of the region.

Doubtless, the expansion of formal education, the increasing proliferation of the notion that education was 'good for girl children too', the challenging ideas of the international women's movement, the development of publishing houses focusing on the work of women, all contributed to the growth in volume of women's writing and have contributed to the increasing availability of work by women (although publishing houses abroad tend to uncover those close to home - Britain, US, Canada). These are vibrant voices; still, the region - smaller islands in particular - awaits that elusive development, which will make paper cheaper and the development of publishing houses more possible. Following the 1988 Caribbean Women

Writers Conference at Wellesley, there have been conferences in Trinidad and Tobago (1990), Curaçoa (1992), and Wellesley (1995).

But what is this word that women are framing? What are the main concerns? The overall concern here is with *gender* and *genre* in Caribbean women's framing of the word. This brings me, of course, to the fact that here we comprise a group of writers, critics, students, all coming from various perspectives. I would submit that Caribbean women writers are usually, not necessarily, but usually not too concerned about analysing whether they deal more with gender or with colonialism, whether they are defined more in terms that are post-colonialist or feminist or whatever. More often than not there is an irritation with questions which seek to effect a neat pigeon-holing of the writing. The concern is with the exploration of experience. Sometimes the critics' efforts at defining or analysing the writer's exploration helps the writer to contextualise efforts; sometimes they might appear to be bogged down in theoretical abstractions that seem to bear little practical connection to the reality.

Caribbean women's writing tends to be concerned with all that has gone into the shaping of Caribbean societies: colonisation and its consequences, the effects of slavery and indenture, the meaning or meaninglessness of independence. There is a concern with formation - formation of the society, formation of the individual - and with reclaiming and revoicing. This revoicing means a re-telling of the story misrepresented by the white male coloniser, a re-voicing of perspectives not adequately voiced by the white expatriate woman would-be liberator, a re-writing of perspectives presented by the African-Caribbean and Indian-Caribbean male writer, a re-voicing of perspectives presented by the male calypsonian in the region, simply a revealing of the stories told by mothers, aunts, godmothers, tanties, nenens, so that many of the themes overlap with themes explored by male Caribbean writers. And Caribbean women, in addition, have a concern with themes of female sexuality and male/female relationships. More often than not, while male/female relations might be openly explored, sexuality is handled cautiously, covertly, or is even conspicuous by its absence. Perhaps it is more openly explored in the work of Caribbean women resident outside of the region. As a critic, Carolyn Cooper has made some pioneering efforts in dealing with oral/sexual discourse in Jamaican popular music. As far as I know, there has been no research to determine why Caribbean women are so cautious about dealing with sexuality as a theme in the writing. It might, however, be pertinent here to observe that in 1831 the missionaries and other white anti-slavery activists had done such a thorough job of transmitting notions of respectability and the type of femininity that would be acceptable to the British public that one has to read between the lines of *The History of Mary Prince* with a powerful microscope in order to try to decode possible references to sexuality and sexual abuse. Mary Prince, perhaps, also spoke another story which no pen wrote. It is not that things were not being said, but that socialisation and circumstance circumscribed the woman's presentation of herself. The internal logic of Caribbean societies, the everyday internal confrontations and revelations, will determine how and when Caribbean women writers will approach the themes that concern their everyday existence. Equally, for Caribbean women living abroad, the internal logic of the societies and the communities in which they live will determine thematic concerns. It is not a question of right and wrong, of exactly what touches us closely but of dynamic responses to the situations that shape the word, that shape our perceptions of what we feel empowered to say and the way we effect our continuing empowerment.

Caribbean women's stories come from a variety of perspectives and I would venture to suggest that the most sensitive critic, the one with the keenest appreciation of the Caribbean woman's story, is inevitably the one who comes to Caribbean literature intent not only on an artistic analysis of the signifying word, or on assessing how much the word conforms to labels constructed outside of its existence but on developing an understanding of the society that has produced the literature.

I move to understanding the society. Just a little example. Consider this hypothetical scenario: a woman in some part of the Caribbean says something like: 'You have to know how to read the Bible. You hear who write them gospel? De Matthew, oh! The Mark, oh! The Luke, oh! The John, oh! What you expect them to say? Don't get me wrong. I believe in the Word of the Lord. But is important who take the word from the Lord and pass it on. You see what I saying, me chile? And is this same Word those preacher and them taking in church promping up man make them think them is king! You have to know who write the word!' And in the next breath this same woman says to her son or to some other man in the house, 'don't go and work for the damn white woman for no fifteen dollars a day. Them does want to take people like rope to tie wood'. This woman is responding to different facets of her experience as woman and as colonised. Both responses would be perfectly logical, and it would also be perfectly logical for her to say, 'I don' living with no man. They too damn bad. But I not into this feminist thing at all'. The power of definition might be with the one who is doing the defining, but, as Leena Dhingra's *Breaking Out of the Labels*[16] so eloquently portrayed, the power of perception is with the one going through the experience who is totally unconcerned with labelling.

I want to leave with you the idea that Caribbean women writers today, whether writing in one or other of the Caribbean Creoles, Papiamentu, Sranan, English, Spanish, French or Dutch, highlight the fact that the Word that they are framing is of them, whatever they might consider to be an individual or collective experience and reflects no-one else. But it is a word, too, shaped by specific experiences of re-formation. Daringly, I placed the Creole languages at the head of the list. Daringly, because to date no Caribbean Creole is an international language. Here in England, there are pros and cons in its use as a literary medium. They might be accepted as exotic languages for literature but not for presentation of a serious academic paper. And this, I hasten to add, would be generally the case in the Caribbean as well. Because what is the modern Caribbean if not a creation of Europe? It is instructive that when we fashion the word in English, Spanish, French or Dutch, it is still our word - the word, that is, not only of Caribbean whites but also the word of the African and Asian people who now largely inhabit the region. So without doubt it is a composite word, and the women and men of the region, with their cooperations and contradictions, are together in their framing of the word.

I leave you finally with two or three quotations, which I hope will amount to two or three lingering thoughts. One which I have quoted elsewhere is from an image presented by Mordecai and Wilson in *Her True - True Name*.[17] It is a quotation from the work of Ana Lydia Vega, a Puerto Rican writer fluent in Spanish, English and French. In an extract entitled 'Cloud Cover Caribbean', Ana Lydia Vega presents three people - a Cuban, a Puerto Rican and a Dominican in the archetypal boat. Initially the Haitian was in the boat alone, escaping Haiti. He helped a Dominican in trouble. They in turn rescue a Cuban and the contradictions and rivalry between them become progressively more apparent as the boat rocks its unlikely way towards Miami. Eventually it overturns and they are rescued by an American ship, where they find a Puerto Rican-American (perhaps a Nuyorican) who puts them immediately to work.

Ana Lydia Vega here sees a 'brotherhood of hunger, the solidarity of dreams'.[18] On the boat, each speaks in his own language. They don't understand each other's words, but they carry on a conversation, because they do understand the tone and tenor of each other's experience. The language goes beyond the mechanics - Creoles or French or English or Spanish.

Then there is a quotation from Marie Denise Shelton, speaking on 'Women Writers of the French-Speaking Caribbean: An Overview' - a piece published in Cudjoe's *Caribbean Women Writers:*

> This discourse (of Caribbean literature)...is produced within a space that has been shaped by slavery, colonialism, creolisation, and insularity...
>
> The literature by women in the Caribbean is inscribed in this general discursive space. Isolating feminine expression does not imply that it can be detached from the conjuncture sketched above. Rather, the attempt here is to determine, within the field of competing voices, what women say and how they

say it. A different 'knowledge' of being Haitian, Martiniquan, or Guadeloupean is expressed in the works by women. At the level of thematics, feminine writing tends to expose conflicts and mutilations that characterise the being-in-the-world of women in the Caribbean.[19]

There is this constant consciousness that, given the region's experience, women's writing is part of a wider discursive space. The 'word' that we are discussing is confident and tentative, assured and hesitant, searching always for the articulation and exploration of the diverse experience of Caribbean women, wherever we may be, physically or psychologically, in our journey towards a deeper understanding of our experiences.

Notes

1. This paper was delivered as a keynote address to the Conference - 'Framing the Word' - at Goldsmiths College, London, 1-2 July 1994.
2 Moira Ferguson, *Subject to Others; British Women Writers and Colonial Slavery, 1670-1834,* Routledge, London, 1991.
3. Mary Prince, *The History of Mary Prince, A West Indian Slave, Related by Herself,* edited with 'Introduction' by Moira Ferguson and 'Preface' by Ziggi Alexander, Pandora, London, 1987.
4. See, for example, Barbara Bush, *Slave Women in Caribbean Society*, James Currey, London, 1990.
5. See for example Maria Christina Rodriguez 'Women Writers of the Spanish-Speaking Caribbean: An Overview' in Selwyn Cudjoe, *Caribbean Women Writers,* Calaloux Publications, Mass, 1990, pp.339-45.
6. Samuel Selvon, *The Lonely Londoners*, Longman, London, 1972.
7. See for example, Kenneth Ramchand, *The West Indian Novel and Its Background,* Faber, London, 1970.
8. Cudjoe, 1990, op. cit, p.16.
9. Lloyd W. Brown, *West Indian Poetry*, Heinemann, London, 1978, p.32.
10. See also Louise Bennett (Jamaica), *Dialect Verses,* Herald, Kingston, 1942 and *Jamaican Humour in Dialect*, Jamaican Press Association, Kingston, 1943.
11. Phyllis Shand Allfrey, *The Orchid House*, Constable, London, 1953.
12. Kenneth Ramchand, 1970, op.cit.
13. Brenda Berrian, *Bibliography of Women Writers from the Caribbean (1831-1988)*, Three Continents Press, Washington, 1985.
14. Anne Walmsley, *The Sun's Eye,* Longman, Harlow, 1968.
15. George R. Coulthard, *Race and Colour in Caribbean Literature,* OUP, Oxford, 1962.
16. Leena Dhingra,' Breaking Out of the Labels' in Rhonda Cobham and Merle Collins (eds.), *Watchers and Seekers*, The Women's Press, London, 1987.
17. Pamela Mordecai and Betty Wilson, *Her True - True Name*, Heinemann, Oxford, 1989.
18. Ana Lydia Vega, 'Cloud Cover Caribbean' in Mordecai and Wilson, 1989, op.cit., p.107.
19. Marie Denise Shelton, *Women Writers of the French Speaking Caribbean* in Cudjoe, 1990, op. cit.

En/Gendering Spaces: The Poetry of Marlene Nourbese Philip* and Pamela Mordecai

*Elaine Savory**

We recognise that what is meant by woman's textuality has to be understood along with knowing that every woman writes out of her cultural placement; ethnicity, race, her class, society, generation. But these facets of self have a complex interaction. Each text, like each individual, is a unique and shifting combination of different intensities of such identities. At the same time, each identity can represent a community, a belonging.

The political meaning of forms of women's writing is therefore not something which can or should be agreed upon, but is rather, valuably contradictory, just as the women's movement, world wide, is often contradictory in a good and productive way. In any case, as Rita Felski argues in *Beyond Feminist Aesthetics*,[1] the political usefulness of literary texts can only be assessed for feminism by the practical effect they have for the condition of women in a given context.

Furthermore, we recognise that language constructs us and our world, as Gayatri Spivak points out when she argues that, whereas we often assume three central concepts contribute to our awareness of human discourse, language, world and consciousness; in fact, language subsumes both world and consciousness as well as being determined by them.[2] We know that feminism has identified how important it is to create language which reflects women's consciousness and deflects the patriarchal world: a woman's text constructs a world in which consciousness of female identity can fully be expressed in language. If a woman's text can contribute to the defeat of forces which inhibit and frustrate women's freedoms and action, it is by constructing an example of the kind of intellectual, emotional and above all linguistic space which precedes effective social change.

Decolonisation is a process which must, therefore, also begin in language. It has to be directed towards regaining a creative cultural space after the confinements of colonisation. Linguistic registers necessarily reflect the struggles of a given community to redefine its own space: Henry Louis Gates examines the difference for example between 'signification' in the international English lexicon and 'signification' in the African-American one.[3] He finds this, of course, to be a political confrontation working itself out in both signifier and signified, i.e. as both relations of identity and difference.

To borrow Gates' words, 'the difference that blackness makes' becomes particularly significant in relation to women's search for freedom of expression. Feminist[4] women writers who have experienced colonialism and decolonisation have a particularly complex awareness of juxtapositions of signifying systems therefore. Black feminist writers have immensely contributed both to our ambivalence about and support for feminism itself. Hazel Carby has described black feminist criticism as 'a problem, not a solution...a sign which should be interrogated, a locus of contradictions'.[5] Carby rejects essentialist notions of black, female language, arguing that the 'terrain of language is a terrain of power relations',[6] in which competing groups are all represented by the process of linguistic change.

As soon as we accept that this is so, we can begin to see more clearly the importance of women's texts which seek to explore complexity as a manifestation of women's space. This paper looks at this in the poetry of two Caribbean women writers, Marlene Nourbese Philip and Pamela Mordecai.

Creating space to write in, for Nourbese Philip, involves nothing less than reorientating consciousness within language, and reshaping the word to reflect another, fuller, freer sense of self and world. Philip searches for a new freedom of language, a new awareness of the possibilities within 'tainted' English for acceptance of wrong and the possibility of redemption. The ways in which racial-cultural and gender-cultural identities are intertwined in this search may be seen in the ways Philip images a mother-tongue as opposed to a father tongue in her essay 'The Absence of Writing or How I Became a Spy' which prefaces her collection *She Tries Her Tongue, Her Silence Softly Breaks.*[7] The father-tongue is the one which imposes colonial culture, formal education, the desire for upward mobility and white hegemony. She quotes from her journal, (and uses the idea later in a poem), that she ought to be writing, not about 'kinky hair and flat noses', but about the language 'that *kinked* hair and *flattened* noses...'.[8] The mother tongue or demotic is full of possibilities, but is also elusive and must be sought by questioning, creative experimentation and desire. She points out that a sense of control and autonomy is essential for the writer, and that this is especially true for the African Caribbean woman writer, for she inherited a language which predetermined her, denied her and distorted even her very personal images of herself, i.e. entrapped her in a series of distortions. But it is the tension between Standard or International English and the demotic tongue of Philips' ancestral community in Trinidad which strengthens her work: English is both mother and father tongue. The greatest challenge to the writer of Caribbean descent then becomes how to:

> ...keep the deep structure, the movement, the kinetic energy, the tone and pitch, the slides and glissandos of the demotic within a tradition that is primarily page-bound....[9]

Her work sometimes recalls the work of Edward Kamau Brathwaite, whose poetic forms and musical rhythms are now and then echoed or transformed within her own original poetic fabric. Brathwaite's concept of 'nation language', or the creation of an original linguistic communal identity by a previously colonised people, and his discussion of the complexity of Creole society in *Contradictory Omens*[10] are also very pertinent to Nourbese Philip's own theories of language and society. Like Brathwaite, Philip theorises that it is not possible to harmoniously fuse all aspects of identity or cultural experience, but it is possible to set up dialogue between them. Whereas Brathwaite images cultural inheritances as mother or step mother, Philip explores very various images of woman as cultural identity.

She remakes also, in her exploration of the nature of the poetic image, the Rastafarian use of 'i-'. She speaks of 'i-mage', a powerful medium for changing the 'way a society perceives itself, and eventually its collective consciousness',[11] and then brings this concept directly to bear on a woman's experience, and not any woman, but a woman descended from African women who were enslaved and violated:

> In the New World, the female African body became the site of exploitation and profoundly anti-human demands - forced reproduction along with subsequent forceful abduction and sale of children. Furthermore, whilst the possibility of rape remains the amorphous threat it is, the female body continues to be severely circumscribed in its interaction with the physical surrounding space and place. How then does this affect the making of poetry, the making of words, the making of i-mages if poetry, as I happen to believe, 'begins in the body and ends in the body'.[12]

Her purpose in this passage is to unlock a space within the word image, for she explains that the power of the artist lies in the ability to create new i-mages which 'speak to the essential being of the people among whom and for whom the artist creates'.[13] Her envisioning of language itself is a striking example of this. She calls English, 'good-english-bad english english, Queenglish and Kinglish - the anguish that is english in colonial societies'.[14] At the root of her work is the sense of wresting i-magery from a language which is both enemy and friend. She speaks, rightly, of the English which colonised and enslaved as 'a language that was not only experientially foreign, but also etymologically hostile and expressive of the non-being of the African'.[15] Thus the 'African learned both to speak and to be dumb', until English could be transformed by a linguistic revolution which could substitute creative power for the Africans severance by the Middle Passage from cultural, spiritual, linguistic, communal autonomy and origins, identity, integrated vision.

Nourbese Philip seeks to win the space for alternative discourses within her own creativity, for dialogue which is not exclusive or absolutely oppositional, but interchanging and intercultural. Edward Said, in discussing the way that monocentrism and ethocentrism 'licence a culture to cloak itself in the particular authority of certain values over others'[16] reminds us of the insidiousness of taking up one solitary ideological position which entrenches itself in a desire to control the way things are perceived.

In a similar way, Pamela Mordecai has articulated an idea of 'prismatic vision' central to Caribbean experience and thought: dialectical thinking becomes therefore identified as alien to the unique complexity of Caribbean identity. 'Prismatic vision' is expressed as a mode of cognition which has emerged out of the particular experience of Caribbean peoples, and is related to African cognitive theory. Mordecai after mentioning Senghor on the symbiosis between African and others, goes on to say:

> It is this palpable sense of diverse others that the prismatic perception tolerates...this habit of cognition proceeds from the reality of cultural syncretism which characterises Caribbean societies and is perhaps most readily expressed in the Caribbean persons habit of operating varieties of linguistic codes and registers.[17]

Mordecai defines 'prismatic perception' as the 'disposition to perceive and construe experience in sometimes unresolved pluralities', which is 'very different from logical/linear methods of knowing'. She puts it another way in identifying images emergent in the collection *Out Of The Kumbla: Caribbean Women And Literature*:

> A thing turns into something else and at the same time retains its identity and intactness. The association-in-disparity and capacity-for-being-confounded both signify.[18]

This image conveys a sense of boundless spatial freedom, a way of defeating the limitations of the literal, the confines of the physical body, the social constructs which attempt to define us.

The intermingling of political realities with a sense of an infinite play of possibilities also marks the theorising of Wilson Harris. He emphasises the loss of vision which ensues from marking off cultural or personal territory in a hard, absolutist manner.[19] His vision of a fullness of creativity, imaged as continuous incarnations of freedom defying the endings, the corporal fixedness of commonplace definitions, has much in common with Mordecai's imagery of the prismatic as characteristic of Caribbean thought. This may also be true of other intellectual traditions grounded in so-called Third World cultures. Trinh T. Minh-ha, in *Woman, Native, Other: Writing Postcoloniality And Feminism*, speaks of a properly told woman's story as a 'gift built on multiplicity'. She dismisses reductive definitions when she says 'Neither black/red/yellow nor woman but poet or writer',[20] though we know that no woman exists outside numerous infinitely changing and intersecting cultural realities such as race, gender, class, nation, generation, sexual preference. Pamela Mordecai offers the idea of the complex multi-faceted thinking of the Caribbean as a strobe light.[21] In a way, a text is an unfinished and open-ended conversation between multiple aspects of experience. The woman's text which consciously sets out to establish such conversation establishes space for female identity to develop freely. Such a text sets out to defeat constructs which limit and divide and which thereby inhibit creativity.

Whereas Philip and Mordecai insist on some of the same awareness of multiplicity established by Caribbean intellectual traditions developed by the great poetic voices of the region, such as Brathwaite, Harris, Cesaire, Walcott and Glissant, their gendered perspectives extend such ideas still further.[22] For example, Kamau Brathwaite's image of Caribbean discourse as 'tidalectics', a clever variant on dialectics, offers a strong sense of the way the ever present Caribbean sea continuously shifts and changes, both dividing and coming together, flowing to the land and away. Philip and Mordecai's poetry and theory could be said to be 'tidalectic', but in a way which extends Brathwaite's image to emphasise the experience and identity of Caribbean women.

The first boundaries of professional space for a literary woman are commonly those established by literary men, mostly of previous generations, and for a woman of African descent who writes in English, even now, these might still be the white men who established European literatures and/or are deeply implicated in imperial adventures. Philip, for example, carries on a dialogue with white male culture, literally carving out space between their words and her own on the page in both. *She Tries Her Tongue* (the cycle 'And Over Every Land And Sea'), and *Looking For Livingstone*,[23] which is mainly written in poetic prose. The quotations from Ovid's version of the story of Prosperpine and her mother Ceres which are superscriptions to Philip's version of the same story, 'And Over Every Land and Sea' provide one side of such a dialogue: Philip's poems implicitly reconstruct the myth as the story of a Caribbean mother losing her child to powerful white male Europe and its language.[24] Sometimes it is the daughter who speaks of her search 'She whom they call mother, I seek',[25] The search is, then, sometimes for language itself, and in the first poem the searcher has a creole voice: 'Before the questions too late,/before I forget how they stay,/ crazy or no crazy I must find she'.[26] The islands themselves are the one who is sought, 'skin green like lime, hair indigo blue', a fitting parallel to the imagery of the original myth, in which Cyane has blue hair as a water spirit, and the story itself tells of the way winter came into the world, through the misery of Earth's loss of her daughter, and the daughter's rape. But the search goes on through the regions where 'north marry cold' , 'but don't look for indigo hair and skin of lime at Ontario Place'. There is a dream sequence, in 'two languages', creole and international English, which brings the goddess, mother and daughter together, vividly to presence: 'lizard-headed/ i suckle her/suckling me'; 'a choosing-/one breast/neither black/nor white', 'wise black and fat she laughs'.[27] The memory of a lost mother haunts:

...the voice of her sound, or didn't I once
see her song, hear her image call
me by name - my name - another sound, a song
the name of me we knew she named
the sound of song sung long past time,
as I cracked from her shell -
the surf of surge
the song of birth.

Nourbese Philip[28]

But searching for her brings knowledge and recognition of 'the many-voiced one of one voice/ours/betrayal and birth-blood/unearthed'.[29] The process of understanding original identity breaks open oppositions and limitations and offers a much greater freedom and space.

In 'Cyclamen Girl', which deals with a young black girl's coming of age in 1960, confirmation and menstruation mark the coming of adult awareness. In the 'ceremony of White' (cultural ideology as well as dress and shoes and prayerbook), first European goddesses (Aphrodite, Mary) give the girl her names, but then she is named for African goddesses as well (Atabey, Oshun, Orehu, Yemoja). Here once again is a sense of spaciousness won by a turning to African origins and a sense of self.

'African Majesty' was provoked by a collection of African art in Ontario, which ends with a pointer to the central theme of this whole volume of poems, 'to adorn the word with meaning/to mourn the meaning in loss'. This poem has images of entrapment, of feet pacing 'the circumference/plexiglass of circle that circles/prisons and prisms the real in once-upon-a-time/there-was/mask reliquary fetish/memory/ancestor'.[30] In this image, the prism is part of an artificial containment of African memory and meaning, the reduction of living, spiritual art into museum artifacts, labelled and imprisoned away from human touch in a display case, which is also, by extension, the intellectual explanation of the meaning of the pieces, ' "the African influence" on-/Braque, Picasso, Brancusi', which 'defies/the blame in absolve...'[31]

'Meditations on the Declension of Beauty by the Girl with the Flying Cheekbones', returns to the question of identity and language: here the spatial arrangement of the poem on the page explores the possibilities which lie in rearranging language to ask the right questions:

If not   If not   If
Not
If not in yours
                              In whose
in whose language
Am I
If not in yours
                              In whose
In whose language
Am I   I am.

Nourbese Philip[32]

This poem leads into a major cycle of poems, 'Discourse on the Logic of Language', 'Universal Grammar' 'The Question of Language is the Answer to Power', 'Testimony Stoops to Mother Tongue' and 'She Tries Her Tongue; Her Silence Softly Breaks'. These present a radical attempt to displace linear containment and order by juxtaposition and dialogue between opposed elements.

Nourbese Philip achieves this by very striking spatial arrangements, including, in 'Discourse on the Logic of Language', text which runs vertically along one side of the page, a page shared also by a poem and 'Edict I', an order to slave owners with regard to preventing slave uprisings by mixing speakers of different African languages together, printed in italic script. The text which runs along the page vertically is entirely in capital letters and describes a mother's tongue licking a newborn child clean of the white substance which covers its body. As she does this, the child falls quiet. Within these two different scripts and meanings, lies the poem, which takes the idea of mother tongue and father tongue and plays them against each other, using Brathwaite's important sound and sense word 'dumb' (with the echo of the African drum silenced by colonial/racial intrusion), as a powerful symbol:

I have no mother tongue
tongue
no mother to tongue

no tongue to mother
to mother
tongue
me
I must therefore be tongue
dumb
dumb-tongued
dub-tongued
damn dumb
tongue.

Nourbese Philip[33]

This collage of meanings, one offsetting the other, is characteristic of the original way in which Nourbese Philip sets about the problem of language and space. The poem is again, on the second page, contained with the mother text and the father text. Here the mother opens her child's mouth and blows her words, which are also her mother's and grandmother's words, into it. A second edict (father text), proclaims that slaves should not speak their native language on pain of having their tongue cut out and displayed. The poem, wresting space for its own words, continues to confront the concept of father and mother tongues internally, until near the end, there is a plea, 'tongue mother/tongue me/mothertongue me/mother me...'[34]

Nourbese Philip also playfully uses multiple choice question forms and grammar book exercises as a frame for her radical and serious questioning: 'Parsing - the exercise of dismembering language into fragmentary cells that forget to re-member'.[35] This line stands alone at the top of an empty page. At the bottom of the same page is a sharp and political dictionary definition of the word 'raped':

...raped-regular, active, used transitively   the again and again   against
women   participled into the passive voice as in 'to get raped'   past
present future-tense(d) against the singular or plural number of the
unnamed subject, man[36]

There are many other examples of Philip's creation of a new spatial relation between familiar elements in a given story or cultural environment, such as the retelling of the story of the three little pigs and the wolf, titled 'How To Build Your House Safe and Right', or the lines from the 'Book of unCommon Prayer', or the Red Queen, screaming 'Banish the word/Off with its head...'[37] At every stage, Nourbese Philip disturbs the dust on the floor of the memory and shakes out associations, redefining, and always creating space for new thoughts and for the flow of long suppressed and intense emotions.

The last poem in the collection is prefaced by another quotation from Ovid's Metamorphoses as translated by Dryden, 'All Things are alter'd, nothing is destroyed', and moves through the sense of loss of ancestor-family and enforced colonial language to the memory of African forms of speech (praise-song, poem, ululation, utterance), to a prayer to the father, inserted between lines of the poet's version of the Christian Communion prayer, 'We do not presume to come to this thy Table...' to a stuttering caused by loss of tongue and then to a moving remembrance of the past as language:

Hold we to the centre of remembrance
  that forgets the never that severs
      word from source
  and never forgets the witness
  of broken utterances that passed
      before   and now
  breaks the culture of silence
  in the ordeal of testimony...[38]

The poem images words as the centres of circles, and then moves to an image of the body as the source of words, a body likened to a drum, a harp, a flute. At last, there is the possibility of 'pure utterance'. This poem is followed by a reference to a custom of returning the skeleton of the first salmon caught in the salmon run, eaten by the elders of an Amerindian community, to the waters where it was caught, to give thanks and ensure future food. Thus language is a memory which must be given back to be sure it is always fresh and inspired by the life of the past community. By reworking the familiar, Philip creates space within it for a new consciousness of linguistic nuance and therefore a new consciousness of experience.

Mordecai's poems, differently but as strongly, also conjure the past and the body as means of escaping confinement. In her poetry, images of growing, planting, nurturing are very central, and often connected to a woman's strength and power, as in 'Up Tropic':

more than I want
to breed you bright
children to tickle
your laughter and
tug at your hair
with lithe toes
more God knows

I want my own
greening.

Pamela Mordecai[39]

Pamela Mordecai's 'Island Woman' is an extended image of the island as a goddess, a 'woman/of a fierce green place', who sings 'many songs', blossoming after the rains each year when 'Kingdoms grow in my dark womb'.[40] Like Nourbese Philip, Mordecai links the body centrally to language and to identity, though they have different tones, Nourbese Philip more intellectual and Mordecai more sensuous. In 'for Eyes To Bless You', there is a play with the body as statement, sometimes open, sometimes reticent:

You will not know how much how
frequently, in that same way, I want
my body back. So do not ask
that what I said a week a month
ago should be what I say now:
the only protest you may make
is that my eyes no longer bless
you: for the rest, the fires
that you lie so quiet against
are me mercurial as hell
and heaven fixed in one
perpetual counterpoise:...

Pamela Mordecai[41]

The sense of a woman looking to find infinite space in which to exist is powerful in 'Walker':

My mother
was a walker
clothes in a brown
paper bag headed
for where under
some car some
bus some
precipice her
whimsy
claimed a place

Pamela Mordecai[42]

Discovering complex space gives autonomy, however oddly placed within social order, and self definition. In Mordecai's 'Breaking Ground', one stanza particularly expresses the need to go in many directions at once:

It is necessary
to walk so many ways
to reach this place
to start from.

Pamela Mordecai[43]

In this image, walking again brings a sense of effort and sense of space, together, and becomes, like the search in Nourbese Philip's poem cycle, an avenue for the female spirit to begin to explore and discover identity.

In Mordecai's poetry, words can be either blessings or curses, for there is a strongly spiritual quality to much of her writing. 'Last Lines' threatens irresponsible occupiers of high positions if they do not take responsibility for the damaged and injured of the community: in this poem Creole strengthens the incantatory quality of the words. The poem flows naturally as if spoken in one vehement breath:

...Every old
twist-up man you see,
every hang-breast woman,
every bang-belly pickney,
every young warrior
who head wrench
with weed, white powder
black powder, or indeed
the very vile persuasion
of the devil - for him not
bedridden you know -
every small gal-turn-woman
that you crucify on the
cross of your sex
before her little naseberry
start sweeten
I swear to you,
every last one shall live...

Pamela Mordecai[44]

Mordecai thus opens up the full power of language, in its old sense as the

'Word', which cleanses, transforms and relates the individual to the moral core of her society. This, too, is a kind of clearing of space, a use of language to dispose of those who confuse moral direction and thereby prey upon and limit other people's lives.

Whereas Nourbese Philip is often explicitly concerned with the betrayals of the Christian church as a woman of African descent from the Caribbean, Mordecai tells of a strong connection with God: in 'Catch the Wind', she flies free in a long wish to escape human confinement. The person wants something which could:

...set me
top of a coconut tree, poised
on the slender stem where I
had blossomed - - a nut
with a tremulous secret
a hard core of jelly
and soft sweetest water.

Pamela Mordecai[45]

In the end, she asks 'And must I cede/these expectations, Lord?'

Mordecai uses Biblical echoes, but rewrites sacred texts to cleanse them of too great a familiarity or distance, thus making them afresh, as poets do with language. In 'Protest Poem', the persona is the poor, collectively. The poem rejects Marxism, ('see me teenager dead from the blows of your/your words that baptise me according/to Lenin and Marx...'). One section revises the Sermon on the Mount: 'Blessed be the proletariat whom/we must mobilize/we must motivate/...' The voice of the poor becomes contemptuous:

Is ole chattel ting again: di same
slavery bizniz, but dis time di boss
look more like we and him does be smarter.
Not a damn soul going mobilize my ass
to rass; dem joking.

Pamela Mordecai[46]

In the end, the voice proposes 'the abolition of you/and us', and goes on 'we propose to share the little/that breeds on these/antilles one mango to one mouth/....' The only possibility to alleviate the prison of poverty is perhaps some space through communal sharing. In the 'Metropolitan Market Conditions', the persona speaks of 'plantation twin-/ingness of view, our primal sin': the oppositional vision which limits is not the same as the faceted vision which frees. In a recent review of *Journey Poem*, Jeffrey

Robinson argues that Mordecai's poems show a creative tension between the masculine or father direction (domesticity, order, security and the mother direction (walking, romantic freedom, impatience with limits). Certainly Mordecai does not indict the father in her poems in the way the father tongue is indicted and censured in Nourbese Philip's: nevertheless, there is a sense in which love in Mordecai's work is defined as *between* one thing and another, like poetry, a space which accepts no single definitions. Thus in one of her finest poems, 'Mongoose', a poem about word making, she says 'Poems are shorter the truth', for the truth disappears as quick as a mongoose into the bush. She explains this: 'the truth (is) elusive and all man's theorising has simply got into the way of our catching it'.[47] The 'certain hunter' in the fourth stanza is Christ, whose grace has been separated from us by empiricism and rationalism.

In 'Going Home', physical love becomes a dimension of expression not able to be found within the fond strictures of domestic life, and therefore known when the 'lists' of domestic ordering are put away. Mordecai's poem 'I Want To Go Up Rivers' is about another kind of space-making - going against the tide, so to speak, where the space is the definition of the person against which the water rushes hard. She identifies this experience, 'ingenious as lust', not the only time in the poems that physical love, sexuality, is imaged as creative potentiality, intimacy as a kind of special space.

Both Mordecai and Nourbese Philip signify on familiar elements of Caribbean culture, constantly presenting the complexities of visions which mark the journey of exploration of the Caribbean woman writer. Spaces, intersections of meaning and perception, constant challenges to hegemonic definitions of any kind are central facets of the poetic themes and forms of Mordecai and Nourbese Philip and so both poets engender spaces, meaning that they create ideas/ ideals of new possibilities which are radical in the sense of breaking conventions, exploring, recreating. Relevant here is Marlene Nourbese Philip's list of questions:

> What happens when you are excluded from the fullness and wholeness of language?
> What happens when only one aspect is allowed you - as woman?
> - as Black?
> ...
> What of celebration?
> What of love?
> What of trust between individuals?
>
> Nourbese Philip[48]

Nourbese Philip says there can be no conclusion to such questioning because language is always changing: nevertheless, if poets, with the power to cleanse and remake language, choose to address such questions, the answers will at least be importantly addressed. In the end, perhaps, the meaning lies now in the fact that we know what the right and vital questions have become for our time - and the last three of Nourbese Philip's questions strike at the heart of our dilemmas. It seems clear that only the defeat of essentialism and the freedom to choose and determine or own complex and developing identities in the world can give us the spaces in which we might, one day, be able to answer those last three questions in an affirmative way.

**Marlene Nourbese Philip currently publishes as M. Nourbese Philip. Elaine Savory has other publications as Elaine Savory Fido.*

Notes

1. Rita Felski, Beyond *Feminist Aesthetics*, Hutchinson Radius, London, 1989.
2. Spivak 1987, p77-78.
3. See Henry Louis Gates, Jr., *The Signifying Monkey*, Oxford University Press, New York, 1988, pp.45ff.
4. By feminist, I mean, of course any woman or man who works towards women's freedom from oppression.
5. Hazel Carby, *Reconstructing Womanhood: The Emergence of the African-American Woman Novelist*, Oxford University Press, New York, 1987, p.15.
6. Ibid, p.17.
7. Nourbese Philip, *She Tries her Tongue, Her Silence Softly Breaks,* Ragweed Press, Charlottetown, 1989, p.20.
8. Ibid, 1989, p.20.
9. Ibid, p.23.
10. E. Kamau Brathwaite Contradictory Omens & Cultural Diversity and Integration in the Caribbean, Savacou, Mona, Kingston, Jamaica, 1974.
11. Philip, 1989, op. cit., p.12.
12. Ibid, p.24.
13. Ibid, p.12.
14. Ibid, p.11.
15. Ibid, p.15.
16. Edward Said, *The World, The Text and The Critic*, Harvard University Press, Cambridge, Mass, p.53.
17. Pamela Mordecai, 'A Crystal of Ambiguities: Metaphors for Creativity and the Art of Writing' in Derek Walcott (ed.) Another Life: West Indian Poetry', Jackson and Allis, College of the Virgin Islands, St Thomas, 1986, pp.106-121.
18. Carole Boyce Davies and Elaine Savory Fido (eds.) *Out of the Kumbla*, Africa World Press, Trenton, NJ, 1990, p.viii.

19. See for example, Wilson Harris, 'The Fabric of Imagination', *Third World Quarterly*, 12(1), January, pp.176-86.
20. Trinh T. Minh-ha, *Woman, Native, Other*, Indiana University Press, Bloomington and Indiana, 1989, p.6.
21. Mordecai, 1986, op. cit., p.106.
22. Mordecai's theory of facets has an interesting tangential relation to Brathwaite's cultural theories of creolisation. Perhaps the most interesting image of Brathwaite's difference in this matter from Mordecai lies in the moving poem in *The Arrivants*, 'The Cracked Mother', which enforced conversion to Christianity on the part of a Carib mother has resulted in her daughter being sent to a convent. The immediate result of cultural change is the image of cracking, disassociation. Mordecai, dealing with a later phase of the creolisation process, images such complexities more fluidly as many-faceted.
23. Marlene Nourbese Philip, *Looking For Livingstone: An Odyssey of Silence*, The Mercury Press, Stratford, Ontario, 1991.
24. Merlin Stone's woman-centred retelling of the story in *Ancient Mirrors of Womanhood* (1989) is an interesting parallel. Here the story is the Greek one, of Demeter (Ceres in Roman naming), and Persephone (Proserpine in Roman naming). But the mythology may have an even older origin, as Stone points out, in Egypt, that is, Africa.

    Probably all readers of this paper know the story in some way, but it is important to retell it to show the way it counterpoints the poems. Essentially the story is of a daughter abducted from a mother by an arrogant and rapacious man, a king, in fact the King of the Dead. The daughter is a Maiden in the service of the Mother Goddess of the Earth, but she is also symbolic of the recurrent grain harvest so necessary to human life. When, after Ceres (Demeter) discovers what has happened to her daughter and has appealed to Jove (Zeus), Proserpine still has to live in Hades for six months of the year, corresponding to the months of winter, since she ate some pomegranate seeds during her captivity, but she is restored to her mother for the balance of the year.

    Susan Griffin, in her *Woman and Nature*, tells the story again, and in it marks the fact that the daughter, being abducted, called on her father, 'not knowing he had blessed this event'. Griffin's version centres on the agony of the mother-daughter separation, relating ecological disasters resulting from indifferent or irresponsible science to the woman being divided within by patriarchal oppression: 'splitting, the chromosome split, spirit burned from flesh, desire devastated from the earth' (1978, p.98). Incidentally, Griffin's book is dedicated to 'those of us whose language is not heard, whose words have been stolen or erased, those robbed of language....'.
25. Nourbese Philip, 1989, op. cit., p.29.
26. Ibid, p.28.
27. Ibid, p.32-33.

28. Ibid, p.35.
29. Ibid, p.36. Subsequent references to 'Cyclamen Girl', 'African Majesty', 'Meditations...', 'Discourse...' etc are to sections of the 1989 collection in the given order of pages.
30. Ibid, p.49.
31. Ibid.
32. Ibid, p.52.
33. Ibid, p.56.
34. Ibid, p.58.
35. Ibid, p.66.
36. Op. Cit.
37. Interestingly, the 'Red Queen' of Nourbese Philip's text speaks in a manner reminiscent of the Queen of Hearts in *Alice in Wonderland*, not the Red Queen of *Through The Looking Glass*. Both Carroll characters are, however, versions of the bossy British nanny, the white woman 'mistress' if you like, and the Nourbese Philip revisioning of the 'Off with their heads!' speeches of the Queen of Hearts finally comes to draw in other British nursery characters which the middle-class child would have encountered:

'The word, the word'
the Red Queen screamed

'Banish the word
Off with its head-
The word is dead
The word is risen
Long live the word!'

'Oh, dear, oh dear', said Alice, 'what will Tigger and Pooh and Eeyore and Mrs Tiggy Winkle think of all this kerfuffle. She does carry on so - that Red Queen' (1989, p.75).

Alice does indeed make sharp retorts in Carroll's work. We see here the playful revisioning of the idea of resurrection - and this piece comes immediately after a strong, powerful passage on the sale and passage of slaves, and is the last piece in the cycle 'The Question of Language is the Answer to Power'.

38. Philip, 1989, op. cit., p.96.
39. Pamela Mordecai, *Journey Poem*, Gandberry Press, Kingston, 1989, p.23.
40. Ibid, p.13.
41. Ibid, p.22.
42. Ibid, p.9.
43. Ibid, p.17.
44. Ibid, p.53.
45. Ibid, p.36.
46. Ibid, p.51.
47. Information provided by Pamela Mordecai to Elaine Savory.
48. Philip, 1989, op. cit., pp.21-22.

Writing for Resistance: Nationalism and Narratives of Liberation

Alison Donnell

The relationship between literature and national identity has been the interest of much post-colonial criticism for, as Edward Said has outlined:

> Literature has played a crucial role in the re-establishment of a national cultural heritage, in the re-instatement of native idioms, in the re-imagining and re-figuring of local histories, geographies, communities.[1]

Certainly Said's suggestion of the imagination as a location for the creation of a post-colonial world is especially pertinent to Caribbean societies for which there was no pre-colonial or established indigenous culture which could be revived and re-valued in order to resist the colonising culture. Although one might argue that this absence has made the role of imaginative forms more vital during periods of nationalist struggle in the Caribbean, it also made their relationship to the projects of cultural nationalism less easily defined.

In order to open up a debate concerning discourses of nationalism and cultural belonging within Caribbean literature, I wish to look at some poetry written by Creole women during the 1930s and 40s and at Jamaica Kincaid's *A Small Place*, published in the 1980s.[2] My argument takes as its point of animation the fact that both of these texts are commonly read as clear statements of national interest - the Creoles' poetry as promoting colonial nationalism and Kincaid's *Small Place* as a document of cultural nationalism, of post-, perhaps anti-, colonial nationalism. Yet my own reading of these texts has alerted me to how unstable the signifiers of nationalism are, and of how these texts mute and blur any confident articulation of cultural positioning. Consequently, the interest of this piece lies in attempting to rethink the cultural politics of these works (both the allegedly securing and elitist notion of colonial nationalism and the supposedly self-defining, even liberatory, narrative of post-colonial nationalism), and their roles in terms of the construction of a national identity.

Perhaps the most contentious strategy on which this piece hinges is the yoking together of Creole women's poetry from the 1930s and Jamaica Kincaid's defiantly non-colonial writing from the 1980s. It is not my aim to point to a transhistorical or transcultural trend which enables us to generalise about women's writing, but rather to focus on two texts which arise in particular historical moments and cultural geographies in order to locate particularly interesting articulations of cultural belonging. However, without forging any easy equivalence between two such different moments and acts of writing, one condition of both a Creole poet and an Antiguan-American writer which might generate productive enquiry is the liminality in terms of cultural identity which both bear in relation to dominant Caribbean culture. This overlap might be instructive in an analysis of their oblique engagement with dominant discourses, but it might more importantly serve to foreground the questions of authenticity, community consensus and claims to belonging which inform constructions of nationalism within the Caribbean region, where arguably all subjects are diasporic subjects. In this way, the playing off of these texts should address the question of whether there can be any unproblematic articulation of nationalism, from either an ex-coloniser or an ex-slave population. I am interested in whether it is perhaps symptomatic that in a culture constructed through a complex matrix of conflict, assimilation and exile, constructions of national identity can only be limited and unstable - and what might the politics of this be.

In order to establish a model for reading these texts which attends to the complex negotiations between cultural identity and modes of representation within the specific Caribbean focus of this paper, I wish to draw on Stuart Hall's article 'Cultural Identity and Diaspora', which advises that:

> Instead of thinking of identity as an already accomplished fact, which the new cultural practices then represent, we should think, instead, of identity as a 'production' which is never complete, always in process, and always constituted within, not outside, representation.[3]

This proposal that cultural identity is not only reflected in, but also constituted by, modes of representation will be explored in my analysis of Creole women's poetry which aims to trace the various modes of cultural identity which are produced, and to explore how the continuum of these cultural identities relate to issues of nationalism and colonialism.

My readings of the poems by Creole women is particularly interested in the ways in which these writers (whose cultural identities could be seen to be as hybrid and as fragmented as those of the colonised populations) demonstrate an interest in the issues of origin, displacement and belonging which are so often perceived to be relevant to colonised peoples, but somehow believed to be confident and stable 'givens' within settler populations.

Both the cultural politics and the cultural forms which need to be discussed with reference to 1930s Jamaican literature are complex. There was no single nationalist ideology in Jamaica during this period, and writers were often sitting uncomfortably between ideas of a colonial nation and a potentially non-colonial or anti-colonial homeland. Certainly the expressions of the need and desire for a distinctly Jamaican culture did not cohere in any easily definable manner during this period, and the lack of consensus over what properly constituted culture in Jamaica, or more contentiously Jamaican culture, during this period can be traced through the poetry produced, as well as through the various debates and positions staged in newspapers and lecture halls.

It might be tempting to think that the clearest statement of cultural politics within this period's poetry can be found in Constance Hollar's title for her 1932 anthology, *Songs of Empire.*[4] Certainly Sir William Morrison's 'Foreword' to this anthology declares its colonial allegiances in an unqualified manner.

> The songs themselves although pitched in various keys and from different outlooks all express unbounded loyalty and devotion of the People of Jamaica to Their Majesties the King and Queen and to the Members of the Royal family and the intense love which all the inhabitants of this ancient and loyal Colony bear to the Motherland.[5]

Yet, while the commitment to Empire as both idea and reality does find strong expression in many of the poems written by Creole women during this period and published in Hollar's anthology, it is not uncommon for works to offer more complex representations of nationalist sentiment. In Albinia Catherine Hutton's 'The Empire's Flag', the Union Jack is given space to 'voice' its achievements, transformed into an oracle of patriotic interest:

> Grown too large for my birthplace they bore me thence afar
> Over the distant seas and 'Neath many a stranger star,
> Seeking the lands that lay far over the silver bar.
> Bought once for all with life-blood, courage that could not flag
>
> 'I fly where'er the birds fly, where'er the sun doth shine,
> I've sons of every colour, in every land and clime
> I witch them all with beauty and make them forever mine
> Crowning earth's highest mountains, Queen of the boundless sea,
> Proudly they walk beneath me, they who are truly free,
> I am the Flag of Freedom where'er my children be.[6]

While the image of the flag bursting through geographical boundaries signalling the 'progress' of Empire and the attendant expansion of British cultural boundaries (consolidated by the references to paternity and possession) may be a clear indication of this poem's colonial cultural affiliations, the suggestion of this emblem as a banner of liberty is less easy to read. Yet, this same image in which the flag of Empire is figured as the flag of freedom, here more 'nativised' by climatic change, surfaces in Constance Hollar's 'Welcome':

See the Meteor Flag of Duty
Streaming in its matchless beauty!
Sun-kissed banner of the free![7]

Again, the possible contradiction between a dedication to the Prince of Wales and Prince George and emphasis on loyalty to Britain, and a representation of the Union Jack as a symbol of freedom is not entertained within the poem. Against a background of rising fascism in Europe at this time, the fact that freedom is associated with Britain and the Union Jack is perhaps not surprising, but the conflation of ideologies suggested by formulations such as 'colonial nationalism' and 'colonial freedom' nevertheless foregrounds the complicated and involved pattern of nationalist thought amongst the 'cultural elite' at this time. In the unresolved tensions between, and of blurring of, cultural frameworks and discourses relating to nationalism (both colonial and Jamaican), the instability and plurality of the points of identification (through which Hall theorises the production of cultural identities) in these work can be located.

To return to Hutton's popular poem, 'The Empire's Flag', it is interesting that the flag itself becomes the colonial mother in the poem's final stanza, evoked in order to praise the protection and glory which the flag affords against an archetypally 'othered' world outside Western civilisation:

When with one voice thy children their loyal homage bring
Draw around us, O, Mother, thy mantle's ample fold,
Let it ne'er leave us naked, out in the dark and cold,
God keep us 'neath thy banner as we have been of old.[8]

This same figuring of Britain as 'mother' appears in Hutton's 'A Plea'. In the absolute antithesis of a call for independence, the poetic persona asks not to be called Colonials, but, in return for their loyalty, to be identified as 'The Britons Overseas':

Britain our Mother, lend to us, thine ear,
Listen to our petitioning to-day!

We are descendants of thy children dear,
Though born in far-off lands, and living there
For generations, love thee, even as they.

We pray thee do not call us 'Colonies'
Nor even say 'The Empire,' nor speak
About 'Colonials,' knowing well how these,
Taught by their fathers, love thee on their knees;
O, Mother, let us love thee cheek to cheek!

Give us thy name in filial pride to wear;
And from that loved but distant land, thy throne,
Extend thy sceptre to thy kindred here;
We know thou wilt not sell thy children dear,
That we are irrevocably thine own.[9]

This trope of the mother as caring custodian works in nationalist terms to signal (or appeal to) the nature of the motherland as guardian, a gendered construction which demands loyalty and attachment as well as offering security and recognition. The image of a powerful and yet compassionate mother within this colonial nationalist rhetoric inscribes an interesting image of maternity and womanhood. It is not clear whether Hutton calls for this acknowledgement for all colonial subjects or only those white 'descendants', however, the notion of subjects being children, somehow 'natural' dependants, which appears in both of these poems by virtue of the maternal allegory, is also strangely reminiscent of a kind of romantic racialism which suggests colonial subjects (like cultural others and women) are children by virtue of their innate simplicity and inferiority. Again, a crossing over of cultural discourses and an indeterminacy in terms of cultural politics can be identified.

This version of nationalism which looks in two directions with the blending (or blurring) of the sentiments of loyalty and love, of pride in power and in freedom is certainly relevant to the majority of Creole women's poetry on the subject of homelands and cultural placings. Yet the level of anxiety regarding cultural identity and the status of belonging which finds articulation in these Creole poems, is clearly matched by the anxieties of a reading population who wish to both simplify and segregate attempts to define nationhood within Caribbean culture. The call for human unity, and a common desire for freedom and for belonging within the Caribbean for the descendants of colonisers which this poetry voices is clearly disruptive to nativist theories of nationalist construction which are often premised upon the colonisers' disinterest in and denial of cultural belonging and the process of cultural redefinition in the face of colonialism's deculturisation.

The tendency of this Creole poetry to establish a sense of belonging and thus to define itself outside of the coloniser/colonised divides of national disinterest/interest seems to stem from an uncertain doubled cultural positioning as both British and Jamaican. Although the political status and written style of Kincaid's text is stunningly self-conscious and self-assured, and thus very different to that of the Creoles, I want to suggest that it is this same confusion concerning cultural identity which creates such a powerful response to questions of nationalism within Kincaid's work.

The question of whose interests the text is speaking may ostensibly be more straightforward in Kincaid's *A Small Place*, which is commonly read as a vituperative attack on tourists and neo-colonial practice generally. Yet, this little book, which has received the least critical attention of all her works, has a far more complex textual and political constitution than such an analysis would suggest.

Following on from Giovanna Covi, who has provided an insightful analysis of the aesthetic strategies of this text, drawing attention to the 'faked, primitive child-like voice' and to what lies 'under the pretended naiveté of the speaking voice',[10] I wish to explore the politics and the ethics of *A Small Place* . Rather than reading this text as a monologic critique of the continuing impact of colonialism on Antigua, I want to suggest that one way to reveal *what lies beneath* is to read *A Small Place* as a consummate work of ventriloquism which deploys a whole series of voices in order to debate the value and limitations of the cultural discourses and positions available to those interested in this small place and its people. Her mimicry with a difference (Louis Gates' 'signifying black difference')[11] denotes the empowerment of her voice, but it is a voice through which she provokes a call for agency and empowerment on larger terms.

Through the process of 'voicing' positions, *A Small Place* not only explores the continuity of corrupt political and economic practice after independence. Kincaid rehearses the rhetoric and idioms of colonial and post-colonial cultures, and their possibilities for self-definition in order to produce both a direct political objection and an ethical, although ironic message, concerning cultural identities.

The irony is possibly most easily traced to a point early in the text during her persistent and persuasive account of the tourist's eye view of the island. The narrator turns with: 'They [the Antiguans] do not like you. *They do not like me!*' [12] Although this second phrase ostensibly functions as an absent echo in the tourist's mind, it is also a strong pointer to the fact that Kincaid herself is a tourist of sorts, an inauthentic national subject, having left Antigua at the age of seventeen for the more comfortable opportunities on offer in the States.

However, this irony is perhaps more significant in its realignment of her readers and their construction of national identities both for self and for 'other'. In terms of uncovering the reader's position, although Helen Tiffin is right when she says that *A Small Place* is 'direct address to Americans, English (or worse Europeans)' who must recognise the implications of colonial culture with which they identify, it is also an exaggerated version of the post-colonial text which plays upon white liberal guilt:[13]

> Have you ever wondered why it is that all we seem to have learned from you is how to corrupt our societies and how to be tyrants? You will have to accept that this is mostly your fault.[14]

I am not suggesting that Kincaid does not mean what she says in literal terms, but rather that the subtext operating throughout this book is a questioning of how to respond to colonialism in any positive way, and a questioning of how ethical it is to position yourself as eternally, unalterably sinner or sinned upon, preserving the 'natural' hierarchy of colonial superior/inferior and consequently stabilising national boundaries around a model of historical conflict and exclusionary practices.

Indeed, Kincaid is not only hard on the liberals amongst ex-colonial societies as well as the tourists (neocolonialists of sorts), it seems to me that she censures the Antiguan people for failing to accept responsibility and critically engage with the forces that shape their lives:

> In a small place, people cultivate small events. The small event is isolated, blown up, turned over and over, and then absorbed into the everyday, so that at any moment it can and will roll off the inhabitants of the small place's tongues. For the people in a small place, every event is a domestic event; the people in a small place cannot see themselves in a larger picture, they cannot see that they may be part of a chain of something, anything.[15]

This small place, small mind equivalence becomes almost a refrain, reflecting on a mindset which cannot free itself from colonial paradigms. Perhaps then the text is critical of the narrative of post-colonial nationalism which adopts the anthem 'of shared exploitation and struggle' and simply involves a reiteration of past oppression, both because it works as an excuse for those who wish to behave as neo-colonialists on their own territory, and because it is an entrapment of consciousness which offers limiting conceptual and ontological possibilities to all national subjects and to the 'subject' of nationalism.

A possible solution to this entrapment presents itself in the text's final statement:

> Eventually, the masters left, in a kind of way; eventually, the slaves were freed, in a kind of way. The people in Antigua now, the people who really think of themselves as Antiguans (and the people who would immediately come to your mind when you think about what Antiguans might be like; I mean, supposing you were to think about it), are the descendants of those noble and exalted people, the slaves. Of course, *the whole thing is*, once you cease to be a master, once you throw off your master's yoke, you are no longer human rubbish, you are just a human being, and all the things that adds up to. So, too, with the slaves. Once they are no longer slaves, once they are free, they are no longer noble and exalted; they are just human beings.[16]

The necessity of unfixing colonially defined identities and the suggestion that cultural and national identities be seen as enablingly contingent rather than negatively so would seem to inform Kincaid's text as well as the Creole poetry.

My suggestion is that *A Small Place* does not just bid for an end to economic imperialism and that the Creole poetry does not simply glorify and consolidate colonial culture, but rather that both texts demand a re-thinking of the ways in which national subjects and cultural identities are constituted. The resistance to 'ready-made' or derivative narratives which both of these examples of Caribbean writing articulate suggests a complexity of both textual and cultural practice which rivals the unproblematic articulation of nationalism as a self-defining and empowering discourse.[17]

Notes

1. Edward Said, 'Figures, Configurations, Transfigurations' in *From Commonwealth to Post Colonial*, Dangaroo Press, Coventry, 1992, p.3.
2. See Jamaica Kincaid, *A Small Place*, Virago, London, 1988.
3. Stuart Hall, 'Cultural Identity and Diaspora' in Patrick Williams and Laura Chrisman (eds.), *Colonial Discourse and Postcolonial Theory; A Reader,* Harvester Wheatsheaf, Hemel Hempstead, 1993, p.392
4. Constance Hollar, *Songs of Empire*, Gleaner, Kingston, 1932.
5. Sir William Morrison Kt, 'Foreword' in *Songs of Empire.*
6. Albinia Catherine Hutton, 'The Empire's Flag' in *Hill Songs and Wayside Verses*, Gleaner, Kingston, 1932, pp.23-25.
7. Constance Hollar, 'Welcome' in *Songs of Empire*, p.2.
8. Albina Catherine Hutton, 'The Empire's Flag', op. cit, p.25.
9. 'A Plea', Ibid, pp.100-101, p.100.
10. Giovanna Covi, 'Jamaica Kincaid's Political Place: A Review Essay', *Caribana*, 1, 1990, pp.93-103.
11. Henry Louis Gates Jr, 'Criticism in the Jungle' in Henry Louis Gates (ed.) *Black Literature and Literary Theory*, Routledge, London, 1984, p.3.

12. Jamaica Kincaid, op. cit., 1988, p.17
13. Helen Tiffin, 'Decolonization and Audience: Edna Brodber's *Myal* and Jamaica Kincaid's *A Small Place*, *SPAN*, 30, 1990, pp.27-38, p.36.
14. Jamaica Kincaid, op. cit., 1988, p.34-35.
15. Ibid, p.52.
16. Ibid, p.80-81.
17. A detailed reading of *A Small Place* can be found in 'She Ties Her Tongue: The Problems of Cultural Paralysis in Post Colonial Criticism', *Ariel*, Calgary, 1995. I am grateful to the Goldsmiths conference for providing a starting point for my thoughts on this text.

Jamaica Kincaid's Prismatic Self and the Decolonialisation of Language and Thought

Giovanna Covi

'If you go to Antigua as a tourist', are the first words of Jamaica Kincaid's book *A Small Place,*[1] whose main purpose is to explain the intricate situation of the island state to a European or American audience. As Moira Ferguson pointedly observes, the conditional that opens the book - 'If you go' - ironically stresses the fact that there aren't tourists who would ask all the fundamental political questions hypothesised in the essay; on the contrary, the common mindless type of travellers 'are 'ugly' human beings who are indulging in hollow pleasures' and thus are, like the colonisers, 'morally culpable' of racism and exploitation of the Third World.[2] I think Kincaid's essay should be made mandatory reading not only for those who are packing their bags for a vacation in the Caribbean, but also for anyone who is interested in the history and culture of these islands and in their relationship to the Western centres that have colonised them. Furthermore, the reading provides a useful introduction to the whole of Kincaid's work. To read Kincaid's stories from the point of view of the perspective taken by *A Small Place*, in fact, enables us to keep the focus on what I consider her main concern - the articulation of the effects of colonialism on subjectivity, specifically on female subjectivity - and account for the strict relation between issues of socio-historical power and her definition of sexualised subjectivity. Kincaid's essay fully meets Virginia Woolf's description of the genre as that writing which 'has for backbone some fierce attachment to an idea'.[3] The passionate stubbornness with which Kincaid pursues her idea certainly gives an impressive 'backbone' to this piece. My critical decision to place this essay in the foreground of her fiction serves the purpose of calling attention to the equally foregrounded interrelationship in Kincaid's oeuvre between the discourse of colonialism - and by implication of race and class - and the discourse of patriarchy. Her writing as a whole passionately and stubbornly hammers the idea that subjectivity emerges when ideologically preconstituted identities, on the basis of such parameters as gender, race, nationality and class, interrupt one another to confront their respective biases and enforce their various powers with reference to a specific political agenda.[4]

As is usual with Kincaid's writing, *A Small Place,* poses a problem of genre definition: it is a political essay for its content, but it reads like fiction, while sounding like a speech delivered with the passion and rhythm of a song. Its slim eighty pages are divided into four parts, each of which is a critical reflection on the socio-political reality of Antigua considered from a different angle. This is the author's native country, one of the Leeward Islands in the West Indies and a former British colony, an independent state, along with two smaller islands, since 1981. Here Jamaica Kincaid was born Elaine Potter Richardson in 1949, of an African, partly Amerindian family. This is the island she left at seventeen to become an au pair in Scarsdale, New York and Antigua is the state that still issues her passport, since she never renounced her citizenship, despite the fact that she has been living in the United States all these years and that she suffered an informal expulsion from Antigua in 1985.[5]

In *A Small Place,* Kincaid's art of writing is at its best. In her previous works of poetic fiction - *At the Bottom of the River* and *Annie John*[6] - the charm comes primarily from shifting the reader's perspective between autobiography and novel, between collection and series of short stories, in a continuous mixture of dream and reality. This rocking-chair effect is obtained through a repetitive, child-like language whose lexicon and syntax are of the utmost simplicity. Here we find the same technique applied to a context even more alien to such treatment; the result is that of a lyrical, powerful essay whose beauty is only matched by Cynthia Krupat's drawings in this little gem of a book. The general effect is that of a pageant told by a ballad-singer.

Yet this song manages to express the most elaborate analysis of a complex and intricate political situation, exactly in the same way as the dream-like perspective of the girl, narrator and protagonist of her previous works, provided a sophisticated and non-dogmatic feminist definition of the identity - rather, dis-identity - of a Third World Black woman. While constantly complaining about the inadequacy of words, Kincaid in all her books succeeds in articulating the contradictions and ambiguities of post-colonialism, rendering in sparkling images the paradoxical and scandalous condition of a well-defined historical place.

This is possible because her use of language is deceptively simple. The transparency of the elaborate political message betrays a *faked* primitive, child-like voice and the reader soon realises that the text functions at multiple levels and the tableaux are indeed multi-layered palimpsests. Under the pretended naiveté of the speaking-voice lays a deeper connotative significance generated by lexical repetitions whose rhythmic effect is counterpointed by the sharp political satire of the authorial voice, now in the foreground and now in the background. The artless simplicity of the syntax is also delusive: right at the beginning, a few basic clauses are tailgated by an elaborate narrative expanding over a two-page long sentence - a construction that no child could possibly master with such balance and stylistic accuracy. The sentences are often chained to add momentum and emphasis to the message, like in the opening twelve-page paragraph of the third part in which the authoritative narrative voice expresses her 'bitterness' and 'shame' at the present state of her island.[7]

Each part is organised around a repetition of sound and lexical patterns slightly but significantly dissimilar, as if the ballad-singer had to address four different audiences from four different perspectives. It is analogous to a jazz composition played on various instruments - always the same theme, but developed in multiple voices. The narrator sometimes repeats and even contradicts herself; at other points she switches back and forth and in so doing turns sameness into difference and vice versa, in an endless movement that refuses to chain her to either a single voice or a fixed point of view. Significantly, the result is not that of a heterogeneous indifferent fluidity; rather, it is that of a message that sustains its temporality throughout the essay. Thanks to the accurate historicisation of the context, difference here always *makes a difference.* The protest voice is enriched by a chorus that contextualises and relativises her rage, thus politicising a reaction which is never allowed to withdraw into a psychological confinement. The sound and word repetitions express the struggle against ideology and dogma, in a way that is no less powerful than the opposition to injustice and racism expressed by the logical organisation of the discourse. Form and content constantly comment on each other, preventing the petrifaction of thought.

Furthermore, each part is organised according to parallel shifts in voice and focus. Reading *A Small Place* is like looking at the sea: the message is carried by the tide, but it is impossible to say upon which particular wave. It is indeed a polyphonic work whose sounds cannot be isolated and whose voices cannot be separated, because their identity is relational - prismatic as it is defined in her fiction. The narrator slides in and out of the events of the story, continuously adopting the perspective of different protagonists.

In the first part, song-like outpouring voices the narrator's relentless, sarcastic disapproval of the obtuse tourist in Antigua. Treated with mocking irony and addressed directly as 'you', the hapless foreigner becomes the focus of the first description of the island. Therefore, this is presented intradiegetically through the narrow and ridiculous point of view of:

> An ugly thing, that is what you are when you become a tourist, an ugly, empty thing, a stupid thing, a piece of rubbish pausing here and there to gaze at this

> and taste that, and it will never occur to you that the people who inhabit the place in which you have just paused cannot stand you, that behind their closed doors they laugh at your strangeness (you do not look the way they look); the physical sight of you does not please them; you have bad manners (it is their custom to eat their food with their hands; you try eating their way, you look silly; you try eating the way you always eat, you look silly); they do not like the way you speak (you have an accent); they collapse helpless from laughter, mimicking the way they imagine you must look as you carry out some everyday bodily function. They do not like you.[8]

The gaze is that of a person who is incapable of thinking. However, by rhetorically pointing out what the tourist misses, the narrator integrates an otherwise limited and biased picture. There's no danger of a narrow perspective in Kincaid's books: the point of view and mode of narration is constantly expanded and stretched to include opposite and diverse foci, as the last sentence in the above passage illustrates.

'They do not like you' anticipates the shift that concludes Part One - a paragraph that turns the perspective to the natives.[9] Just like the tourist who 'ordinarily' is 'a nice person',[10] they are not unblemished heroes. They both suffer from a life of 'banality and boredom and desperation and depression', the difference being that the tourist can escape it, while the natives are 'too poor' to do so.[11] This reversed focus serves a double function; it dismantles the binary opposition tourist/native and connects the First to the Second Part.

Here the narrator concentrates on her own past - a history of slavery and colonisation - which she tells again in a double voice. The first is the candid eye of the colonised girl she was, the second the outraged opinion of the author she has become, a person full of indignation for having been forced 'to see the world through England'.[12] The English filter seems as blinding for the native protagonist as the tropical sun is for the tourist. It takes the intervention of the extradiegetic voice of the authoritative narrator to explicate what the girl calls the 'bad manners' of the various colonisers: 'No one ever dreamed that the word for any of this was racism'.[13] This line invites the reader to translate the term 'ill-mannered' with 'racist' each time it appears in the previous pages: now we understand that it applies to the English as well as to the Americans, and even to those Europeans who have themselves suffered discrimination, like the Czech doctor who fled from Hitler and the Northern Irish headmistress, who should certainly know about British colonialism. A passage like this meets San Juan's call for a 'socially oriented semiotics...committed to the elimination of the hegemonic discourse of race'[14] and cannot be silenced nor subsumed under the generic label of 'post-colonial discourse'. This is a voice which uncompromisingly moves through poetry to stretch and reach the actual political fight for those cultures inhabiting the cutting edge of survival.

Therefore a contrapuntal structure transmits the contradictions and injustices undergone by a colonised, enslaved people. Three pages before the ending, two narrative voices - one external and one internal to the events - merge in a fugal stretto passage in which a focal reversal turns again on the intradiegetic addressee. The 'you' has become a 'master' and is blamed for post-colonial corruption derived from the imposition of the 'English' view of the world:

> But then again, perhaps as you observe the debacle in which I now exist, the utter ruin that I say is my life, perhaps you are remembering that you had always felt people like me cannot run things...[15]

And a few lines later we find the explanation:

> Do you know why people like me are shy about being capitalists? Well, it's because we, for as long as we have known you, *were* capital, like bales of cotton and sacks of sugar, and you were the commanding cruel capitalists, and the memory of this is so strong, the experience so recent, that we can't quite bring ourselves to embrace this idea that you think so much of.[16]

A cutting statement then concludes this analysis:

> Even if I really came from people who were living like monkeys in trees, it was better to be that than what happened to me, what I became after I met you.[17]

This outburst of anger leads nicely into Part Three, which opens with a speaking-I focusing on herself and her addressee. The native invites her white interlocutor to imagine how she feels when telling about the corruption of post-colonial Antiguan government; this is how, in the longest section of the essay, 'rage' becomes 'bitterness and shame'.[18] But only one-third of the way through this section, the intra-homodiegetic narrator leaves room for an impersonal external voice recounting what 'the people in a small place' do.[19] In the narrative tide, this is no distinct wave either: the autobiographical voice soon intrudes[20] to cast a judgement on the people of the island, in what is a complete reversal of the roles assigned to intra- and extra-diegetic voices in the First Part. This time, in fact, it is the speaking-I who shows more knowledge than the omniscient narrator wondering who her people are. She concludes that they must be 'a combination' of 'children', 'artists' and 'lunatics', and then lets them speak for ten pages, 'in a voice that suggests all three'.[21] This tri-tonal voice lists some of the major scandals in Antigua: drug dealing and its connection to offshore banks; members of the government engaging in such business as importing

Japanese cars (the main market being the government itself), prostitution and gambling; government corruption such as 'electric and telephone poles' also carrying 'the heavier wiring for cable television' at public expense,[22] special ammunition being tested in Antigua to be shipped to the government of South Africa,[23] or meat 'contaminated by radiation' distributed in Antigua,[24] political crime committed by Syrian and Lebanese real estate owners as well as by the US Army based on the island,[25] robberies, like the disappearance of French developmental aid funds,[26] and finally the fact that the country's ministers are legal residents of the U.S.[27] Facts are named, and it is this practice of naming which renders Kincaid's discourse a political engagement in the decolonisation not only of the nation-state but also of its culture and people, rather than a mere contribution to the all-encompassing academic debate on 'post-coloniality'. In fact, the list of the scandals in the newly independent state of Antigua brings us directly from the British old empire to the US new empire, and *A Small Place* moves rapidly from the articulation of slavery and colonialism to the discourse of the neo-coloniality of American hegemony and the domination of multinational capital.

Pointed, serious, and specific as these accusations may sound, they do not seem effective enough to the impersonal voice who intrudes twice to spin out the political implications of this state of affairs. Of the two parenthetical statements - one concerns banks and the other gambling - the first cannot be overlooked. Here the narrator ironically points out the relationship between Swiss neutrality and Antiguan corruption:

> ...not a day goes by that I don't hear of some criminal kingpin, some investor, who has a secret Swiss bank account. But maybe there is no connection between the wonderful life the Swiss lead and the ill-gotten money that is resting in Swiss bank vaults; maybe it's just a coincidence.[28]

International political and economic connections are spelled out very clearly and the philosophy supporting them is not understated either. Here is what follows the quotation above:

> The Swiss are famous for their banking system and for making superior timepieces. Switzerland is a neutral country, money is a neutral commodity, and time is neutral, too, being neither here nor there, one thing or another.[29]

The complicity of a linear concept of time in the violent mastering of the world is underlined not only by a sustained, non-logocentric development of the story, but also by continuous references to the cultural meaning of a Euro-centric, metaphysical structure of consciousness. In these parts, the essay insists on the importance of re-membering, dis-covering the radical temporality of Being that a spatial, metaphysical orientation has domesticated and silenced in its effort to master existence. But what makes Kincaid's discourse more convincingly and genuinely political than most philosophical debates is her anchoring these observations to a historically defined situation. We are made aware of the fact that the 'small place' in the following apparently universal statement is Antigua: 'To the people in a small place, the division of Time into the Past, the Present, and the Future does not exist'.[30] The political implications of the spatialisation of time are pointed out already in Part One, when - with reference to the library constantly under repair - the ironic voice assuming the thoughts of the tourist comments: 'you might see this as a sort of quaintness on the part of these islanders, these people descended from slaves - what a strange, unusual perception of time they have'.[31] But the issue is too fundamental to be hinted at only in passing, and in the next page the narrator spells out how 'the West got rich' by exploiting the people and resources of the Third World: 'what a great part the invention of the wristwatch played in it, for there was nothing noble-minded men could not do when they discovered they could slap time on their wrists just like that'.[32]

Therefore, in one of the most important themes of *A Small Place*, Kincaid provides an instance of a temporal treatment both of structure and of theme: a historical - as opposed to mythical - repetition characterises the entire discourse; memory interacts with the present, rather than freezing into a nostalgic paralysis; the recurring pattern is not a litany, but a way of showing connections on a larger and larger scale. Repetition opens up the discourse to new possibilities, like at the end of the tale by three Antiguan voices, who explain their need for expansion in these terms:

> And it is in that strange voice, then - the voice that suggests innocence, art, lunacy - that they say these things, pausing to take breath before this monument to rottenness, that monument to rottenness, as if they were tour guides; as if, having observed the event of tourism, they have absorbed it so completely that they have made the degradation and humiliation of their daily lives into their own tourist attraction.[33]

And yet, one more time we shouldn't believe that the new voice is superior to the previous one, nor that it proposes to replace it. The nature of this essay is profoundly dialogic: the narrative is resumed by the impersonal narrator to attack the national as well as the international scene, to establish connections between Antigua's depression, the US invasion of Grenada and the Baby Doc scandal in Haiti; nevertheless, the comparative political analysis is reported as the making of those same natives that in the quotation above have been scolded for their political passivity. It is 'them' who 'anchor' the events together and see what sort of dictatorship their independent government has turned into, a dictatorship likely to face 'death, only this time at the hands of the Americans'.[34]

This naturally leads to the omniscient narrator of the last section in which paradox and opposites are accepted and in which the 'you' and the 'I' blur into a mutual 'human being'.[35] Here the tone is more sombre and balanced; it describes the present situation of Antigua, declaring that there are no longer masters to be angry at and slaves to be proud of. The new situation is rendered through the oxymoronic repetition of descriptions of the beauties and miseries of the land,[36] a land that is both real and unreal and for that reason it is a prison of beauty. Indeed this is the best metaphor to describe the post-colonial condition: 'the unreal way in which it is beautiful now that they are free people is the unreal way in which it was beautiful when they were slaves'.[37] The 'prison of beauty' is the oxymoron of post-colonialism, a situation that is often one of a freedom received as a gift from the enemy, rather than won. Kincaid points this out:

> No Industrial Revolution, no revolution of any kind, no Age of Anything, no world wars, no decades of turbulence balanced by decades of calm. Nothing, then, natural or unnatural, to leave a mark on their character.[38]

The conclusion serves as a logical explanation of the tidal movement of the whole essay:

> Of course, the whole thing is, once you cease to be a master, once you throw off your master's yoke, you are no longer human rubbish, you are just a human being, and all the things that add up to. So, too, with the slaves. Once they are no longer slaves, once they are free, they are no longer noble and exalted; they are just human beings.[39]

And once our mode of thinking by a binary logic has ridded itself of the Hegelian dichotomy of Master and Slave, we are left with what Thomas Pynchon has called the 'bad shit' of the 'excluded middles' and a whole new world-picture to re-invent - tentative, fragmentary, relative but thankfully dynamic and dialogic and certainly historically grounded.[40]

Kincaid has engaged the creation of this new episteme, re-thinking mostly sexual and racial differences in *At the Bottom of the River, Annie John* and *Lucy*, and relationships between the so-called Third World and Post-industrialised countries in *A Small Place* and 'On Seeing England for the First Time'. In both cases, she has articulated the issues in terms other than those of a complementary opposition, by way of adopting a repetitive logic which adds, modifies, but never outrules the previous positions. In her fictional works, she criticises the very existence of sexual and racial difference, rather than the modes of their existence: her approach leaves no room for reform, invoking a radical change of structures, not simply of guards. The same is true for her political essay: it moves far beyond the protest pamphlet, into a deep analysis and exploration of new frames for social and human comprehension.

The syntax, sounds and structure of the essay imitate this new process of understanding. Her inquiry requires logical thinking to move back and forth, in order to avoid the traps deriving from a reduction to a linear progression - which would result in the glorification of slaves who no longer exist - or to a binary opposition - which could only interpret the corruption of the slaves who no longer exist - in terms of the old masters. Repetitions and parallelisms enhance the importance of her circular *and* linear logic - an example of how the process of Deriddian repetition and *trace* can be put into practice and acquire political significance. Kincaid's voice provides a radical instance of a monumental, multileveled history. Here *différance* produces not only many differences, but enhances their possibility of making a significant difference in the distribution of power in the world.

In *A Small Place* repetition is never a repetition of the same. It is deeply grounded in the celebration of what Iris Murdoch has called the 'messiness' of existence: only the interaction between Past and Present, the memory of a reality governed by masters and slaves can fully comprehend a situation in which such a dichotomy has ceased to function. In its dismantling of the symmetrical, linear tale of the metaphysical interpretation of the world, Kincaid's book inevitably deviates from the literary canon. More importantly, it does so by clearly enhancing the inevitable significance of memory and history, therefore placing itself beyond - and not against or above - metaphysics. For Kincaid, her slave ancestors are there at the bottom of the Caribbean sea for us to remember - rather, to re-memory, as Toni Morrison's *Beloved* has emphasised. In Antigua, the recollection of British colonialism becomes a Foucauldian counter-memory and it permits us to draw a connection between post-/neo-colonialism and post-/neo-capitalism, allowing a better understanding of international politics. This is why a ten-by-twelve-mile island becomes emblematic of the role imposed on the so-called Third World by contemporary capitalism and its culture. I insist on the potential radicalness of a resistance postmodernism, such as that advocated by bell hooks and theorised by William Spanos's *Destruktion*, and wish to point out how it may help us to fully understand the implications of Kincaid's discourse.

The insistence on an ontological philosophy, of a concept of human being as thrown in the midst of a worldly chaos, casts a philosophical light on her experimental treatment of the essay. Here is what a traditional 'objective' reporter of political facts would never say:

> ...an exact account, a complete account, of anything, anywhere, is not possible. (The hour in the day, the day of the year some ships set sail is a small, small detail in any picture, any story; but the picture itself, the story itself depend on things that can never, ever be pinned down.) The people in a small place can have no interest in the exact, or in completeness, for that would demand a careful weighing, careful consideration, careful judging, careful questioning. It would demand the invention of silence, inside of which these things could be done.[41]

It represents an effort to say things from outside the tradition of the 'Age of Enlightenment', which has done us 'very little good'.[42] The protest against a world that excludes and discriminates is uttered without, in turn, excluding and discriminating -that is, *silencing* - other voices. Kincaid has indeed invented a silence in which all the Others, those excluded by the phallic identity of the Western tradition, have found a voice - the voice of a Woman, of an Afro-American, of a Caribbean, of a radical militant, of a tender child, and possibly of many more that I don't recognise. Furthermore, she has created a polyphonic sound which unites but never assimilates the various melodies. In this music, the One and the Other are no longer polarised, and a search for a post-/neo-colonial and a feminist/womanist identity - instrumental for a radical engagement in the present historical conjuncture - is not incompatible with the rejection of a teleological picture of the world.

In this commitment, Kincaid's fiction is fundamentally similar to her essay. For example, in her series of short stories, *At the Bottom of the River,* we find a multiplicity of voices and an identity expressed in a 'silent voice'. The opening story, 'Girl' reads like a list pounded out by the beat of drums, which provides the only comment to the message that, in a world in which 'ends' are meant to 'meet', girls are 'bent on becoming sluts'. At the end we are left with nothing else but a series of imperatives, prohibitions and directions, culminating with 'this is how to make ends meet'.[43] This is a prelude to the final condemnation of the girl as 'a slut', not surprising in a story that is almost a chronicle of a slut foretold. The practice of making ends meet is the primary target of this ferocious critique which manages to expose the very origin of sexual role division - the rational construction of an ideology of symmetry. The 'uncivilised' Lack-of-Reason - the sound of the African drums that beat within the lines - serves as a political commentary, as a cry of protest against the predetermined destiny of the girl. It serves the same function as repetition does in the political essay.

Of particular interest is the story 'Blackness', in which the disruption of binary oppositions is overwhelming: everything is ambiguous, multiple, fragmented. Blackness is the night that 'falls in silence' as well as a colour of skin. But above all it is what cannot be defined - a signifier that escapes its signified by a continuous shifting, 'for I see that I cannot see'.[44] It is identity together with annihilation of the self, a celebration of a narrative 'I', who ends its song with the words, 'I am no longer 'I''.[45] Just like the tourist in *A Small Place* who is 'a whole person' at the price of being 'not too well equipped to look too far inward',[46] the narrator in 'Blackness' disrupts the concept of identity as One - of phallic identity. Like the ambivalence of the mother's body that is One *and* Other at the same time (herself and the child she bears), this 'I' can say: 'the blackness cannot be separated from me but often I can stand outside it'.[47] It is neither the silence of the repressed Slave, nor the voice of the Master because, like the silent voice, 'conflict is not part of its nature'.[48] And her child can stand in front of the mirror looking at her skin without colour,[49] while the speaking-voice rests in the oxymoron of the 'silent voice'. The silent voice could be defined as that which 'lingers in post-coloniality in the space of difference, *in decolonised terrain*', to borrow from Spivak. As she says of Mahasweta Devi, this is a space that cannot share in the reversal of the colonial logic as it is being adopted by the new, independent nation; on the contrary, it is 'the space of the displacement of the colonisation-decolonisation reversal...[which] can become...a representation of decolonisation as such'.[50] To reiterate this in the terms I like to borrow from Angela Carter, this 'silent voice' is that of a decolon*iali*sed subjectivity, one that participates in 'the slow process of decolonialising language and thought',[51] one who speaks in the new language which Luce Irigaray deems necessary in order to avoid repeating the same story; finally, one for whom 'poetry is not a luxury', as Audre Lorde clearly defines the condition of the subaltern woman.

A Small Place is an echo also of the conclusion of *Annie John*, where she dismantles the very dialectics of colonialism by noting:

> Of course, sometimes, what with our teachers and our books, it was hard for us to tell on which side we really now belonged - with the masters or the slaves - for it was all history, it was all in the past, and everybody behaved differently now...

She says so, adding with revolutionary anti-colonial pathos:

> ...if the tables had been turned we would have acted differently; I was sure that if our ancestors had gone from Africa to Europe and come upon the people living there, they would have taken a proper interest in the Europeans on first seeing them, and said, 'How nice', and then gone home to tell their friends about it.[52]

This provides a further example to support the comparison of Kincaid's discourse with Spivak's. The position occupied by the subaltern voice of Mahasweta - the only voice which can really speak for decolonisation, since it is situated beyond and outside the binary opposition empire-colony - is similar to that occupied by Annie John. It is worth recalling that the quotation above is placed in the wonderful Chapter 'Columbus in Chains', where under a picture of an imprisoned Christopher Columbus, Annie prints in Old English lettering: 'The Great Old Man Can No Longer Just Get Up and Go'.[53] The passage could find its explanation in the essay where the Native tells the Foreigner: 'there must have been some good people among you, but they stayed home. And that is the point. That is why they are good. They stayed home'.[54]

The episode of Columbus recalls the fundamental role played by the educational system within a colonised situation. This function is stressed in *A Small Place* in relation to the discussion of the Old Library and the New Library, this being a building under repair since 1974. The library here serves as a perfect metaphor for colonial as well as post-/neo-colonial conditions: the Old Library - from which the narrator 'stole many books'[55] - contained 'the fairy tale of how we met you, your right to do the things you did, how beautiful you were, are, and always will be',[56] whereas the New Library does not exist yet - a perfect symbol of the devastation which exists for a people deprived of their own culture. It symbolises a state that needs also a Minister of Culture - a need explicitly condemned by Kincaid through her comment: 'in places where there is a Minister of Culture it means there is no culture'. These places must be like 'Countries with Liberty Weekend',[57] she continues, clearly relating Antigua's neo-colonial misery to US imperialism, which is perpetrated in the name of liberty but entails the systematic violation of liberty.

Grounded on personal experience, Kincaid's writing nonetheless defies a realistic interpretation of her voice; it challenges any possibility of deciphering a single meaning by emphasising multiplicity in what Roland Barthes has called 'an anti-thelogical activity', which is 'truly revolutionary since to refuse to fix meaning is, in the end, to refuse God and his hypostases—reason, science, law'.[58] It is in an anti-teleological narrative that Kincaid keeps engaging a devastating critique of Colonialism and Patriarchy in the forms they have assumed in the contemporary power system. To the tourists in Antigua, Kincaid's books may provide the right glasses to see what is at the bottom of the Caribbean Sea: not only the contents of the lavatories which the developers of today have failed to connect to a proper sewage-system, but also the 'large number of black slaves' whom the past exploiters have kidnapped across the ocean.[59]

Moreover, Kincaid achieves such results in a language so new that the whole history of colonialism undergoes a radical revision. Kenneth Ramchand has pointedly discussed the following passage in Kincaid's *At the Bottom of the River* as exemplary of her 'literary orality'.[60]

> I leaf through the book, looking only at the pictures, which are bright and beautiful. From my looking through the book the word 'thorax' sticks in my mind. 'Thorax', I say, 'thorax, thorax', I don't know how many times...Oh sensation. I am filled with sensation. I feel - oh, how I feel. I feel, I feel, I feel. I have no words right now for how I feel.[61]

I would suggest this passage is analogous to the following scene in Kincaid's novel *Lucy*:

> ' ...Let's go feed the minions' [said Mariah].
>
> It's possible that what she really said was 'millions', not 'minions'. Certainly she said it in jest. But as we were cooking the fish, I was thinking about it. 'Minions'. A word like that would haunt someone like me; the place where I came from was a dominion of someplace else. I became so taken with the word 'dominion'...[62]

The insistent focus on signifiers throughout her books invites me to play with the title word 'Lucy'. Lucy as she who brings light/enlightenment, insight; as the brightest morning star Venus, which also stands for sexual desire; as female Lucifer - and this is in the title story - the proud, rebellious archangel, Satan; Lucy also as the female skeleton of the hominid found in Ethiopia in 1974 and named after the Beatles' song 'Lucy in the Sky with Diamonds;' finally, Lucy as a Lucy Stoner advocating the retention of maiden names through marriage, or as a Lucy Terry, North America's first Black poet.

But who is Lucy in the book *Lucy*? 'Lucy is the only character drawn directly from life',[63] declares Kincaid in an interview, allowing the equation, suggested by one name, of Lucy Josephine Potter with her own real name, Elaine Potter Richardson. Also, Lucy is the protagonist of the five stories which read as the continuation/repetition of the life of the nameless speaking-I in *At the Bottom of the River* and of Annie John in the second book. The title itself already draws our attention to the fact that things are more simple and yet more complicated - more simple and more complicated than a choice between either fiction or autobiography. The specification that continues Kincaid's declaration about Lucy points towards such complexity by a masterful ironic use of the double negative: 'but I would never say I wouldn't write about an experience I've had'.[64]

That a simple title like *Lucy* triggers such an intricate network of interpretations should not surprise. Throughout Kincaid's work, the use of language is *deceptively* straightforward, as in the declaration above about the autobiographical nature of her novel. The transparency of her primitive, child-like voice exposes the elaborate politics at the core of her writings, making us soon realise that her texts function as palimpsests. The artless simplicity of her oral syntax is delusive: irony as well as lexical and phonetic repetitions chain her sentences together into a literary composition that engages in an endless movement between sameness and difference, beyond both fixed identity and heterogeneous indifferent fluidity - a movement back and forth that keeps difference always already significant by anchoring its identity on the historical temporality of being-in-the-world. Not surprisingly and like other of Kincaid's works, *Lucy* poses a problem of genre definition. The attraction of *Lucy* lies in the foregrounding of the definition of an identity which is posed in terms of survival strategy - an oxymoronic identity/dis-identity which transcends the polarity Sameness-Difference and which we already find expressed in the eloquent 'silent voice' of the nameless prismatic 'I' in *At the Bottom of the River*. When placed within the rhetorical and structural frame of autobiography, this postmodern, open, fragmentary, multiple and paradoxical subjectivity - a decolonialised subjectivity - precipitates the self-consciousness of the woman's place both as the cultural construct 'woman' and as author. As Sidonie Smith states in her seminal study 'autobiography' no longer makes sense culturally', because new ideologies of selfhood have fractured its form and 'women writing autobiography in the twentieth century explore alternative scenarios of textuality and sexuality', disrupting the notions of author and woman alike.[65]

I like to think of the 'alternative scenario' explored by *Lucy* as a quilted autobiographical narrative, with the five stories being the larger pieces of material forming the central pattern. As such, they demand to be viewed closely, to examine the fine work of their stitches, and also from afar, to capture the total effect of the quilt. This metaphor suggests that a linear reading will be unproductive, despite the ordered chronological development of the events which bring the protagonist to her economic independence.

The five stories stretch exactly over the period of one year, beginning with 'Poor Visitor' and the narrator's first day in her new place (unnamed, but seemingly New York), where it is as cold 'as it was expected to be in the middle of January';[66] then the speaking-I is experiencing her first spring in the story 'Mariah' and her first summer vacation by one of the Great Lakes in 'The Tongue', after which she returns to the city in October where the story 'Cold Heart' begins; finally, she takes us back to January - 'a new beginning again'[67] - in the opening scene of the last piece, the title-story. The seasonal cycle also functions as the sound-track of the plot. This takes the protagonist from a village in the West Indies to a city in the US - in a geographical movement from the colonies to the actual core of the empire; at the same time, it shows her hatred for the new place growing to match her hatred for the home she has left behind. It is a psychological movement from opposition to sameness within difference characterising the two worlds. In the end, spatial and emotional movements merge to express and to accept the oxymoron of post-coloniality, which blurs while it emphasises the difference between the so-called Third and the First Worlds.

During the passing of the four seasons, Lucy decides that being an au pair still means living with a family - defined alternatively as 'the millstone around your life's neck',[68] or the locus of 'untruths that I had only just begun to see as universal'[69] - and by the end of the year she moves into a rented apartment and finds a secretarial job. In the process, she learns to appreciate her mother's principle that 'Everything remains the same and yet nothing is the same'[70] - a principle which governs the structural, rhetorical and thematic organisation of her discourse throughout *Lucy*. 'Everything remains the same' - just little pieces of flowered material forming a quilt - in that January is just as cold and unpleasant in the first piece as it is a year later in the last, and the conflictual relationship between mother and daughter is expressed in the writing of letters full of lies in both. Yet, 'nothing is the same' - if we look carefully, the flowers in each patch have different colours - and not only because Lucy has left Mariah's family.

One significant difference which is also a sameness is Lucy's attitude towards her own name. She is nameless until the last story, but the final act of naming herself in the piece 'Lucy' doesn't entail any more knowledge of herself: 'The person I had become I did not know very well',[71] she states in unquestionable terms. In 'Poor Visitor' she refers to herself merely as a 'young girl' with 'colour brown' skin and eyes, adding that her host family calls her 'the Visitor', and declaring, 'I was very unhappy'.[72] Otherwise, she only defines herself in negative clauses, as in the following examples: 'something I had always known [her race and name] ...was not so. I was no longer in a tropical zone...',[73] and 'I was not cargo...I was not even the maid'.[74] Emblematic of her choice of utterances which must affirm their subject in order to negate it is the recurrence of the word 'untruth', in lieu of 'lie', 'fiction', 'story', or 'invention', as if a veiled/masked truth were less real, faithful than a falsehood. Her self-definition through the sameness/difference of the negative clause continues and gains full significance in the next story, 'Mariah', where Lucy explores the ways in which she is different from the mother of her host family - somebody 'beyond doubt or confidence', since 'the thing she wants to happen happens' to her. Mariah can best be captured in the last, irresistible scene of the story:

...she turned and said 'I was looking forward to telling you that I have Indian blood...But now, I don't know why, I feel I shouldn't tell you that. I feel you will take it the wrong way'.

This really surprised me. What way should I take this? Wrong way? Right way? What could she mean? To look at her, there was nothing remotely like an Indian about her. Why claim a thing like that? I myself had Indian blood in me. My grandmother is a Carib Indian. That makes me one quarter Carib Indian. But I don't go around saying that I have Indian blood in me. The Carib Indians were good sailors, but I don't like to be on the sea; I only like to look at it. To me my grandmother is my grandmother, not an Indian. My grandmother is alive; the Indians she came from are all dead. If someone could get away with it, I am sure they would put my grandmother in a museum...

Mariah says, 'I have Indian blood in me', and underneath everything I could swear she says it as if she were announcing her possession of a trophy. How do you get to be the sort of victor who can claim to be the vanquished also?[75]

The comparison with Mariah is emblematic of a positing of her identity in relational terms. Like the other authors discussed in this study, Lucy's question is never, 'Who am I?', but 'Who am I in relation to an Other?' Crucial in this regard and relevant to 'the Woman question' is the confrontation of the speaking subject with the mother - her actual mother and the mother-figure Mariah. Moreover, the passage is also a clear example of the I-Thou mode of narrative, fully explored in *A Small Place*, which rhetorically multiplies the possibilities of meaning by inviting the reader to participate. Finally, this scene brings to the foreground the tissue of repetitions that constitute Kincaid's prose. The dilemma directed at the reader - 'How does a person get to be that way?' - appears with the insistence of a refrain in *Lucy*, but its numerous variants take into account the direct construction of the personalities of Mariah, Dinah, the mother and Lucy.

The focus on Mariah, who is an American liberal feminist, brings along a comparison with her own mother, a 'traditional' Black housewife in the West Indies, so that two apparently different types of women merge into sameness:

Mariah wanted all of us, the children and me, to see things the way she did... But I already had a mother who loved me, and I had come to see her love as a burden...I had come to feel that my mother's love for me was designed solely to make me into an echo of her...I felt that I would rather be dead than become just an echo of someone.[76]

In 'The Tongue' Mariah continues to be a negative model for the still nameless young girl. Nevertheless, here Lucy repeats how much she likes her, shifting her self-definition from rejection to acceptance of differences. This is an important step towards her confrontation with the mother, fully explored in the following section. Conversely, 'Cold Heart' starts out with an acceptance of the past:

> I could see the sameness in everything; I could see the present take a shape - the shape of my past.
>
> My past was my mother...I was not like my mother - I was my mother.[77]

And yet, this recognition doesn't prevent her from stating 'I am not like my mother',[78] when her resemblance is pointed out by the much despised cousin Maude. The contradiction is made even more explicit in the final words of the story, where she refers to her trauma at the birth of the first of her three brothers when the unconditional love of her mother was taken away from her forever: '...for ten of my twenty years, half of my life, I had been mourning the end of a love affair, perhaps the only true love in my whole live I would ever know...'.[79] This conclusion makes absolutely clear that the complications she struggles against in defining herself are associated with her unresolved problematic relationship with her mother.

It is in the story 'Lucy' that the focus on the autobiographical voice is sharpened - namely, where Lucy declares: 'I understood that I was inventing myself...'.[80] This statement clearly challenges the notion of referentiality and authenticity of the self, shattering a milestone of traditional autobiography. Placed within a context that articulates a conflictual mother-daughter relationship, this sentence exemplifies what Smith has called 'a poetics of women's autobiography'. Lucy is a female autobiographer who 'traces her origins to and through, rather than against, the mother whose presence has been repressed in order for the symbolic contract to emerge'.[81] She has now rejected the models of her own mother and of Mariah, and she is getting ready for 'a new beginning'. However, her task is still difficult, as the following reflection shows:

> I was born on an island...I know this: it was discovered by Christopher Columbus in 1493; Columbus never set foot there but only named it in passing, after a church in Spain. He could not have known that he would have so many things to name, and I imagined how hard he had to rack his brain after he ran out of names honouring his benefactors, the saints he cherished, events important to him. A task like that would have killed a thoughtful person, but he went on to live a very long life.[82]

Because she is a very thoughtful person, she finds it very hard to find a name even for herself, let alone the whole of the 'new world'!

And it is again because she is a very thoughtful person that her self-'invention' culminates in the acceptance of the name that is printed on her documents. This is so, despite the statement that 'your past is the person you no longer are, the situations you are no longer in'.[83] In fact, from photography she has learned that language and reality are not interchangeable:

> I would try and try to make a print that made more beautiful the thing I thought I had seen, that would reveal to me some of the things I had not seen, but I did not succeed.[84]

So she finally is Lucy Josephine Potter, even though she 'used to hate all three of those names' - Potter, because it belonged to the Englishmen who owned her ancestors when they were slaves; Josephine, because it came from an uncle who was supposed to leave some money for her in his will but lost it all, and Lucy because 'it seemed slight, without substance'.[85]

Potter reflects the history of her race and nation, and Josephine that of her class and family. But, again, what about Lucy? Lucy certainly gains a powerful substance in these pages. Lucy first tells us she 'felt like Lucifer, doomed to build wrong upon wrong' in a furious rejection of Mariah's suggestion that she may feel guilty after her father's death.[86] And after she has revealed and explained her three names, Lucy remembers her mother's reply when she asked the reasons for naming her so: 'I named you after Satan himself. Lucy, short for Lucifer. What a botheration from the moment you were conceived'. To which the daughter reacts:

> I was transformed from failure to triumph...Lucy, a girl's name for Lucifer. That my mother would have found me devil-like did not surprise me, for I often thought of her as god-like, and are not the children of gods devils? I did not grow to like the name Lucy - I would have much preferred to be called Lucifer outright - but whenever I saw my name I always reached out to give it a strong embrace.[87]

Lucy embraces her slight/powerful, inherited/invented full name in the final scene where 'everything remains the same and nothing is the same':

> I wrote my full name: Lucy Josephine Potter. At the sight of it many thoughts rushed through me, but I could write down only this: 'I wish I could love someone so much that I could die from it. And then as I looked at this sentence a great wave of shame came over me and I wept and wept so much that the tears fell on the page and caused all the words to become one great big blur.[88]

Not only because Kincaid's autobiography is told in the form of five stories, but also because it focuses on the definition of the speaking subject on the problematic issue concerning the communication between mother and daughter, it recalls another contemporary quilted autobiographical narrative - *The Woman Warrior* by Maxine Hong Kingston.[89] Kingston too *uses* autobiography to show that identity is an 'invention', a process of creation that is always in progress. Yet, such creation - despite its linguistic origin - provides a fundamental grounding for experience and social agency. I thereby read 'identity' in Kincaid's fiction in the terms she uses to describe the process of writing:

> It's just walking...on empty space. Every step you take you have to build something under it. Sometimes it would take me days to build up a sentence, and I would have to come back because it had gone too far. I was always somewhat frightened...I had points of reality that I *had* to have...[90]

Similarly, identity is that 'something' we build in order to walk along - the necessary scaffolding for constructing a house - but in the case of *Lucy*, the scaffolding is still there, a sort of Pompidou Centre which addresses directly and visibly the question of female subjectivity, and in so doing undermines the very humanistic foundation of the androcentric contract of autobiography. Following the indication of Smith, especially in her interpretation of Kingston's novel, I read *Lucy* as part of the tradition marked by Gertrude Stein's *The Autobiography of Alice B. Toklas* and *Everybody's Autobiography*.[91] Like *The Woman Warrior, Lucy* reads as five confrontations with the fiction of self-representation and with the autobiographical possibilities embedded in the cultural fiction of gender roles; each book is composed of five stories which have fractured formal autobiographies beyond recognition; in addition, each work expresses the complications of mother-daughter relations within patriarchal culture. There is in both novels a cyclical movement, an apparent line of progress which in the end returns to the beginning. Both rooted in the working class and the ethnic margins of American culture, the Chinese-American Kingston and the Antiguan-living-in-the-US Kincaid bring to the autobiographical project complicating perspectives on the relationship of woman to language and to narrative, by embracing a definition of the gendered subject in all its complex relation to the symbolic order.

The 'gendered subject Lucy' brings an important contribution to the current debate among feminist theorists on the related concepts of 'woman' and 'gender'. She shows that an identity can actually be asserted and denied at the same time, that the oxymoron of the woman speaking within, while existing only outside the Symbolic can in fact be accepted as politically significant. In Lucy we find a consciousness such as that theorised by Linda Alcoff in terms of 'a positionality within a context', or a speaking subject which Teresa de Lauretis would define as 'a dynamic process', semiotically constructed through practice and experience; Lucy is what Spivak calls 'a questioning subject', only 'strategically' committed to essentialism, or what Trinh Minh-ha calls a woman expressed in terms which 'baffle definition', because gender is 'a social regulator as well as a political potential for change'. Lucy's self is imbued but not overdetermined by race, gender, class and nationality. Her subjectivity is always already de-essentialised, and yet defined by the assumption of a definite positionality within different contexts. Lucy's identity is the strategic consciousness kept in fluid interaction and constant motion by a practice of self-analysis. Lucy's self is relational to a moving context and yet also a locus for the construction of meaning - an example of how feminist theory and practice can avoid the impasse imposed by the obligatory choice between either the essentialism of liberal and cultural feminists' conception of 'woman' as a biologically grounded subject, or the nominalism of poststructural feminists' rejection of the concept 'woman' as semiotic discourse.[92] It is precisely because she both rejects Mariah's essentialist explanations and accepts to name and write herself, that Lucy shows how the polarised terms of this controversy can be made to coexist. *Lucy* embraces what has all too often and too simply been stigmatised as the double bind of feminism - namely, that its existence is justified only by the existence of women's submission and alienation, which is precisely what feminism is meant to expose as a delusory imposition upon reality. Kincaid's discourse proves it is not necessary to exclude in order to affirm: Lucy can be 'other' and yet 'love' Mariah. Just as her mother and Mariah are always present in Lucy's struggle for self-affirmation, so is 'the other woman' never forgotten in this text, which follows Jane Gallop's forcible recommendation to hold onto 'the rifts in feminist plenitude' in order to avoid the danger of effacing the differences among women.

Lucy repeats that her life cannot be explained by the books which Mariah treasures,[93] and the emphasis with which she differentiates herself from 'women in general' is parallel to that by which she rejects her own mother who - by marrying a man who left her in debt and by having had children - 'had betrayed herself' and 'her own intelligence'.[94] Neither the American 'liberated feminist' nor the Antiguan 'oppressed housewife' can provide her with a suitable model of identity. And yet, the alternative is not that of a dissolution of consciousness into the indifferentiated self of pure signifiers. The name she 'invents' for herself is nothing other than the name she was given at birth - a choice that grounds her identity in the temporally mutable but un-erasable occasions of history.

The next question is, in what voice does Lucy speak? In contrapuntal fashion, and precipitates both representation and self-representation. Although she declares that the Brontës are 'the authoresses whose books I loved',[95] and although she states that the 'invention' of herself is 'performed more in the way of a painter than in the way of a scientist',[96] Lucy doesn't think of herself as an artist. And yet the contrary is also true, because this indeed is a portrait of an artist, as Kincaid explicitly tells us: 'This is not about race and class. This is a person figuring out how to be an artist, an artist of herself and of things'.[97] Similar to the existing category of 'woman', that of 'artist' doesn't offer her a desirable identity:

> [T]hey seemed to take for granted that everything they said mattered. They were artists. I had heard of people in this position. I had never seen an example in the place where I came from. I noticed that mostly they were men. It seemed to be a position that allowed for irresponsibility...Yes, I had heard of these people: they died insane, they died paupers, no one much liked them except other people like themselves. And I thought of all the people in the world I had known who went insane and died, and who drank too much rum and then died, and who were paupers and died, and I wondered if there were any artists among them. Who would have known? And I thought, I am not an artist, but I shall always like to be with the people who stand apart.[98]

Lucy is *not* an artist - once again the double talk of the negative clause - because she doesn't fit in the model provided by Western bourgeois culture. Lucy is not 'the excluded' who feels rejected by modernity's economic values in the various personae of the romantic, modernist and avant-gardist artist, and yet she likes 'to stand apart'. Borrowing John McGowan's argument, all the artists of modernity express their desire, commitment, or dream to transform the existing world by situating themselves in oppositional autonomous terms vis-à-vis society, and in so doing providing a liberating ground for art. It is this willed separateness, I suggest, that makes Lucy remark that she doesn't belong, despite her liking to be apart. In these terms, on the contrary, Lucy *is* an artist: she creates her own discourse, speaking in a voice under erasure that does dissolve her own identity 'in a big blur' only after she has presented it as a clear picture but never without presenting a clear picture - 'Lucy Josephine Potter'. Again, here is how Kincaid puts it: 'I'm trying to discover the secret of myself. If that's connected to the universe, I'm very grateful. But for me everything passes through the self...'. This is how she has figured out 'how to be an artist, an artist of herself and of things'.[99]

Kincaid's writing is neither the teleological variety of the androcentric, linear and unitary self constructed for and by the genre 'autobiography'; nor is it the tangles, cuts and silences theorised by Kristeva as the writing of the maternal. *Lucy* moves a step beyond *Annie John* where the longed-for pre-Oedipal unity of the undifferentiated selves of mother and daughter is predominant. By bringing the maternal into the Symbolic, the discourse of the father, by showing that identity - once posited - is unbearable and must be continuously blurred, Lucy speaks from and to a place situated beyond the dichotomy of gender opposition. This does not mean that she speaks in a mythic androgynous voice. Lucy is a sexualised subjectivity in the same way as she is an artist - with a difference: she stands for what Elisabeth Badinter would label 'the unopposite sex'. Referring back to the description of modernity provided by McGowan, I can also say that she is a postmodernist with a difference: Lucy continually moves 'between truth claims and the deconstruction of truth'.[100] The space which she forces us into attacks the 'various versions of autonomy and integrity' which have so far characterised the relation between culture and society, and focuses instead 'on the alternative strategies for social action that postmodernism proposes as appropriate responses to foundationalism's demise and as adequate protections against the static social orders that have arisen in foundationalism's stead'.[101]

Similarly, by bringing the colonies to the metropolitan centre of the empire, by showing the displacement of the master-slave reversal, Lucy speaks also beyond the colonisation-decolonisation binarism. Lucy's voice comes to occupy a space that Shakespeare couldn't even conceive of, not even in terms of desire. In *The Tempest* the only woman is Miranda, who becomes the signifier of 'the Woman' or 'women in general', the monolithic entity that triumphs in Mariah's books. Even in his dreams, Caliban is allowed to long only for her. Lucy's voice is that of a character whom even Mary Wollstonecraft Shelley had to confine to the space of desire. Lucy speaks for 'the equal companion' so longed for by the Monster and destroyed by Dr. Frankenstein right after her creation. Lucy is Caliban's woman, a monstrous female whose identity shakes the boundaries between subject and object, by continuously challenging the boundaries of its own narrative. And yet, she does speak her identity—having no choice.

Her voice is monstrous because it combines elements considered incompatible before, like the 'monstrous' combination of a lesbian and a mother we find in the Grenadian-American poet Audre Lorde, who expresses the present condition of Caliban's woman in the following terms:

> ...living in the european mode...we rely solely upon ideas to make us free.
>
> But as we come into touch with our ancient, non-european consciousness..., we learn more and more to cherish our feelings and to respect those hidden sources of our power from where true knowledge and, therefore, lasting action comes.
>
> ...the possibility for fusion of these two approaches [is] so necessary for our survival, and we come closest to this combination in our poetry...

For women, then, poetry is not a luxury.[102]

Indeed Kincaid's poetry shows the need - not the luxury - of bringing together what Lucy calls the 'good idea' of New York and the 'bad feelings' associated with her island to create a fusion which brings her 'to love the idea of seasons', as they 'give the earth a character with many personalities'.[103] Multiplicity and change characterise Lucy with the same flexibility and determination as the seasons do in the temperate zones of the world.

She constantly warns us against grounding her discourse upon any presumed external foundation, and the passage in which she rejects a Freudian interpretation of her dreams is eloquent in this regard. The conclusion of 'Poor Visitor' makes clear that Western culture is not adequate to understand her. When she relates her dream of being chased by Mariah's husband and falling down a hole filled with blue and silver snakes, she expresses her bafflement at her host-family's reaction:

> I did not know who Dr. Freud was. Then they laughed in a soft, kind way. I had meant by telling them my dream that I had taken them in, because only people who were very important to me had ever shown up in my dreams. I did not know if they understood that.[104]

With this straightforward rejection of the need for the external grounding characteristic of humanism, the first story sets the pace for the whole novel, inviting us to turn the presumed ground of human experience into an object of anxious interrogation, like the signifier itself. This way Lucy's dreams enter the outside world to fuse with it in 'a big blur' - like the tapestries in Remedios Varo's paintings. Her voice is a quilt - she stands for God as well as for Satan, but also always already Lucy stands for 'a slight' signifier, 'without substance', thus providing a most effective example of the fundamental postmodern subsumption of signifiers back into the system of meaning and allowing through a provisional, relational 'prismatic identity' for the decolonialised subjectivity to be heard and defined.

Aptly, Lucy's voice is followed in Kincaid's publications by the cutting irony of the voice of the narrator in the short story, 'On Seeing England for the First Time',[105] which provides a powerful commentary on the quincentennial's emphasis on Columbus's voyage of discovery. I would define Kincaid's venture as a voyage of 'recovery'.

The recent anti-colonial views of the discovery have also served to recover one Columbian phrase - quite possibly second only in importance to the Admiral's celebrated claim that the world is round. I am thinking of Christopher Columbus's *Account of the Third Voyage to the Indies*, in which there is a figuration of the 'otro mundo' as a nipple on the swelling breast of the world.

The recovery of this image has become the focus of feminist socio-cultural readings of the Columbian texts of discovery. Among these is Margarita Samora's insightful, *Abreast of Columbus: Gender and Discovery*, which provides the Columbian grounding, as it were, for my own reading of Kincaid's story.[106]

Samora observes that in Columbian writing the dichotomy Spaniard-Indian is ideologised in terms of the dualist opposition feminine-masculine and is articulated through the rhetorical feminisation of the term *Indian* that is contrasted to the masculine term *Spaniard*. In the process, the sign 'Indies' is subjected to two seemingly contradictory operations - one of denigration and one of idealisation. It is in this way that Columbus's dialectics inscribes 'the other world' as feminine within Western culture. Thus, 'the other world' becomes assimilated, annihilated by a discourse incapable of letting difference be, and powerful enough to obliterate the autonomy of otherness. Columbian texts of discovery interpret, rather than describe difference - they co-opt the new cultures into a political economy which defines otherness in terms of an identity related to sameness. Hence, everything gets reduced to the dichotomy of masculine and feminine, in which the latter is granted only an exchange value. Samora's analysis demonstrates that such discourse inscribes 'the other world' as feminine within a patriarchal culture which equates femininity to exploitability. In other words, the essay successfully shows how exploitation is determined and justified by a gendered epistemological politics.

Kincaid's texts provide a devastating subversion of Columbian hermeneutics not simply by reversing Columbus's gender-specific view, and not even by opposing the voice of the colonies to that of the empire. The previous discussion has already underlined how her voice is unquestionably anti-colonial and anti-patriarchal, but more precisely and incisively, I contend, hers is a voice that corrodes Columbian discourse because it situates her anti-colonial and anti-patriarchal stance within a radical critique of a binary logocentrism which also constitutes the grounding of the concept *gender*. She expresses the voice of the decolonialised subject who is journeying back and forth between empires and colonies of the past and the present, always refusing to adopt the language of either the vanquished or the victors and yet never pretending, in contrast with Mariah in *Lucy*, to be both and thus dissolving their difference. Her repetitive logic spins a thread that adds, modifies, but never rules out its previous positions; it demonstrates the political vitality of a feminist thought whose power is pathos, and which consists of knowing - as Rosi Braidotti claims we should - that all knowledge rests on affective and corporeal, which is to say libidinal ground. Kincaid's critique of that social thought which is dependent upon the dichotomy empire-colonies, and upon the opposition center-periphery, is counterpointed by her relentless rejection of the dualistic vision which derives from accepting *gender* as a hermeneutical concept.

Columbus's voyages were of *discovery* (from the Latin *discooperire*) in that he took off the veil, the mask, of something not known before, something which never belonged to him and which he must strip off in order to grasp, to comprehend. His voyages were of possession - the rape of America - also because his rhetoric adapted the new reality to his pre-existing ideas and words. Kincaid's voyages, on the contrary, are of *recovery* (from the Latin *recuperare*) in that she gains back something she previously had - her right to be a non-identity. Hers are voyages of cross-cultural encounters and as such they do not require a discourse of inscription, as suggested by Trinh Minh-ha, but are grounded instead on the endless process of re-naming the world in order to un-name it.

Literally and figuratively, Kincaid's voyages are voyages of *recovery*: her heroines go from the colonies to the centres of the empire - New York and London - in order to 're-depart' - as Trinh Minh-Ha would put it - from the colonies after having recovered the colonial view, in a continuous process. Minh-Ha's definition helps us to understand the significance of Kincaid's voyages: 'Re-departure: the pain and frustration of having to live a difference that has no name and too many names already'.[107] Kincaid's naming is always a process of simultaneously re-naming and un-naming; her identity - effaced for so long in order to survive - must today be named first, must declare, as Minh-Ha says, 'solidarity among the hyphenated people of the Diaspora'. By this she means that identity can dare say its plurality, that identity can be redefined as 'the necessity of re-naming so as to un-name'.

Kincaid's commitment to infinite progress - where 'infinite' undermines linearity and rationality - and her spatial-emotional movement between advancement and regression make the name of Lucy Josephine Potter *different* from, and not *other* than the name Christopher Columbus. Such distinction is the fundamental mark of a discourse that refuses to articulate the other side of the same coin. In fact, the Admiral thought it was pre-ordained that he should be the carrier of Christ (Christoferens); moreover, in Spanish he was Colòn - the populator, while the name Columbus recalled the Holy Spirit. Thus, by virtue of his name, his quest became the product of a celestially-revealed certainty that he was the designated instrument of a providential design to locate the Earthly Paradise. In addition, his act of naming the new discoveries was always performed as a baptismal or conversionary rite underlining the redemptive purpose of his enterprise. But it was proper of Christian eschatology, as Greenblatt points out, to assume a linear destiny in which the whole world would be consumed by fire and sword before a celestial age would dawn.

Kincaid, on the contrary, is fully conscious of the devastating consequences of this attitude, and she makes this clear in 'On Seeing England for the First Time' when she declares with lapidary concision: 'the idea Christopher Columbus had was more powerful than the reality he met so the reality he met died'.[108] This sentence casts light on her incredible capacity to view Columbian naming ironically in *Lucy*. With a loud laughter, she shows that the colonised woman does not speak to respond to a figuration of the world that has oppressed and excluded her; rather, she speaks to do away with that episteme and start re/un-thinking the world anew. Lucy puts it precisely in terms of intellectual skills, when she observes that Columbus's task of naming 'would have killed a thoughtful person, but he went on to live a very long life'.[109] The difference between the patriarchal and the feminist position vis-à-vis language, and hence reality, is not a switch in point of view, nor a shift from center to margin. The process of de-westernisation that the contemporary episteme is undergoing is actually another Copernican revolution presenting us with a vastly altered world. The un-telling of the stories of marginality recovers marginality as a condition of the center, as a displacement involving the invention of new forms of subjectivities and implying the continuous renewal of critical work.

I suggest that displacing as a living in-between, as a way of surviving, is creatively expressed in Kincaid's works by the act of writing 'sentences'. A sentence (from the Latin *sentire*) is a feeling: it is an encounter, a passion, an identity which exists for a moment and then becomes, like Lucy, 'a great big blur' - a sentence *is* Lucy, a corporeal intelligence, a 'body that matters' to paraphrase Judith Butler. A sentence is also that which Annie John writes under the picture of a chained Columbus in her textbook: *So the Great Man Can No Longer Just Get Up and Go*. She thus captures in one gesture the relationship between patriarchy and colonialism: she attacks the explorer with the very same words that her mother used to criticise her own father - with the words of women's resistance against patriarchy.

But it is probably 'On Seeing England for the First Time' which best enhances the complex significance of Kincaid's focus on 'sentences' in her writings. Like Lucy, the speaking-I of this essay discusses 'the space between the idea of something and its reality'; she observes that it is 'always wide and deep and dark' and that, although initially empty, it gets 'filled up with obsession or desire or hatred or love'.[110] Kincaid's subaltern subjects inhabit this in-between Foucauldian space and speak the feelings that fill it. In this piece, the first England 'seen' is 'an idea', pure language - a map on which the country looks like 'a leg of mutton'; the words 'Made in England' printed on almost everything; phrases such as 'having troubling thoughts at twilight',[111] which are baffling and preposterous in a tropical country where day and night alternate abruptly, just as incongruous as her father's felt hat or a big British breakfast in a hot climate. By the time the England 'seen' has finally become a reality, the in-between space has become so filled with hatred that Kincaid writes: 'I wished every sentence, everything I knew, that began with England, would end with 'and then it all died; we don't know how, it just all died'.[112]

The quotation foregrounds the complex character of Kincaid's interpretation of the world - a complexity which allows no simple reversal of imperialistic, racist and sexist rhetoric. It is the prismatic validity of the word *sentence* together with its facticity that enhances the significance of Kincaid's un-writing. A 'sentence' is 'everything' she knows of England, an overwhelming 'idea' that is nevertheless the reality in Antigua, a country reduced to 'conquests, subjugation, humiliation, enforced amnesia'.[113] Yet, all she juxtaposes it with is another sentence - her wish 'that it all died'. The comparison shows the abyss existing not so much between word and world - since human beings can only inhabit the space between language and reality - but rather the abyss existing between a sentence that has a force behind it and one that is powerless. This fundamental difference is best illustrated by the observation that:

> I may be capable of prejudice, but my prejudices have no weight to them, my prejudices have no force behind them, my prejudices remain opinions, my prejudices remain my personal opinions...The people I come from are powerless to do evil on grand scale.

In addition, there is also the 'reality' of England after her voyage, which is described as 'a jail sentence'.

Significantly, it is at the moment when she sees the cliffs of Dover that she realises the need to rid herself of all these sentences and recover the strength for a re-departure:

> The white cliffs of Dover, when finally I saw them, were cliffs, but they were not white; you would only call them that if the word 'white' meant something special to you; they were dirty and they were steep, the correct height from which all my views of England, starting with the map before me in my classroom and ending with the trip I had just taken, should jump and die and disappear forever.[114]

Notes

1. Jamaica Kincaid, *A Small Place*, Farrar, New York, 1988.
2. The books on Kincaid by Ferguson and by Diane Simmons are not comprehensively discussed here, but they are implicitly meant to stand as primary interlocutors. See, for example, M. Ferguson, *Jamaica Kincaid, Where the Land Meets the Body*, University Press of Virginia, Charlottesville, 1994.

3. Quoted in Robert Atwan, 'Foreword' in Susan Sontag (ed.) *Best American Essays*, Ticknor and Fields, New York, 1992, pp.i-xi
4. In this respect, I would take issue with the perspective privileged by Simmons, who argues that betrayal and loss by a beloved mother and by the British colonial power is the main theme which 'permeates Kincaid's work' (1). Simmons's study maintains that this sense of betrayal further develops with issues of power; nevertheless, this otherwise interesting study finally places the emphasis on a faulty key, since the vindication of her rights to identity as woman and as colonised subject is articulated in more than oppositional terms or mere nostalgia for a paradise either lost or dreamed, as my own reading is meant to demonstrate.
5. For further details about her life, see Moira Ferguson, op. cit., 1994.
6. Jamaica Kincaid, *At the Bottom of the River*, Farrar, New York, 1983 and Vintage-Random, New York, 1985a; *Annie John*, Farrar, New York, 1985b and Plume-New American Library, 1986.
7. Jamaica Kincaid, 1988, op. cit., p.41
8. Ibid, p.17
9. Ibid, pp.18-19
10. Ibid, p.15
11. Ibid, pp.18-19
12. Ibid, p.33
13. Ibid, pp.27, 29
14. San Juan, 'Racial Formations', p.96 (Giovanna's paper brings in the essay)
15. Jamaica Kincaid, 1988, op. cit., p.36
16. Ibid, pp.36-37
17. Ibid, p.37
18. Ibid, p.41
19. Ibid, p.51
20. Ibid, p.57
21. Ibid, p.57
22. Ibid, p.58
23. Ibid, p.61
24. Ibid, p.61
25. Ibid, p.63
26. Ibid, p.66
27. Ibid, p.68
28. Ibid, p.60
29. Ibid, p.60
30. Ibid, p.54
31. Ibid, p.9
32. Ibid, p.10
33. Ibid, p.69

34. Ibid, p.74
35. Ibid, p.81
36. Ibid, p.78
37. Ibid, pp.80
38. Ibid, p.79-80
39. Ibid, p.81
40. Thomas Pynchon, *Gravity's Rainbow*, Viking, New York, 1973.
41. Jamaica Kincaid, 1988, op. cit., p.53.
42. Ibid, p.36.
43. Jamaica Kincaid, 1983, op. cit., p.5.
44. Ibid, p.46.
45. Ibid, p.52.
46. Jamaica Kincaid, 1988, op. cit., p.16.
47. Jamaica Kincaid, 1983, op. cit., p.46.
48. Ibid, p.52.
49. Ibid, p.49.
50. Gayatra C. Spivak, 'Woman in Difference: Mahasweta Devi's Douloti the Bountiful' in Ross et al. (eds.), *Nationalism and Sexualities*, Routledge, New York, 1991, pp.96-117.
51. Angela Carter, 'Notes from the Frontline' in Michelene Wandor (ed.), *On Gender and Writing*, Pandora, London, 1983, pp.69-77.
52. Jamaica Kincaid, 1985b, op. cit., p.76.
53. Ibid, p.78.
54. Jamaica Kincaid, 1988, op. cit., p.35.
55. Ibid, p.45.
56. Ibid, p.42.
57. Ibid, p.49.
58. Roland Barthes 'The Death of the Author' in Stephen Heath (ed.), *Image, Music, Text*, Fontana, London, 1977.
59. Jamaica Kincaid, 1988, op. cit., p.14.
60. Kenneth Ramchand, 'West Indian Literary History: Literariness, Orality and Periodization, *Callaloo*, 11(1), Winter, 1988, pp.95-110, quotation p.110.
61. Jamaica Kincaid, 1983, op. cit., p.61.
62. Jamica Kincaid, *Lucy*, Farrar, New York, 1990.
63. Quoted in Leslie Garis, 'Through West Indian Eyes', *New York Times Magazine*, 7 October, 1990.
64. Ibid
65. Sidonie Smith, *A Poetics of Women's Autobiography: Marginality and the Fictions of Self-Representation,* Indiana University Press, Bloomington, 1987, pp.174-75.
66. Jamaica Kincaid, 1990, op. cit., p.66.
67. Ibid, p.133.

68. Ibid, p.8.
69. Ibid, p.77.
70. Ibid, p.78.
71. Ibid, p.133.
72. Ibid, p.9.
73. Ibid, p.5.
74. Ibid, p.7.
75. Ibid, pp.39-41.
76. Ibid, pp.35-36.
77. Ibid, p.90.
78. Ibid, p.123.
79. Ibid, p.132.
80. Ibid, p.134.
81. Smith, op.cit.
82. Jamaica Kincaid, 1990, op. cit., p.134-35.
83. Ibid, p.137.
84. Ibid, p.160.
85. Ibid, p.149.
86. Ibid, p.139.
87. Ibid, p.152-53.
88. Ibid, p.162-63.
89. Maxine Hong Kingston, *The Woman Warrior,* Vintage, New York, 1976.
90. Quoted in Garis, op. cit., pp.80, 91.
91. Smith devotes Chapter 8 of her book to an analysis of Kingston's text, which she reads as a postmodern work challenging the ideology of the individual, of gender, and of the dominant culture; she convincingly shows how the text functions as 'five confrontations with the fictions of self-representation and with the autobiographical possibilities embedded in cultural fictions, specifically as they interpenetrate one another in the autobiography a woman could write', and she emphasises the importance of 'the mother, who, as her point of origin, commands the tenuous negotiation of identity and difference in a drama of filiality that reaches through the daughter's subjectivity to her textual self-authoring' (p.151).
92. For a critical exposition of the terms of this argument, see Linda Alcoff, 'Cultural Feminism vs Post-Structuralism: the Identity Crisis in Feminist Theory', *Signs,* 13(3), 1988, pp.405-36.
93. Jamaica Kincaid, 1990, op. cit., p.131-32, 142, 163.
94. Ibid, pp.127-128.
95. Ibid, p.149.
96. Ibid, p.134.
97. Quoted in Louise Kennedy, 'A Writer Retraces Her Steps', *Boston Globe*, 7 November 1990.

98. Jamaica Kincaid, 1990, op. cit., p.98.
99. Quoted in Kennedy, 1990, op. cit.
100. John McGowan, *Postmodernism and Its Critics*, Ithaca, Cornell UP, 1991.
101. Ibid.
102. Audre Lorde, *Sister Outsider*, Crossing, Trumansburg, NY, 1984.
103. Jamaica Kincaid, 1990, op. cit., p.51-52.
104. Ibid, p.15.
105. Jamaica Kincaid, 'On Seeing England for the First Time', *Translations*, 51, 1991, pp.32-40.
106. Margarita Zamora, 'Abreast of Colombus: Gender and Discovery', *Cultural Critique,* Winter, 1990-91, pp.127-149.
107. Trinh T. Minh-ha, *When the Moon Waxes Red: Representation, Gender and Cultural Politics*, Routledge, New York, 1991.
108. Jamaica Kincaid, 1991, op. cit., p.37.
109. Jamaica Kincaid, 1990, op. cit., p.135.
110. Jamaica Kincaid, 1991, op. cit., p.37.
111. Ibid, p.34.
112. Ibid, p.40.
113. Ibid, p.36.
114. Ibid, p.40.

This paper has been re-worked from previously published papers.

VIEWS FROM WITHIN AND BETWIXT GENRES

Part two brings together writers, critics and teachers with a multi-dimensional interest in the literature. A range of perspectives from the 'academy' to the infant classroom; from the academic essay to the writer's personal view or the teachers' discussion is represented in this section. Out of the intersecting space, therefore, various interpretations are offered which contribute to the on-going debate.

The discussion focuses upon texts of broad generic classification - poetry, short story, novels, and romances - as well as genre mixed texts such as song texts, poetry-song texts, collages of postmodern texts and children's literature. Questions arise which concern relations within and betwixt genres and meanings to be found in terms of aesthetic resistance of the emergent literature to established forms. Central to much of the debate is the question of orality and its function in the literature. The two final papers, however, shift the focus to the imposition of popular genre within the region and to comparison, beyond the Caribbean, of treatment of genre.

David Marriott's essay 'Figures of Silence and Orality in the Poetry of M. Nourbese Philip' explores the generically compounded text 'She Tries Her Tongue Her Silence Softly Breaks'. Through this work David Marriott discusses Nourbese Philip's use of 'psychoanalytic terms in her reading of silence and language'. Investigating the dialectical nature of Nourbese Philip's position on silence, one which appears to transcend the oral-scribal split of 'nation language' accounts of Caribbean culture', David Marriott highlights particularly the way in which Nourbese Philip encodes meanings in voices, the body, fantasy and psychic effects. Nourbese Philip's 'liberatory poetic' text is shown to be profoundly dialogic in its figuration of silence and orality.

When the discussion moves to 'black femininity and the social bond', the focus turns to the confrontation central to Nourbese Philip's poetics. That confrontation: 'colonialism's narcissistic fantasy of the white male tongue-penis-word and the disarticulation and fragmentation of the black female body as silence-in-words' is highlighted through a reading of 'Looking For Livingstone'. The 'issue of orality and discourse in black feminist discussions of voice, identity and mothertongue' is addressed and Nourbese Philip's figuration of the tongue and body of the black mother and the silencing of black women in the enslavement colonial experience is explored. Nourbese Philip's 'poetological and dialectical reflection' is interrogated to reveal 'colonialism as sexual pathology' with black femininity itself a 'writing-in-pieces' in the signifying of psychic trauma of the black colonial experience. Marriott shows how Nourbese Philip's use of 'demotic figures' has reinscribed both voice and body of the African Caribbean woman into the literature.

Morgan Dalphinis' 'Caribbean Traditional songs: Saint Lucian Lawòz and Lamagwit Songs within the Caribbean and African Tradition' is, in contrast, grounded in orality derived from rootedness in the orature, a performance aspect of oral culture, of the region. The role of women in song related performance is explored and while song texts and Saint Lucian Chantwel or Female lead singers are of central concern, illustration is given of the generic range of 'traditional ' songs and the use of songs in poetic forms in Caribbean oral and emergent scribal culture. Ways in which the song/poetry of Merle Collins functions variously as social criticism or, for purposes of emphasis, or, 'to remember' or store 'Creole within musical memory' are indicated.

Folk songs of the work song genre are discussed and linked to dance and spirit possession which surface in the literature. Magwit and Lawòz songs, derived from 'old negro societies' yet present in forms which are manifested in contemporary St Lucian Creole are a particular focus. Implications of the 'flower societies' are drawn out to indicate ways in which they carry 'traces of previous power' as well as ethnic and social rivalries still exploited contemporaneously by local women.

In 'Keeping Tradition Alive', Jean Buffong, like Morgan Dalphinis similarly steeped in the oral culture seeks to define for the writer a role akin to that of the traditional storyteller. Within her vision of the woman writer's role, the mothertongue, Creoles of the region, vitalise the emerging women's literature imbued with a range of features drawn from the orature of the region, its traditional tales, proverbs, riddles and so on.

The conversation between Susanna Steele and Joan Anim-Addo, 'New Encounters: Availability, Acceptability and Accessibility of Caribbean Women Writers' articulates the dialogue that is often not represented between colleagues concerned with the teaching of the new literature; teachers at the 'cutting edge' of practice in literary studies determining the status of new works vis à vis courses and programmes of study within the higher education curriculum. The textual focus of the piece is Merle Collins's

The Walk, foregrounded in the discussion of three issues: availability, acceptability and accessibility of the new literature critical to the teaching of Caribbean Women's writing.

In 'Children Should Be Seen and Spoken To: Or Writing For and About Children' Thelma Perkins focuses on the writing of children's literature as well as upon the writing of childhood. Whether or not children's literature represents a separate genre, it has been an area affording publication openings to many Caribbean women writers. Thelma Perkins indicates this and relates publication to the extending of oral communication with children within families and classrooms. The discussion concerning the process of researching and writing includes a focus upon memories. Illustrating the process, Thelma Perkins draws upon her experience of writing for publication and the 'sense of history' with which this connects.

Jane Bryce's 'A World Of Caribbean Romance': Reformulating The Legend of Love' is concerned with how 'romance formula' in the tradition of Mills and Boon is appropriated and rewritten by Caribbean writers. The question encoded in the subtitle - 'Can a Caress Be Culturally Specific' - lies at the heart of the essay which focuses on the emergence of Caribbean romantic fiction through the 'popular' Heinemann series, 'Caribbean Caresses'.

The discussion, located within the context of both 'western romance fiction and feminist theory' draws upon 'other postcolonial appropriations' notably the romance genre in Nigeria. Formulaic representation, derived from European discourse of 'chivalry' and notions of a 'lady' is problematised in the Caribbean context, a site of negative stereotyping of black female sexuality and where the region itself is represented as an exotic 'paradisiacal' location. Jane Bryce considers in the light of this, the dynamics of a form shaped by such paradoxes. Valerie Belgrave's *Ti Marie* is examined as a precursor to the romance series and Jane Bryce surveys six published 'Caribbean Caresses' titles, assessing the extent to which the writers have become entrapped by the formula or, alternatively, through fantasy rewritten women's desire locally.

Part two closes with Mary Condé's *'Houses and Homes:* Elizabeth Jolley's *Mr Scobie's Riddle* and Beryl Gilroy's *Frangipani House'* . The essay offers a critical comparison of the two works with particular reference to the treatment of old age and guilt. In drawing out differences and similarities between the texts, both written by contemporaries who left their respective homes at a similar period in their lives, Mary Condé considers also the significance of houses and homes in much Caribbean women's writing. In addition, the connection between the activities of reading and writing and the old people's homes in the two texts is highlighted.

Figures of Silence and Orality in the Poetry of M. Nourbese Philip

David Marriott

> While I continue to write in my father tongue, I continue the quest I identified in 1983 to discover my mother tongue, trying to engender by some alchemical practice a metamorphosis within the language from father tongue to mother tongue.[1]

Writing of her attempts to inscribe, in poetry, the multiplicity of voices that compose her 'dark continent of silence' - a racialised and feminine figure denoting something mute and voiceless within nineteenth-century European discourses of race, gender and psyche - the African Canadian Caribbean poet, M. Nourbese Philip, goes on to ask a series of questions central to her poetics:

> Is the polyvocular the natural voicedness of women and Blacks? Is it because our sense of self is constituted of so many representations - the gaps, the silences between those selves - the many selves presented to us as African or woman. The disjunctures between. What we know ourselves to be; what others say we are. Do we fall between the gaps of these objective selves - the selves presented?[2]

The lingual structure of those gaps in the black and feminine unconscious, in whose absence an unsublatable indeterminacy in the structure of speech emerges as a voiceless voice, receives an extensive elaboration in Philip's third book of poetry, *She Tries Her Tongue; Her Silence Softly Breaks*.

absenceloss tears   laughter   grief
in any language
                                                      the same
only larger
                                   for the silence
                                                      monstrosity
obscenity
tongueless wonder

blackened stump of a tongue
torn
out
withered
petrified
burnt
on the pyres of silence
a mother's child foreign
made
by a tongue that cursed
the absence
in loss
tears laughtergrief
in the word

M. Nourbese Philip[3]

What could it mean to say that the spacing between words in this poem is the same as that of silence? That there is an immanent muteness and illocutionary interruption of 'black' tongues as a result of the 'middle passage' and the lingual dismemberment of African language communities? And what could it mean to construct the tongue and body of the black mother as the privileged figure of this silence, as the key to the rememory of those excluded 'archaisms of the semiotic body' within New World cultures?[4] The identity of the maternal-feminine resulting from the conjunction of silence and an abject femininity viewed as the excluded 'instance of all culture'[5] is frequently construed as an engendered rather than racialised position, for example, the work of Julia Kristeva, and more generally *écriture féminine.*[6] Philip's attempt to identify the black mother tongue as the privileged figure of what Julia Kristeva terms the 'semiotic', which refers to the difficulty of a subject's entry into language and which privileges the maternal body as the key to the pre-Oedipal sexuality of the female child, associating such maternity with the spacing of language and poetic practice, raises an altogether different series of questions when the semiotic concerned emerges in the unconscious gaps of a colonial experience and one which seemingly valorises black femininity within the social symbolic as a selfhood based largely on abjection. In both her poetic and critical work, Philip, by trying to articulate a *figure* or *image* 'about women, words, language and silence' and the colonial and slave 'edicts that established the parameters of silence for the African in the New World',[7] has sought to interrogate the relationship between black femininity, negativity and silence at the heart of recent debates in both psychoanalysis and feminism concerning racial and sexual difference, language and culture.

If one of the most important themes or series of themes in these debates has been the expressive qualities of silence, in the sense of exile and marginalisation, abjection and learning to speak 'otherwise', then one of the least interrogated - but ultimately more far-reaching in its effects and implications - has been the continued interest in the interaction between word and silence as a metatrope for signifying the complex interrelations between language, race and gender.[8] The proposition that language, as a product of desire, is also an inescapably gendered and racialised phenomenon, expressing a lack that can never be fulfilled, raises important issues concerning any poetics employing silence to signify racial and sexual difference. Gayatri Chakravorty Spivak, criticising the theorists of *écriture féminine* for an inability or disinclination to discriminate clearly between deconstructing a metaphysics of identity and masculinist ideologies, argues that the Caribbean subaltern women must be able to 'make audible what...suffers silently in the holes of discourse'.[9]

Such an attempt to make the subaltern woman speak could be counterposed to Julia Kristeva's more nuanced claim that 'in 'woman' I see something that cannot be represented, something that is not said, something above and beyond nomenclatures and ideologies'.[10] If the signifier 'woman' presents an impossible signification rather than a representation, constructed so as to signify or figure an essential negativity introduced into the symbolic order, then 'woman' can only be made audible through the silences she leaves in discourse, she can only signify as the negativity of semiotic transgression. If this is the case, then the question of how to challenge the very form of 'self-definition without losing the possibility of speech' becomes all the more pressing for a liberatory poetic attempting to reinscribe the maternal-feminine inside the interrupted interval between speech and silence.[11]

In her impressive narrative in poetry and prose, *Looking for Livingstone; An Odyssey of Silence*, the question of how 'woman', as the signifier *par excellence* of silence held together by 'the invisible but necessary word',[12] constitutes an impossible signification which is, in turn, a manifestation of extreme dereliction in the social bond, is also intimately linked to an attempt to uncover the psychic pain and aggressivity of 'woman' in the social order. Consigned to a position of abjection in the symbolic realm as an empty signifier but one constantly written over, erased, and reread, the signifier 'woman', Philip argues, needs to be repossessed of her 'silence' as desire, as a wordless flow of drives and appetites, as a fecundity passed on to the child through the mother's tongue. The question of how men and women identify or disidentify with the symbolic domain of a culture is thus, for

Philip, interchangeable with a poetological and dialectical reflection on the interrelations between language and silence. If the signifier 'woman' is nothing more than the articulation of the withdrawal of subaltern silence - a withdrawal which nonetheless leaves its traces - from the social symbolic, then, no longer capable of designating herself than as 'other' within herself, 'woman' becomes what Irigaray terms the 'other meaning' of language and culture.[13] If the other meaning of silence defaces the word, translating the signifying function of 'woman' into negativity and death, so too, the social symbolic is infected as it were by this disfiguration, leaving room for the subaltern voice to signify an altered form of speech and to connote an interruption of any poetics of identity based on speech itself.

Philip's intervention into the ongoing debate concerning the status of orality and gender in Caribbean poetry and culture is thus an important rereading of black femininity in terms of psychic negativity, silence, disfigurement and death. In the readings that follow, I will be discussing Philip's use of psychoanalytic terms in her reading of silence and language. But first, I will address the issue of orality and discourse in black feminist discussions of voice, identity and the mother tongue. In particular, I want to investigate how Philip's position on silence seems to be a dialectical one that, rather than simply reproduce the oral-scribal split of 'nation language' accounts of Caribbean culture,[14] depends rather on a deep understanding of the relation between voice, body, unconscious fantasy and psychic affect.

Transcribing the Archive: Rememory and the Caribbean Demotic

> seek   search and   uproot
> the forget and remember of root words
>
> M. Nourbese Philip[15]

If in order to understand 'woman' as silence we have to understand this silence as neither an ethics of responsibility nor as a beyond of language, it may be good to know what this silence comes down to. Rather than proceed too quickly to the conclusion that such silence refers directly to the lack of words capable of speaking the events of colonialism and slavery, however we read this silence it cannot be dissociated from the working through of memory and mourning in those racial catastrophes of European history. In other words, such silence is an archive of alterity and difference, of loss and violence - an archive containing the silences of 'woman' and of blacks. The question then becomes how one writes and remembers this silence given that it cannot be either easily written or read. Uncovering such silence becomes the work of writing as a process of memorialisation and of the working of the poetic as already other, naming the foreignness of self. This task takes on a particular urgency given the traditional historical excision and exclusion of women and blacks from the archive that is writing.

In *She Tries Her Tongue*, Philip privileges a hearing and reading of the poem which can 'keep the deep structure, the movement, the kinetic energy, the tone and pitch, the slides and glissandos of the demotic within a tradition that is primarily page-bound'.[16] Philip's own reading of her attempt to write into the body of her writing the multiplicity of New World voices, whilst preserving 'writing as the most intimate relation of the body of the woman to itself',[17] emphasises the corporeality of language and of the mother's tongue as both emerge in the irremediable gaps of the silent printed text. In this view, scribalised oral form, resisting the hermeneutic separation of sound and sight in the hearing of the poem, attends to the full spectacle of the poetic word as a scribal-oral event rather than to just phonetic transcriptions of voice. These written figures of orality open onto a caesura between the linguistic and phenomenal worlds, a caesura whose name is that of 'woman' and whose figure is that of 'silence'. Under the sign of the 'Caribbean demotic', to which she assigns a complex, multifaceted and polysemic array of dialects and discourses - and one opposed to the cultural univocality of 'English', Philip strives to avoid the two extremes of a solely English-oriented transcription of voice - which would reduce the orality of desire, of remembering, to that of an hegemonic linguistic code - and a radical phonetic departure from the English acrolect - which would transform orality into an illusory presencing of a non-discursive authenticity. This attempt to preserve the interval between speaking and the hearing of a text, is also an attempt to preserve the distinctiveness of the Caribbean demotic as a double archival symbolic.

In its syntax and morphology the demotic is structured by a radical diasporic genealogy with African, East Indian, European and Ameriindian word roots; and in its preponderantly English-derived vocabulary it negotiates the gap between memory, violence and the social symbolic. In a reflection that reminds one of Edouard Glissant's theory of *ántillante*, a cultural syncretism based on transnational and translational differences, Philip writes: 'the linguistic rape and forced marriage between African and English tongues has resulted in a language capable of great rhythms and musicality; one that is and is not English, and one which is among the most vital in the English-speaking world today'.[18] There can be no limit to what Glissant terms the polysemic and 'unlimited *métissage*'[19] of the Caribbean demotic and its cultural genealogies, there can be no return to a fixed monosemic origin which escapes the dialectic of archive and loss, rootedness and diaspora. The linguistic continuum of the Caribbean demotic is not therefore reducible to a univocal conception of identity; nor can it be the self-realisation of a cultural exclusivity. In the figures of silence and orality which Philip uses to 'i-mage' or denote demotic variants, the Caribbean archipelago emerges as a complex, polyvalent network of languages fundamentally hybrid in structure. Like the place of language in memory, repetition and recollection, the place of the demotic in the Caribbean writerly text is thus not a primary fact of closure, but the secondary working through of multiple silences that inhabit the unity of the text itself.

Philip's notion of the demotic is thus a rememoralisation of the silent black body and its figuring through interlectal hybridity which disfigures and disrupts the monosemic body of the imperial word. There are two central figures in her poetry which may be taken as key demotic tropes - the dual unity of mother and child as a unity of tongue and mouth and the black maternal body as a 'body-in-pieces'. Both figural tropes involve a radical rereading of psychoanalytic feminist accounts of the maternal body in its interface with language. The examples chosen derive from 'Discourse on the Logic of Language'.

> WHEN IT WAS BORN, THE MOTHER HELD HER NEWBORN CHILD CLOSE: SHE BEGAN THEN TO LICK IT ALL OVER. THE CHILD WIMPERED A LITTLE, BUT AS THE MOTHER'S TONGUE MOVED FASTER AND STRONGER OVER ITS BODY, IT GREW SILENT - THE MOTHER'S TURNING IT THIS WAY AND THAT UNDER HER TONGUE UNTIL SHE HAD TONGUED IT CLEAN OF THE CREAMY WHITE SUBSTANCE COVERING ITS BODY.[20]

> THE MOTHER THEN PUT HER FINGERS INTO HER CHILD'S MOUTH - GENTLY FORCING IT OPEN; SHE TOUCHES HER TONGUE TO THE CHILD'S TONGUE, AND HOLDING THE TINY MOUTH OPEN, SHE BLOWS INTO IT - HARD. SHE WAS BLOWING WORDS - HER WORDS, HER MOTHER'S WORDS, THOSE OF HER MOTHER'S MOTHER, AND ALL THEIR MOTHERS BEFORE - INTO HER DAUGHTER'S MOUTH.[21]

In both passages, the child's instinctual orality is essentially passive, the figures of forcing and violence through which the transgenerational maternal unconscious (embodied in the mother's words and tongue) is transmitted, pass over the infant's body reducing it to silence. However there is no suggestion here of what Julia Kristeva calls 'abjection,' the primordial fear situated at the point where the infant first splits from the body of the mother, 'finding at once in the body and in the terrifying gap that opens up between them the only space for the constitution of its own identity, the only distance which will allow it to become a user of words'.[22] For Philip, on the contrary, if there is a void to be filled between mother and daughter it is not one of abjection, in which language functions as a counter-phobic object, but a violent gift of orality from the maternal unconscious to that of the child's. Accordingly, Kristeva's representation of the mother-daughter relationship as one of abjection - an account running the risk of placing the mother-daughter outside of any social-symbolic contract thereby reinstating sexual differentiation into the socialising process[23] - is revised by Philip in order to reinvest the maternal-feminine as the site of inheritance, knowledge and law rather than as abjection vis-à-vis paternal authority. The question of whether this is or is not an idealisation of the maternal should therefore be secondary to two issues or problems: the mother's blowing of words into her daughter's mouth could indeed be a warding off of anxiety, a metaphorisation of a more primordial fear, as Kristeva contends. On the other hand, the fact that the child's mouth must be forced and held open - whilst contradicting any naive phenomenological dream of a meaning-laden imbrication of body and word, subject and language, in which there is an elective affinity between black mothers and daughters prior to any entry into a racist symbolic - nevertheless points to the fact that writing is violence - that there can be no liberation of orality from the strictures of discourse. Accordingly, Philip's account of the dual unity between mother and female child, defining it essentially in terms of its functions as reparation and symptom, does not stop there but moves on to consider the psychic identification of orality with metaphors of the body, with the gaps of desire experienced in the physical production of speech. In other words, the psychic dynamic of orality, writing and speech cannot be dissociated from the act of symbolising an identity at the point in which it first constitutes itself in speech. Philip writes: 'When I was done with *She Tries*...I could point to the exact place on my body from which it had come from - the right abdominal area. For months after I felt a sensation - not pain, but akin, I suppose, to the ache of the missing or phantom limb'.[24]

If Philip's figure of demotic writing - which one could name a phantom haunted by its own negativity - is accepted, then the printed word becomes the carrier of its own 'amnesiac blow',[25] produced by, but also productive of, a notion of the Caribbean demotic as the image of its own interruption, as an event of identity and difference within the production of speech. And if the dual unity is thus an image of the way in which the black female subject can relibinidise the word as psychic object, the irreparable shattering of the tongue into withdrawal and silence - 'the grief sealed in memory'[26] - is no less a symbol of narcissistic injury and psychic dereliction. Interrupting the two passages cited above Philip introduces a poem which is itself a symbolisation of narcissistic catastrophe resulting from the incorporation and encryption of a racist symbolic.

English
is my mother tongue.
A mother tongue is not
is not a foreign lan lan lang
language
l/anguish
anguish
- a foreign anguish.

English is
my father tongue.
A father tongue is
a foreign language,
therefore English is
a foreign language
not a mother tongue.

What is my mother
tongue
my mammy tongue
my mummy tongue
my momsy tongue
my modder tongue
my ma tongue?

I have no mother
tongue
no mother to tongue
no tongue to mother
to mother
tongue
me

I must therefore be tongue
dumb
dumb-tongued
dub-tongued
damn dumb
tongue
[.....]

Nourbese Philip[27]

In *She Tries Her Tongue*, the poem as a textual body-in-pieces comes itself to signify a cycle of meta-metaphorical movement - in the sense of a meta-troping and turning on language as act, resistance, voice, and translation - from negativity to an extreme form of regression. This dialectic between demand and desire - desiring a psychic integration with the mother tongue and demanding such representation be integrated into the social body - is also a dialectic between power and sign which opens in the poetic speaking a meta-metaphorical movement of inversion and regression symbolised through the chiastic figures of mother and tongue, foreignness and anguish. The poem itself, relatively straightforward in its performativity and almost antinomian in its construction, seems to reenact the eradication of ethnolinguistic difference symbolised by the loss of a mother tongue, a loss construed as a catastrophe of the black body in its relation to words. Such a catastrophe opens a deformative spacing of the word that cannot be reversed into the topos of a father tongue. The resulting phobic dereliction is that of a silence that needs must remain unattainable even for the fragmented self, and becomes instead translated into the problem of repairing the internal object (the good memory of the mother's words) which has been damaged by the negativity of colonial-masculine social death and violence. In other words, the trauma resulting from maternal loss represents a failure of symbolisation which cannot be incorporated as such, which cannot be fully incorporated into the meaningful context of the poem.

Therefore rather than turn to art as a form of sublimation or satisfaction - a process Freud termed 'regression in the service of the ego' - in *She Tries Her Tongue* the disjunctive logic of the poems locate the split and anguish associated with the loss of the maternal body at the point where the subject discovers her racial dereliction and silence; a splitting and negativity that cannot be overcome and that shows itself in a bodily experience that cannot be reintegrated into an ordinary notion of self. In her 'Afterword' to *She Tries Her Tongue*, Philip discusses the problematic of being in language in terms of the ways in which the body can be directly translated into psychical and textual process: 'there was a profound eruption of the body into the text of *She Tries Her Tongue*'.[28] Philip's poetry attempts to speak out of the materiality of the body as writing; but within psychic figures of silence and orality that, as much as they are buried in the disfigurement and deformation of the morphological and lexical denigration of the black female body, still remain the nexus of a figural eruption of unconscious desire and fantasy into the surface discourse of the text. Discourse is disrupted because the originary fantasy of the maternal tongue is not that of ordinary language or representation, but that of the work of desire. Figures of orality in *She Tries Her Tongue* are nothing other than the negativising of a translation of desire into patrilineal linguistic terms and, by the power of that negativity, they also work to preserve the detotalised body of the maternal word. In other words, these figures are determined by a continuity of negativity that 'writes' itself within itself, enclosed like a word on the tongue. This absorption of the unintegrated word by figural desire itself passes away into silence of a thing or the 'body-in-pieces' and into every word that intends that thing; the word - or the name - itself cut by a process of negativity by which psychic events come to register in the writing down of a word. In the next section my discussion of this process of negativity will centre on Philip's rereading of black feminity and the social bond.

'A Body in Pieces': Black Feminity and the Social Bond

Reflecting on the role of language within colonialism, Philip writes: 'only when we understand language and its role in colonial society can we understand the role of writing and the writer in such a society'.[29] The figures of orality and silence would therefore not be, in this sense, enclosed in a self-referential aestheticism or metaphysics of the poetic work. Rather, they relate to a politics of orality and sexual difference in relation to colonialism and language. Having sketched the determining power of the figure of mother, mapped out with reference to the tonguing of the mother identified both as site of difference and as oral void in which the subject may be effaced, the dominant image of orality which emerges is that of a figure of inversion which collapses both an inside and outside of the body within the subject's psyche. One could demonstrate the fantasmatic affect of the mother's mouth understood as both oral void and transgenerational gift in terms of both its obsessional recurrence - as a substitutive trope always retraceable to metaphors of silence and orality - in Philip's *She Tries Her Tongue* and her poetic work generally. Strikingly, the oral void experienced by the black woman in these works also emerges as a hole in colonial textuality. The stakes - and the eventual outcome - of the confrontation between colonialism's narcissistic fantasy of the white male tongue-penis-word and the disarticulation and fragmentation of the black female body as a silence-in-words is thus central to Philip's poetics, as a reading of *Looking for Livingstone* makes clear. Recounting two recurring dreams in which the colonial-masculine tongue is incorporated as a foreign body into the silent mouth and vagina of the black woman, Philip writes:

> HE - LIVINGSTONE - AND I COPULATE LIKE TWO BEASTS - HE RIDES ME - HIS WORD SLIPPING IN AND OUT OF THE WET MOIST SPACES OF MY SILENCE - I TAKE HIS WORD - STRONG AND THRUSTING - THAT WILL NOT REST, WILL NOT BE DENIED IN ITS

SEARCH TO FILL EVERY CREVICE OF MY SILENCE - I TAKE IT INTO THE SILENCE OF MY MOUTH [....]

IN MY SECOND DREAM I AM HUGE AND HEAVY, BLOWN UP LIKE A SOW ABOUT TO FARROW - THE FRUIT OF HIS WORD. PREGNANT FOR ONE THOUSAND AND TWO YEARS - MY LABOUR AN AGONY THAT LASTS FOREVER AS I STRUGGLE TO BIRTH - NOW SQUATTING, NOW KNEELING, NOW SITTING, NOW WALKING - I GROAN AND GRUNT LIKE THE ANIMAL I AM, KEENING AND WAILING I TRY TO BIRTH THE MONSTROUS PRODUCT OF HIS WORD AND MY SILENCE - CONCEIVED IN THE SILENCE OF MY OWN, MY VERY OWN WOMB

M. Nourbese Philip[30]

Undoubtedly, it is the non-relation, the absence of a relation, or something other than a relation that is being recounted in this thrusting of words into vaginal and oral silence, a scenario represented in terms of a foreignness inhabiting the female body and as a form of psychosis resulting from the painful psychic splitting of the female body in its pregnant state. The incorporation and ejection of the colonial-masculine word yields to a rhetoric of dejection - 'a monstrous product' - figured through a grotesque embodiment of possession by a foreign anguish, or word. However it would not be enough to define the alterity of Philip's 'dark continent of silence' as a beyond of words, as an absolute otherness negativising, as it were, the 'invagination' of colonial discourse. The figure of invagination is here yoked to the logic of colonialism as sexual pathology which may be understood to yield arguments based on psycho-sexual accounts of political identification. Hortense J. Spillers has described the total objectification of the captive body under enslavement and colonisation as a cultural ungendering of the black female body and a violent rewriting of black maternity: 'under conditions of captivity, the offspring of the female does not 'belong' to the Mother, nor is s/he 'related' to the 'owner,' though the latter 'possesses' it, and in the African-American [and West Indian] instance, often fathered it, and, as often, without whatever benefit of patrimony'.[31] In this reading of familial kinship in terms of legal property relations and commodified exchange the reproductive uses of the black mother may result in the maternal body becoming a 'body-in-pieces' for the enslaved child and its earliest affective processes in two main ways. Firstly, in the traumatic recollection of kinship loss by adult slaves, phantasies of the subject's own ego fragmentation and psychic aggressivity associated with her social death as a person are transferred onto the *imago* of the mother as a fragmented body. In this sense the maternal body acts as a metonymic figure for the child's own sense of pre-Oedipal distintegration. Secondly, mother-child separation results in the child's introjection of corporeal dislocation as the mother's own unconscious aggressivity and sense of loss is intrapsychically passed onto the child - a dual movement aptly described by Frederick Douglass: ' For what this separation is [sic] done, I do not know, unless it be to hinder the development of the child's affection toward its mother, and to blunt and destroy the natural affection of the mother for the child'.[32] The psychic dereliction of black maternity thus has - as the mode of relation, of primary affect - an intimate link to the 'profound natal alienation of the slave'.[33]

What is unspeakable and left unspoken in the violent histories of black women under colonialism and slavery, a cultural symbolic riven by trauma and mourning, is both the singular event of black maternity representing its own death to itself as spectacle, theatre, sacrifice, in which the maternal was hollowed out, encrypted, in a derelict kinship unable to name itself as such; and the impossible working through of such an event in the kinship relations of ancestral ties and communities.[34] Hence the dual unity between mother and child in which the mother's unconscious was secretly passed on to the child, involved a secret which said (silently) black maternity was essentially one of negativity, bringing death into the world as represented by the social death experienced by black infants in order to feed the maternal death symbolised by the 'peculiar institution' of slavery. In both the body of slave narrative writing and the racist social symbolic the fragmentation of the black body occurs retroactively for a post-Oedipal subject, i.e. the white symbolic gaze is always already in the black mother's unconscious which she then passes on to the child in the forcing open of its mouth and the blowing of words into it. The child's mirror stage is thus refracted through her own dereliction, i.e. the black maternal body is already a body in pieces and the child's oedipal complex is already a symptom, an inherited irresolution whose form is passed on from the mother.

To the extent that black Caribbean women writers use Creole locutions to figure the two deaths outlined above, ranging from basilectal Creole to allegorise and veil the violence of unspeakable things - a semiocentric inversion of any ability of language to simply 'represent' psychic trauma as such - to inversions and appropriations of the acrolect, such heteroglossic figures of orality are not straightforwardly interlectal as some linguists would suggest.[35] These figures signify a use of language which no longer refers to something absent, but is itself the process of an impossible signification rather than representation, since the history of those two deaths - death of maternity and death as a person - can not be easily brought into everyday language as an experience used to represent a self. In both *Looking for Livingstone* and *She Tries Her Tongue* Philip uses such impossible signification to suggest black feminity is itself a writing-in-pieces, a rupture that intersects and disrupts a self-presencing of self, a fissuring and fragmenting of the body of the word by an écriture of mutilation, sacrifice and death. In other words, there is a phobic remainder at the surface of her texts which actively resists any recuperation into a centre, or narrative, and one which actively resists any limit to its own labour of the negative as a self-presencing of self. Finally, Philip suggests the possibility of a further recuperation of the 'symbolic' relationship between black maternity and feminity at the level of a nonlinear genealogy, a possibility she represents as a maternal orality passed on from the mother's mouth to the daughter's tongue.

If Philip's reading of black feminity as a palimpsest of orality makes writerly presentation itself impossible (and yet bases itself on writing as its own condition of possibility), does this not make her attempt at reclamation of a black maternal silence itself impossible? Against the exclusivity of an either/or position my reading of Philip has tried to show how her use of demotic figures of silence and orality construes black feminity as the *interdict*, or interruptive figure of the mutual imbrication of language and culture, voicing and silence in colonial and neo-colonial discourse. In her attempt to invert the historical exclusion of the black woman's voice and body from both the nationalist and neo-colonial texts of reason - texts which have traditionally consigned her to an 'elsewhere' of governmentality, of law and of nation - Philip has tried to reinscribe this voice in all its materiality and difference, to make it once again 'readable' in all its heterogeneity and difference as a dialogism of silence and orality, of mouth and tongue.

Notes

1. Marlene Nourbese Philip, *She Tries Her Tongue, Her Silence Softly Breaks*, The Woman's Press, London, 1993, p.90.
2. Marlene Nourbese Philip, 'The Habit of: Poetry, Rats, and Cats' in J. Spahr and M. Wallace et al. (eds.) *A Poetics of Criticism*, Leave Books, New York, 1994, p.211.
3. Ibid, p.66
4. J. Rose, 'Julia Kristeva: Take Two' in K. Oliver (ed.) *Ethics, Politics, and Difference in Julia Kristeva's Writing,* Routledge, London and New York, 1993, p.49.
5. Ibid, p.51.
6. See for example, Helen Cixous and C. Clément, *The Newly Born Woman*, Manchester University Press, Manchester, 1986. See also translation by Betsy Wing, Manchester University Press; J. Kristeva, *Powers of Horror. An Essay in Abjection*, Columbia University Press, New York, 1982; J. Kristeva in T. Moi (ed.) *The Kristeva Reader,* Basil Blackwell, Oxford, 1986.

7. Marlene Nourbese Philip, 1994, op. cit., p.212.
8. See for example, G.C. Spivak, 'French Feminism in an International Frame', *Yale French Studies*, 61, 1981; Mohanty, C., 'Under Western Eyes: Feminist Scholarship and Colonial Discourses', *Feminist Review*, 30, 1988, pp.65-88; b. hooks, *Yearning: Race, Gender, and Cultural Politics*, Turnaround, Boston, Ma, 1991.
9. G.C. Spivak, 1981, op. cit., p.165.
10. J. Kristeva, 'Woman Can Never Be Defined' in E. Marks and I. de Courtivron (eds.) *New French Feminisms: An Anthology,* University of Massachusetts Press, Amherst, 1981, p.137.
11. J. Rose, 'Julia Kristeva: Take Two' in K. Oliver (ed.) *Ethics, Politics and Difference in Julia Kristeva's Writing,* Routledge, London and New York.
12. Marlene Nourbese Philip *Looking For Livingstone: An Odyssey Of Silence*, The Mercury Press, Canada, 1991, p.55.
13. L. Irigaray, *This Sex Which Is Not One*, Ithaca, Cornell University Press, New York, 1981, p.29.
14. See for example E. Brathwaite, *A History of the Voice; the Development of Nation Language in Anglophone Caribbean Poetry,* New Beacon, London, 1984.
15. Nourbese Philip, 1993, op. cit., p.60
16. Nourbese Philip, 1988, op. cit., p.89
17. J. Rose, *The Haunting of Sylvia Plath*, Virago Press, London, 1991, p.30.
18. Marlene Nourbese Philip, 1988, op. cit., p.89.
19. E. Glissant, *Poétique de la Relation*, Gallimard, Paris, 1990, p.46.
20. Nourbese Philip, 1993, op. cit., p.30.
21. Ibid, p.32.
22. Rose, 1991, op. cit., p.33.
23. V. Lebeau *Lost Angels: Psychoanalysis and Cinema*, Routledge, London, 1995, pp.107-8.
24. Marlene Nourbese Philip, 1994, op. cit., p.210
25. Derek Walcott, 'Laventville', *The Castaway*, Jonathan Cape, London, 1965, p.35.
26. Marlene Nourbese Philip, 1993,op. cit., p.72.
27. Ibid, p.30.
28. Ibid, p.90.
29. Ibid, p.77.
30. Marlene Nourbese Philip, 1991, op. cit., pp.25-26.
31. H.J. Spillers, 'Mama's Baby, Papa's Maybe: An American Grammar Book', *Diacritics*, 1987, p.74.
32. F. Douglass, *Narrative of the Life of Frederick Douglass An American Slave, Written by Himself*, Signet, New York, 1987, p.22.
33. See O. Patterson, *Slavery and Social Death*, Harvard University Press, Harvard, 1982.
34. See for example Toni Morrison, *Beloved*, Picador, London, 1988.
35. See for example R.B. Le Page, 'Dialect in West Indian Literature', *Journal of Commonwealth Literature*, 7, 1969, pp.1-7.

Saint Lucian Lawòz and Lamagwit Songs Within the Caribbean and African Tradition

Morgan Dalphinis

This article briefly outlines the place of Lawòz and Lamagwit songs sung by Saint Lucian Chantwèl (Female lead singers) within the African Caribbean traditions. The focus here is on song texts.

While the oral tradition itself is a universal in human cultures, there are a number of features that are characteristic of the African and the Caribbean oral tradition. These include the use of praise epithets/poems and songs, for example from praise shouted to the Housa Emir *Babba Giva!* (Big Elephant!) to the praise of great cricketers *Mi Boy!* and the use of song/poetry to describe and criticise social reality. For example, from the Hausa singers' analysis that civil war followed the granting of independence in many parts of Africa '...dark sun fada sunkashe yan uwe' (..they all quarrelled and fell upon [and killed] their brothers) to Merle Collins's clear social criticisms on the invasion of an independent Grenada by America and its aftermath:

...time passing
who in the prison frustrating
who done dead disappearing
who alive remonstrating
nuff people still mix up and hesitating
and time
just passing...

Merle Collins[1]

In some parts of the song tradition, aspects of the link with Africa are extremely clear, for example the Saint Lucian Kèlè ceremony in which the names of the dead are shouted out and the spirits of the African ancestors are called to bear witness:

Nou Jiné ka kwiyé pou fè
We Guineans are calling to tell you
Sat you mè isi
One (of us) has died (in Saint Lucia)...

Cowley[2]

As with many of the other literary genres, in both the Caribbean and African literary tradition, the content of the genre, in this case a song, can reappear within another genre such as poetry. The genres are also closely juxtaposed in the literature, for example with proverbs being characteristic of the prose used in Chinua Achebe's novels and song as a feature of the poems of Merle Collins, for example 'She Sits on the Train and Sings Inside':

'She Sits On The Train And Sings Inside'

She sits on the train and sings inside

Las abété mwen, Naporinden
Las abété mwen
Las abété mwen Naporinden
Las abété mwen
Las abété mwen Naporinden
Las abété mwen

She sits and sings snippets of remembered songs
to keep her feelings company

Oy o yoy! Lord! Look at me crosses!
They want to kill me ...

Merle Collins[3]

Amongst the 'remembered songs' are the Creole 'Las abété mwen, Naporinden', the repeated 'Oy o yoy! Look at me crosses!', 'Sad to Say I'm On My Way' and so on throughout the poem.[4] The songs are used repeatedly as a means of emphasising the theme of unhappiness and pain expressed in the poem.

Such repetition for emphasis is typical of the African Caribbean literary tradition and also features in the juxtapositioning of Creole song with English writing.[5] In Derek Walcott's poem 'Iona: Mebonye Valley', the song narrative about Ma Kileman, in Creole, is juxtaposed within the poem, in English. Ma Kileman's over-religiousness is juxtaposed, with the repeating and emphasising of Iona's lack of fidelity to men, let alone God.[6]

The use of music to reinforce the poetic text or song text is also a key device of memorisation in oral literature. This allows the Merle-like griot to remember the long king lists and descendents of Sunjate. Similarly, this allows many of us to remember the words of Sparrow's 'Melde Woi' and the modern (mis)application of our oral literature to memorizing advertisements, for example Desmond Dekka's 'Israelites' becomes the memory agent for Vitelite and Sabba Ranks' music becomes the memory agent for 'bombastic' denim jeans.

The use of song for the Creole French words in the poem 'She Sits on the Train and Sings Inside' is also a means of storing Creole within musical memory in the bilingual situation of Grenada where English is dominantly used, but Creole (French) is the traditional language of Grenadian culture.

This is comparable with the Trinidad situation in which older calypsos are in Creole (French) and modern calypsos are in Creole (English) with a number of refrains in Creole (French).

Caribbean Traditional Songs

The traditional music of the Caribbean reflects the histories of particular islands as well as forming the historical record of the Caribbean past for celebrations such as Carifesta, the Caribbean wide festival of the arts, and for the more 'culture on demand' performances for tourists at hotels. The music includes folk songs and can be classified by content and by social function. Belizian folk songs, for example, give us a clear picture of the logging and boating activities of Belize in the recent past, 1930-70.[7]

Some Jamaican folk songs also fit into the work song genre inherited from Africa and adapted within Caribbean slavery. In this genre, the song leader leads with the main song while those performing the collective work sing in chorus while carrying out collective labour or the collective motion within a piece of work e.g. chopping or pulling:

Leader	*When I was in America I hear de soldiers groaning*
Men	*Oo pullaway*
Leader	*Sally ha one steamboat a run over yanda*
Men	*Pullaway Yankee pullaway*
Leader	*Pullaway to London pullaway oh*
Men	*Pullaway Yankee pullaway.*[8]

Traditional songs are tied to a number of Caribbean dances often reflecting the slavery period as well as African religious ideas, such as spirit possession in which spirits possess the dancer/singer, at times to the accompaniment of music.

Calypso remains the dominant modern realisation of such past musical form, reflecting the critical tradition of the African griots and the social commentary of past calypsonians on slave and then colonial societies. Caribbean music carries with it the soul and experiences of the Caribbean people and carry with it periods of hope and despair loss and gain. Periods of 'nationalist' Caribbean song by Bob Marley and Jimmy Cliff were part of the demands for social justice also demanded in the sixties by people of Caribbean descent in the Americas, for example Stokely Carmichael from Trinidad and the part Grenadian Malcolm X.

Some folk songs also carry with them resonances of the past which remain very much part of the present living culture. For example, the Saint Lucian Magwit and Lawòz songs are both part of the St Lucian present and past. In the past, the songs may have expressed differences between Africans traceable from Africa itself cited in conflicts between the Fante and the Ashanti in Ghana or between the Bamabara and their Mandinka overlords in Mali. They may also have expressed Caribbean based conflicts between Black (French) revolutionary Saint Lucians and the English. In the present day, they express instead the satirical conflicts between two 'flower societies' representing the rose for Lawòz and the marguerite for Lamagwit. Both societies have their 'kings and queens and soldiers'. They ridicule each other and praise themselves in song:

Liminé Lawòz liminé
Enlighten Lawòz enlighten
Liminé Lawòz liminé
Enlighten Lawòz enlighten
Se Lawòz ki èdiké
Its Lawòz who educates
Lamagwit pa konèt ayen
Lamagwits society is not educated
Lamagwit ka tchen dèyè
Lamagwit holds people back (in ignorance).[9]

In the above song Lamagwit is criticised by Lawòz. In songs of Lamagwit the opposite trends are evident.

As in other St Lucian songs these 'flower society' songs are led by a Chantwèl (female lead singer), in the same way that Christian burial hymns when sung by modern Saint Lucians, for example in the singing of *Abide With Me* will also 'informally' recognise the Chantwèl as the one to take the lead initiatives in tone, chorus and pitch when such songs are sung.

The Role of Women

In order to better recognise the implications of these flower societies it is necessary to examine the role of St Lucian women generally in the society and to note their particular roles in the flower societies. As in their traditional African societies, St Lucian women retained the roles of keepers of cultural tradition and healers. This is not to say that these roles are not occupied by men in the society also, but to underline instead the important roles that St Lucian women play within them. When one wakes up in St Lucia, the first sight at dawn is the oldest woman of the house with the 'sacred' cup of coffee. She wakes everyone up and gives them coffee. We then shower and have breakfast which she may have cooked. The family then go to work, which traditionally meant farming. On return to the home in the evenings it was again the eldest woman in the house who began the storytelling session with *Ting, Ting, Bwa Chèz*, one traditional formulae signalling the beginning of a story.

If one fell ill, it was again the elder women who knew the herbs, how to mix them and for what illness. Should one have had a dream, it was again the eldest woman who identified what was significant in the dream and what warnings one should draw from the dream, including those of adults in the house.

When one sought to marry, it was the elder women who told whether the bloodlines were too close to marry or whether the proposed in-laws were potentially friends or foes. The elder women also told you who was who in St Lucian society, for example that Derek Walcott's identity was really 'Roddy Walcott Brother, Teacher Alexis son'.[10]

The elder women also connected you to other bloodlines, for example that others with other names than St Just were really relatives because of the links of older ancestors or that other friendships had been so long established between families that they operated as one wider family.

The location of Lawòz and Magwit as societies in which the women would dance, enter trance-like states, drink and help define those who were to be 'princes and princesses' in the society is itself an expression of the past power of women in Caribbean and African societies.

Williams summarises the power of Caribbean women as follows: 'Combine the woman's cultural role with her roles as peasant, labourer, trader, urban domestic and usually head of a matriarchal home and we understand why she is so often portrayed as the strong, survivalist Caribbean woman'.[11]

Indeed Caribbean women play a dominant role also in the transmission of non-formal cultural skills such as basket weaving.[12] Women also play an important role in agricultural production in modern Caribbean society: 'they produce 60-75 per cent of the food for the local market, and are responsible for over 80 per cent of its distribution'.[13]

Because Lawòz and Lamagwit societies were 'old negro societies',[14] it is likely that such traces of previous power continued within the Saint Lucian social system. Flower society membership allowed the Chantwèl and other society members to temporarily adopt social roles such as magistrate, higher than those of their daily lives and to enjoy finery and jewellery on loans given by the larger stores on an annual basis:

> .... these parties and dances entail considerable expense upon their partisans for the purchase of finery and jewellery...indulged in tastes and habits far beyond their means to satisfy, and to be credited with fine stuff, etc even by the large stores, equal in the aggregate to the year's entire income.[15]

Bearing in mind the possible divisions in St Lucian society between French Revolutionaries and the English who had defeated them, plus the acknowledged two divisions between Africans in St Lucia, that is, Ti Jiné (Guinea Africans) and Ti Kongo (Congo Africans), it is likely that the wider divisions that the two societies marked between all ethnic and social groups in St Lucia, would have included the flower societies. Like the stick fighting groups within Trinidad of both French or English affiliations (1700-1834), as described by Cowley,[16] it is likely that the support given by the various store owners to the Chantwèl (Lawòz or Lamagwit) may have also indicated an affiliation related to the French or English ancestry of the store owner.

Traces of these conflicts remain in the songs of at least one older Saint Lucian woman, singing the following extract from what appears to be a French revolutionary marching song:

> Adieu chèri
> Goodbye darling
> Adieu péyi
> Goodbye country
> Mwen ka alé
> I am going
> Ma sav si ngay viwé...
> I don't know if I'll return...[17]

Notes

1. Merle Collins, extract from 'Nearly Ten Years Later', *Rotten Pomerack*, Virago, London, 1992, p.42.
2. D.J. Cowley, 'Song and Dance in Saint Lucia', *Ethnomusicology*, 9, 1957, pp.4-14, also cited in Morgan Dalphinis, *African Language Influences in Creoles Lexically Based on Portuguese, English and French*, PhD Thesis, School of Oriental and African Studies, University of London, 1981, University Microfilms Intl, 1986.
3. Merle Collins, *Rotten Pomerack*, Virago, London, 1992, p.25.
4. Ibid, p.25, line 36.

5. See Morgan Dalphinis *Caribbean and African Languages*, Karia Press, London, 1985.
6. See Derek Walcott's *Sea Grapes*, Jonathan Cape, 1976, pp.48-52.
7. See E. Beck, *Caribbean Quarterly*, 29(1), March, 1983.
8. Olive Lewin, *Caribbean Quarterly*, 29(1), March, 1983.
9. Recording of song in St Lucia in April, 1979.
10. Derek Walcott, 1976, op.cit.
11. Cheryl Williams, 'The Role of Women in Caribbean Culture' in P. Ellis, *Women of the Caribbean*, 1986, Zed Books, London and New Jersey, p.109.
12. Beryl Carascoe, 'Women's Participation ion Non-Formal Educational Activities' in P. Ellis, 1986, Ibid, p.105.
13. P. Antrobus, in 'Crisis, Challenge and the Experiences of Caribbean Women', *Caribbean Quarterly* , 35 (1 and 2), 1989, p.21.
14. See *The St Lucian* (newspaper) 1865 in P.A.B, Anthony, 'The Literature in the Flower Festivals of St Lucia', *Bulletin of the Folk Research Centre*, 1(1), Castries, St Lucia, 1974, pp.7-14.
15. See *The St Lucian* (newspaper), 1865.
16. Cowley, Personal Communications, 1995.
17. Recording of song in St Lucia in April, 1979.

Keeping Tradition Alive

Jean Buffong

It is age old knowledge that women, in particular African and Caribbean women are 'master' storytellers. This goes back to time immemorial to the days when 'men' decreed a woman's place to be the kitchen with a baby on her shoulder and another on her back. It was during those times that the art of storytelling manifested itself in full strength as a form of entertainment. Speaking of the Caribbean context, our grandmothers before us were indeed grand 'master' storytellers. Through storytelling, our traditions were handed down the generations.

Keeping tradition alive...we cannot talk about keeping tradition alive without talking about storytelling and we cannot talk about storytelling without talking about language. Language is the centre of a culture. If we do not hold on to our language we find important aspects of our culture phasing out and our language becoming a museum piece, if we are that lucky.

With the modern advent of technology, that age old tradition of storytelling is slowly being killed off. Oral storytelling with all its cultural 'semmi demmi' is being extinguished. That's where the role of Caribbean women writers comes in to play in keeping tradition alive. In earlier years it may be observed that some Caribbean women writers, away from their homeland, tended to adapt the language of the country of abode when writing about their country of origin. They then created a second class language of their mother tongue. Reading the language used then by Caribbean writers, one would be forgiven for thinking that the writer felt guilty for using a word or phrase of the local language, I refer to patois, Creole or whatever the name of the specific Creole may be.

In the case of some early writers the words or phrases used came across in a mocking tone. Those were the days when it was cemented that only the 'master's' language was a proper language, therefore any native tongue in the 'English' Caribbean was unwritable. In that atmosphere, writers and particularly women writers were of 'a certain calibre'. They were not the true authentic storytellers displaying their talents in written form. This is evident from the early years when there were very few Caribbean women writers as only a few fitted into that certain calibre. A limited few outside that framework 'magically' got their work published. To enjoy their writing one had to search through archives for a copy of such work.

Today more and more women are shaking off that age old 'ism' as kitchen sink owners and Caribbean women writers are playing their part, taking up their position. More publishers are waking up to the fact that Caribbean women writers do indeed have something to say. Publishers are beginning to accept that women are not only saying it but saying it loud and clear in the language of the culture to which they belong.

Those Caribbean women writers tuned into oral culture do not only put words on to paper but record 'visual' sounds and 'going ons' of the people they write for and about. Listening to the language, the reader, even if not acquainted with the 'word' or languages, sees images of Caribbean life past and present. The reader is transformed from being an observer and becomes a participant in the story.

In keeping tradition alive, Caribbean women writers are anthropologists, historians, and so on. As born storytellers Caribbean women writers are maintaining the art of storytelling which is being phased out by modern technology. We are preserving the culture of the people for future generations.

Rain Darling,[1] a book of short stories by Merle Collins, is an example of how traditions are kept alive and handed down through generations. Most of the traditions glimpsed in these tales are still practised throughout the islands; others are recorded as folk history by Caribbean women writers. In *Rain Darling* there are many examples. For instance, in *Gran*, we witness the old customs of keeping 'wake'. After Gran's death, all before the funeral, there was hymn singing and praying:

> They get a lady from the Catholic church to pass the chaplet. Even though Grannie was an Anglican... and everybody was singing.[2]

Afterwards they pass coffee, they pass sandwiches, they pass cocoa.
One gets an insight into the love affair between the character Gran and the island:

> ...she (Gran) body must be hurting her, yes, because all she strength in the cracks in the road in this country. And when she wasn't walking fixing roads, she baking bread.[3]

In *My Sister Cherish* Merle Collins has recorded some of the traditional beliefs in the 'supernatural entwined with religion'.
After Cherish's funeral:

> And Aunt Cleopatra said, 'the Lord giveth and the Lord taketh away'. And Auntie Magdalene said, 'Yes, this one is his angel for sure. Never did a bad thing in her life'. Daddy said, 'She wasn't for this world. I never see a prettier child'.[4]

Added to this, Cherish's sister gave her thoughts:

> And I'm always afraid of thinking about things like spirits and so, but Mammie is right, if Cherish is really a spirit, then she is a good spirit, but still, I don't want to see her, because I can't handle the idea of seeing any spirit, good or bad. So let me cross my fingers and stop this story. And make the sign of the cross.[5]

My idea of 'keeping tradition alive' continues in *The Walk*. Customarily one 'bites the finger if one accidently points to a grave for fear of the fingers dropping off'. Queenie's Cousin Liza chastises her for pointing not to a grave but to something unnameable: '...Don't point', she whispered hoarsely. 'Bite your fingers' she remembered to add.[6] This practice, like many others travelled from Africa through the middle passage.

Throughout the book the language of the people is very prominent thereby keeping the characters and places alive, real and undeniably authentic.

Caribbean women writers are also seen as forerunners to other women who have the talent but are reluctant to expose themselves because in most instances the question of language is still a setback.

The language of a people is the foundation of its culture. Through the language of a people tradition is handed down, thus keeping a culture alive. Take away the language from a people and they are nothing. They lose the very essence of their being. They adapt someone else's language because the mother tongue is not considered 'good', thus birthing themselves a second class people and their language a second class language and so extinguishing aspects of their culture. When a people lose aspects of their culture in this manner how do they communicate with each other? 'Within a second dimension'.

As 'master' storytellers Caribbean women writers are not only recording the history of the Caribbean but also keeping tradition alive, tradition with all its cultural 'semmi demmi'. Caribbean women writers are preserving an existence in their writing which will otherwise be lost. They are cementing their cultural identity for future generations.

Notes

1. Merle Collins *Rain Darling*, Women's Press, London, 1990.
2. Ibid, p.64.
3. Ibid, p.54.
4. Ibid, p.181.
5. Ibid, p.182.
6. Ibid, p.91.

New Encounters: Availability, Acceptability and Accessibility of New Literature from Caribbean Women

Susanna Steele and Joan Anim-Addo
In Conversation

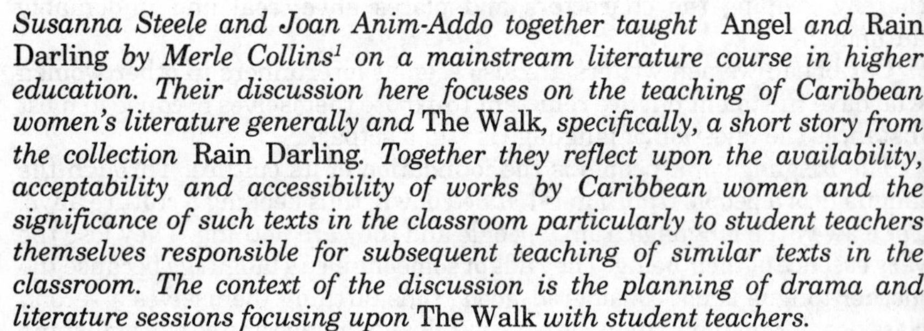

Susanna Steele and Joan Anim-Addo together taught Angel *and* Rain Darling *by Merle Collins*[1] *on a mainstream literature course in higher education. Their discussion here focuses on the teaching of Caribbean women's literature generally and* The Walk, *specifically, a short story from the collection* Rain Darling. *Together they reflect upon the availability, acceptability and accessibility of works by Caribbean women and the significance of such texts in the classroom particularly to student teachers themselves responsible for subsequent teaching of similar texts in the classroom. The context of the discussion is the planning of drama and literature sessions focusing upon* The Walk *with student teachers.*

Availability

J: *Rain Darling* is fairly readily available in bookshops and this is more than can be said for other Caribbean women's writing on the booklist.[2] Nonetheless, we seem to be faced with several difficulties. As well as the students who are reluctant to read specific titles, we also have a majority of students who expect to read all the set texts, but, in trying to purchase or borrow the books, they suddenly and dramatically find themselves in the situation of being in a minority group. They find that they have to go into specialist bookshops, they have to search the shelves of black literature or black women's literature,[3] they have to order the books and wait a very long time to get their orders through. They seldom find the set books in mainstream bookshops and many find this surprising.

S: Or on the library shelves. This can be pretty exasperating. For some it is the first experience of finding themselves more or less marginalised. Amongst the groups we teach are people who, despite belonging to minority groups have never had the experience of feeling marginalised, or, alternatively, do not recognise their marginality. This is why, I think, some students react negatively to being asked to read black literature - they think it has nothing to do with them; they feel marginalised by it in the way they do not, say, by *Jane Eyre* which they understand to be a 'classic' - so, there's not only the barrier of availability. First get hold of your text! We also have to address notions of acceptability. It happens to black writing in general. It happens to women's literature and it happens to gay and lesbian literature.

J: Yes! I have had white students write graphically in their reading journals of 'entering minority ground' just from having gone through the process of finding the text. Buying a book from the black fiction section, separate from the other literature, can itself be for some students an uncomfortable and challenging experience.

Acceptability

S: The fact is that bookshops and libraries effectively marginalise literature such as Caribbean women's. I say 'such as' because this marginalising process does not only happen to Caribbean women's writing.[4] However the students who react against being asked to read black literature in the belief that it has nothing to do with them, also feel excluded by a sense of 'otherness' about the literature.

J: Of course, the 'otherness' perception is double edged. Some readers are motivated precisely because this separating on the bookshelves signifies literature with a *difference*.[5] For other readers the isolating of the books as 'black' or 'black interest' contributes to a sense of 'otherness' difficult to reconcile with prevailing notions of literature as the 'best' of high culture, as a canon of specific works.

S: So, they also marginalise the literature. They accept it as being outside 'the canon' which is accredited with high cultural status. To have read within 'the canon' gives, it is believed, a cultural acceptability which does not come, for some readers initially with, say, a work by Merle Collins. Black literature, particularly Caribbean literature and more specifically women's writing is dismissible as belonging to a particular identifiable group.

J: There follows with this reasoning the belief of limited appeal for some literature in direct contrast to canonical works. Canonical literature is understood to have more 'universal' applicability than 'lesser' literatures. But the concept of the universal is used in effect to dismiss or exclude some literatures at the expense of justifying certain more readily appreciated inclusions. The universality of experience encountered in say, Caribbean women writers is often a surprise to students. Occasionally a student makes a remark such as 'but its crosscultural because I can understand that in my own culture even though the writer is saying it in words that are slightly different'. She refers to the meanings gained as 'cross cultural' but what registers is her surprise and readers are often surprised. Such students do not initially expect the experience to be that meaningful to a wide readership. They are not expecting the experience to translate into something that is known or understood.

S: This is similar to the challenge that we have when we introduce Shakespeare to students who have never read any of his work before. But Shakespeare has a cultural status that means he cannot be set aside or dismissed in the same way as Caribbean women writers.

J: And this is why enabling students to engage with literature is so important. Both the breadth and depth of their reading is so vital. This is less related to who students are as individuals but vital for the future because they make decisions significantly affecting the literary 'diet' of others for whom they become responsible.

S: Indeed. They therefore need to be aware of the subjectivities that we bring to a text and how this can be both enabling and discouraging. Students gain by having a positive experience of texts which may be considered 'outside' their personal literary and cultural boundaries. We all do. At the same time, it is also about confirming some students in their cultural heritage. But, professionally, it is so valuable to develop a range of ways of approaching texts that cross boundaries. These texts can then be confidently used with the students they teach. Otherwise, a real danger is that from higher education down to Primary education level, what gets read does not stray far beyond notions of mainstream culture.

J: ...with the result that the pupils or students they teach subsequently are impoverished. So, the 'how' of reading, the range of strategies which may be used for encountering the text begins to be critical in the case of teachers.

S: Reading a text always requires more than just a response. We need to encourage levels of engagement in audiences new to Caribbean women's literature. So, yes, how we go about this is important. Some students do pick up the key meanings spontaneously, perhaps because they recognise that it relates to their culture or because they're experienced and confident readers. But we also need to consider the question of how to support student teacher confidence in approaching texts with which they feel unfamiliar.

J: Particularly in light of the knowledge that feelings of unfamiliarity may well lead to justification for not including lesser known texts such as, in this case, Caribbean women writers. There is an argument which goes: 'I don't know the text well enough therefore I can't teach it'.

S: On my part I have sometimes had a sense of not doing the works justice because I appreciate that the reading brought to the text by someone who is within the culture, possibly has more depth than someone who is an outsider. There is the difference in being able to talk about 'we' rather than 'they' that is about knowing the culture from the inside. But on the other hand I can see how that can become an excuse for not approaching these texts at all. Yet I can see as many connections, for me, with the works of Merle Collins as I can in Jane Austen...perhaps more!

J: Keen stprytellers among us can really enjoy the way Merle Collins draws so strongly on the oral tradition. That is part of what makes Merle's writing so vibrant: her use of oral Caribbean culture, or orature in the literature, her use of story form, oral retelling and the Creole voice. Yet this, too, can contribute to the barrier of acceptability. It may well be that issues of accessibility are entangled here. And that is part of what concerns us, making texts accessible to students whatever the texts may be, whether it's *Midsummer Night's Dream* or *The Walk* both of which we teach.

Accessibility

S: Yes. This takes us into strategies which allow entry into the many worlds that literature offers. It is about learning to be an open reader; it is about learning to come to the text willing to be taken in and finding points of entry into the text. Drama strategies offer us invaluable flexibility in this.

J: It offers ways of working which are useful for a whole range of texts from very new literature such as the collection *Rain Darling* to well established literary icons - Shakespeare's texts.

S: That's right! It's not specific to teaching Merle Collins's work. It's a way of approaching text that foregrounds personal response, an active world to text encounter, before, or even alongside, exploring the work through more formal literary methods.

J: What makes for a very special response or variety of responses is the way in which drama methods acknowledge, even privilege, the personal world into text encounter more than literary studies usually allows. It is useful to remember that it is precisely the individual's personal world and quality of experience of that world, whether at first hand or through a variety of secondary sources, which serves to regulate access to, in this case, literatures signalling *difference*. The clue to that difference is, use of language. In the case of Merle's work, the use of Creole, for readers reluctantly approaching new literature, can initially act as a barrier to interpretations or meaning.

With drama we can leap over such barriers which language can create into the world created by the language.

S: Yes, and yet it doesn't mean that we side step the issue of the language of the text, but as teachers ourselves with a particular interest in drama, we can choose to use ways of working that are representational as a way to explore the text...

J: ...it takes the discussion, for a time, away from the way the story is written to the events that it contains and the ways in which those can be shown.

S: ...When we work with the collective representations that drama encourages, it enables us to respond to a range of different interpretations in a much more profound way than by simply responding to the written text. Take the opening of the story for instance:

> Faith reached up and unbuttoned the apron at the back. Let it drop to the front. Reached back and loosened the knot at her waist. Pulled off the apron and dropped it on to the barrel behind the door. She slumped onto the bench just inside of the kitchen door. She looked across at the fireside, at the scattered bits of wood, at the ashes, cold and grey around the wood. Her eyes moved automatically towards the coalpot, where a yellow butter-pan rested on partly burnt out coals. She wondered whether Queen had prepared anything. To tell the truth, she was too tired to really care. She turned and looked at the bucket of water on the dresser, at the two pancups hanging from a nail above it. She took a deep breath, released it and let her head fall forward on to the rough board of the kitchen table.[6]

Even if you simply take part in acting out the scene as it is being read, following the actions of Faith as she comes home from work and finally sitting 'as if' you are Faith with all her tiredness, you're drawing not only on the words and images created by Merle's writing but also on first hand experience of all the times you have known yourself to have been tired at the end of a day. It becomes a meeting of worlds. The personal world of the 'reader' with the world of the story. And to respond to questions from Faith's point of view, 'as if' you are Faith, brings your understanding to bear in ways that are not easy to develop if you are only talking about the text.

J: And watching another group's response can shape, challenge or confirm your own interpretation. A visual interpretation allows you to take in so many different levels of meaning because Faith's tiredness at the end of a hard physical day takes you into the real world of Caribbean rural poverty at the same time as you encounter that other reality which is equally part of the story. Powerfully evoked are trees which, linking their branches and 'caressing' in the pale moonlight are key symbols to another world at least as ancient as humanity itself. This world, negotiated by Queen and Liza, we are reminded, is one which is immediately appreciated by those whose journeys 'would have to be made in darkness, when the sun was down'.

S: In selecting and presenting 'still' images of moments in the texts, we encounter, for example, a whole area of significance relating to the cockerel in that section of *The Walk*. It may seem initially as if this is a bizarre and 'exotic' experience until students are questioned about their own experience of superstition and its manifestation. It helps to be able to link into ideas which are not readily understood or these may remain 'exotica' and therefore dismissible.

J: You referred to 'still' images. For some, what we do with drama, that is, the creating of a new visual text that is an interpretation or series of interpretations of *The Walk* counts as a weakness of this way of working. However, while it is true that the drama work can evoke or invoke a power that is more related to the drama itself than the text upon which it originally drew, this process can also be said to be in keeping with notions of the text as an ongoing 'production', source of a plurality of meanings.[8]

S: Also what you do get is a personal engagement with the world of the text. For the time of the drama you are part of that world...it doesn't preclude studying it in different ways once that connection has been made. And of course in working within drama you are always going back to the text itself, to both language and events. If you are working on the moment when Queenie is praying for help on the walk in order to explore her feelings and attitudes to what she has been asked to do you go back to the text to shape your work, to give you information about the setting, to give you dialogue:

> Queen changed quickly, knelt down, bent her forehead to touch the sofa, and prayed aloud: 'Gentle Jesus meek and mild, look upon a little child!'
>
> She lifted her head and looked at the crucifix over the bed.
>
> 'Papa God, help me to grow up into a big strong girl for me please. Bless Mammie and Cousin Dinah and Maisie and Mark. Make the walk tomorrow not hard please and don't let me and Cousin Liza meet anything on the road. Bless Cousin Liza too and let me have a lot of money when I get big please God. Amen.[9]

To show that event in a dramatic form allows you also to include the spectres that haunt her prayers or the fears and terrors that are part of her anticipation of the trip to pay the society. It may not happen in the written text but you can also explore Queenie's responses to her daughter's fears...drawing out for example, for Queenie, the significance of the trip to pay the money. Using drama as a way of working enables us to respond to the possibilities inherent in the world of the text and in doing so create a 'need to know' about the actual world within which this story is set.

J: And ultimately, when students leave the drama space, they take the written text with them and it is this original text to which they return. In the process the text has been mediated by drama strategies in ways that have brought it alive, lent it a heightened reality. This textual encounter with a new audience is critical to new literatures. The visibility of the body of texts depends, in part, upon new audiences.

Notes

1. We refer to: Merle Collins, *Angel*, Women's Press, London, 1987; Merle Collins, *Rain Darling*, Women's Press, London, 1990.
2. Published works by Caribbean women writers enjoy notorious 'invisibility' in libraries and mainstream bookshops. See, for example, 'Woman Words' in *Mango Season*, 3, Summer, 1995.
3. Even sections categorised as 'Black Women's Writing' can be a source of disappointment for students of Caribbean women writers since Caribbean writers do not neatly fit the category 'Black' as the body of writing includes Caribbean writers from different racial groups. In any event, 'Black Women Writers' often focus on the more highly profiled African-American women writers.
4. Caribbean literature generally suffers from this kind of marginalisation. Other bodies of literature, for example, women's literature and lesbian literature have made a similar case. This is not an exhaustive list.
5. That is, different cultural contexts and possibly 'exotic'.
6. Merle Collins, 1990, op. cit., p.86.
7. Ibid, p.93.
8. We refer to the Roland Barthes notion of text as on-going 'production' rather than product cited in Steven Cohan and Linda M. Shires, *Telling Stories: A Theoretical Analysis of Narrative Fiction*, Routledge, London, 1988, p.26.
9. Merle Collins, 1990, op. cit., p.89.

Children Should Be Seen and Spoken To: or...Writing For and About Children

Thelma Perkins

There was a time when children were not included in conversations. Adults either talked as if they were not there, sent them out of the room or, as my mother and my aunts did, used 'back-slang', an invented adultspeak.

'Speak when you are spoken to', was the rule. This really meant that the topic of conversation was either not suitable or intended for little ears.

The result of this lack of communication between adults and children is that very few of us know about our parents' childhood. We know even less of the family history and some of us virtually nothing of our place of origin.

I once heard Diane Abbott MP talk of 'knowing' where we came from. She said how important it is for parents and grandparents to talk about 'home' and, if possible, to make it a duty to take your grandchildren back home. 'Back home' is an important part of the story for children of the Caribbean diaspora. For how else can we go forward if we don't know where we come from?

To take an example from outside of the Caribbean, Somali and Ethiopian cultures are strong story telling cultures with an oral tradition which makes it possible to trace familial roots back over four hundred years. Clan relationships can be linked and deeds infamous and famous may be recalled through conversation, stories and poetry. A growing number of authors from the Caribbean and of British Caribbean origin have begun to include their memories of childhood in both poems and novels. How else could Merle Collins write so vividly of childhood, extended families and story telling in *The Colour of Forgetting,*[1] if she hadn't been part of it herself?

Lakshmi Persaud writes of her own childhood in Trinidad dominated by her grandmother who massaged her from head to toe while discussing her good points as if she was a separate entity from her body. *Butterfly in the Wind*[2] is an example of how stories from one's culture eventually affect our own understanding of life and in some ways help to interpret the actions of our parents.

Cecil Foster's *No Man in the House*[3] recreates life in Barbados prior to independence. However, the political background is only part of the story for surely the little boy being raised by his grandmother in acute poverty is the author himself. The boy longs for his parents who have gone to England to send for him. He feels that there is not one person who understands his longing. Having grown up in care I could empathise with Howard. Similarly, Pauline Stewart's 'Goodbye Granny'[4] must cause many of those who were left with their grandparents to recall the day they left the Caribbean to meet once again with their parents.

Pauline Stewart, Valerie Bloom and Lyn Joseph[5] use poetry to recapture their childhood in the Caribbean. Sometimes humorous, occasionally sad, their work can be used with children to encourage discussion and inspire creative writing through comparisons.

A Jamaican author I recently discovered, Hazel D. Campbell, has cleverly used her mother's tales of life in rural Jamaica along with her own experience of childhood in Kingston to create a collection that is a historical record both socially and linguistically.

I feel certain that women of Caribbean origin who read *Tilly Bummie,*[6] could not fail to recall similar events. If only more women would tell or write them down for their own families. I believe that everyone has a story inside them waiting to be told. There are many ways of telling and we owe it to our children to record our past and their present.

What begins as an anecdote can soon develop into a time of reminiscence and one memory brings forth another. When families are together, each one will tell the same story in a different way, through their own eyes. The incident will be argued over, outcomes and consequences will vary but the essence of the story will remain the same. However, if this conversation goes on above or around children and they are not included, it will eventually be lost to the family and part of their history will be gone forever. Young children learn to switch off when not included in conversation, perhaps if they could listen with one ear, then the stories of childhood that should really be told to them instead of around them, would remain within the family.

My sister and I began writing for ourselves. We had no family history that we knew of, only a childhood of growing up in care. We both began our search for different reasons but came together to share the few memories and compare the similarities which turned out to be greater than the differences. Through this talking we began to write and as we wrote about our experiences memories came flooding back, many of which we recorded in *In Search of Mr McKenzie.*[7]

For me, memories that had seemed like dreams became ideas for stories. I realised that I too had not been telling my own children of my childhood. Yet some of the things I did with them were as a direct result of my upbringing. The long walks in the Kent countryside during the summer holidays, the nights spent under canvas close to the sea; and the stockings they woke to before daylight on Christmas morning, were all part of this. It was those same stockings that influenced my first 'stand alone' story for children,*Wishing On A Wooden Spoon.*[8] I wrote for my children and for all children as well as for myself. Mine is a history still within living memory. Something to which parents and children can relate. I write about being the only black child in a totally white environment. About being a child who had a Mother and for while a Father who were far away but still loved. I wrote of my need but of not being able to express a reason. Why did I want twin baby dolls? And how did those dinner ladies whose conception of black children could have only been the same missionary views that I held, know to give me a black doll?

Is this the reason that adults write of their childhood? To seek out answers? I know that writing about my childhood has enabled me to look back and with hindsight attempt to analyse the actions of those who contributed to my upbringing. Racism was not a word when I was a child. Yet today when I do readings followed by a discussion, I can guarantee that someone will ask if I encountered racism as I was growing up.

Should I include the word when I write? Was it part of childhood? And if I did, would it change the whole context and nature of my work?

I have chosen to write about my memories and how it was for me then. I was not aware of racism. I know that I was different and that I was treated in some respects differently to the others in the home. I was spoilt as a baby and toddler up until I began school. Even then I still received special treatment from some of the staff and the parents of my school friends. However in other ways we were all treated the same. No equal opportunities policies then, routines, visiting days and punishments!

So I write for children. I write with a sense of history because I want all children to know of the past. Not the past that lies beyond the mists of time. But the past that their parents or grandparents can recall and relate to. The past that they link to their own lives and perhaps I might stir up enough memories for them to begin telling their tales. I want adults to talk of what they were told and where their family came from; for children to want to go back and explore the playground, the woods, the seasons and, in turn, tell their own stories: stories that have been told to them by their relatives.These children are our next generation of writers of history.

For some, the process of writing about one's own childhood can be a painful experience. It can be a journey that causes rivers of tears to flow, anger to erupt, sleepless nights and days of questioning. And then when the journey is over, the healing can begin. Writing down those memories in a journal can be therapeutic. The author may want to continue keeping them locked away but what has happened while they were being written will have changed the author. And in the meantime part of a history has been documented for a family to find in years to come.

Mine was a legacy of silence; a jigsaw with many pieces missing. There are still pieces to be found and while others fall into place as I recall my childhood I have to resign myself to knowing that death silenced the storyteller before she ever took up the pen, as in my mother's case.

When I write stories for children who are not related to my own life, I am still drawing on real life experiences. I look at the children that I work with. I observe their parents and the traits that contribute to their culture, for culture changes, influenced by circumstances sometimes beyond anyone's control. I create a story around what I observe.

I write stories about everyday life, about what happens to the children, about the questions they ask that demonstrate their perception of the world and the strange things that adults do and say. I don't create fantasy worlds where animals wear clothes and speak, or where amazing creatures are confronted by mythical characters or where children have adventures. This is not because I disapprove. Every child needs to escape into the realms of fantasy and should be able to create their own world away from reality from time to time. But I am not able to do this. Instead, I weave stories around the world that children know. Like the nursery teacher I am, I begin with where the children are. So in a way I am still creating history, not personalising it but putting today into a permanent form.

Like all writers I hope that what I write will one day be published. I want the rest of the world to know that the little people I work with and my grandchildren who are most often my inspiration are individuals. They may come from other ethnic groups. Their cultures may not be the same. They all have different experiences but, the similarities outweigh the differences.

When I write about the children who are looked after in extended families, who go to visit relatives in India or Ghana, who have never been on a train, who want to be part of a carnival band, I am writing about the children that I know. I try to inject humour as well as truth into the stories and if they don't always have a happy ending they do end on a positive note. Unlike fairy tales there is not always a moral in the story or a sting in the tale but there will be truth and an element of real life.

We owe our children their history and which ever way we choose to record it, what ever it does for us on a personal level, whether we write, talk or paint, the future depends on our history and the way we interpret it.

Notes

1. Merle Collins, *The Colour of Forgetting*, Virago, London, 1995.
2. Lakshmi Persaud, *Butterfly in the Wind*, Peepal Tree Press, Leeds, 1990.
3. Cecil Foster, *No Man in the House*, Ballantine Books, New York.
4. Pauline Stewart, 'Goodbye Granny' in *Singing Down the Breadfruit*, Bodley Head Poetry, London, 1993.

5. See for example, Valerie Bloom's, *Duppy Jamboree*, Cambridge; Lyn Joseph's, *Coconut Kind of Day*, Picture Puffins, Middlesex, 1992.
6. Hazel D. Campbell, *Tilly Bummie*, Kingston Publishers, Kingston.
7. Isha McKenzie-Mavinga and Thelma Perkins, *In Search of Mr McKenzie*, Women's Press, London, 1991.
8. Thelma Perkins, *Wishing on a Wooden Spoon*, Mantra, London, 1992.

'A World Of Caribbean Romance' Reformulating the Legend of Love or: 'Can a caress be culturally specific?'

Jane Bryce

> In the historical memory of European people, there is the image of a brave young knight kneeling solemnly, not before the altar of God, but before a beautiful, white-bosomed maiden, his mistress, in defence of whose honour he would attempt the impossible and hazard his life. Centuries after the age of chivalry, the European male's attitude to the female sex continues to be conditioned by the ideas of chivalric romance surviving in the historic memory of the race.
>
> E. Obiechina, *An African Popular Literature.*[1]

This statement by the Nigerian critic, Emmanuel Obiechina, forms part of his discussion of the evolution of romantic love and romance fiction in the context of Nigeria. As a case study of a literary and social phenomenon which is both post colonial and syncretic, heir to the missionary influenced ideals of chastity, romantic love and monogamy in a context which traditionally privileges fertility and polygamy, Obiechina's work makes a useful point of reference for the more recent emergence of romantic fiction in the Caribbean.[2] In analysing the ways in which the peculiarly Christian, individualistic and fetishistic conventions of romantic love have been indigenised and altered in the process of appropriation by an African readership, Obiechina stresses several key divergences. Firstly, the African chivalric knight-romantic hero seeks the endorsement, not of the individual lady, but of the community, and wins the 'lady' 'in recognition of his justification of his manhood'. Rather than 'integration and fusion of individualities in love and marriage', he maintains, the African couple seek 'complementarity', not 'one body and one flesh', but as 'collaborative individuals whose autonomy is attested to and constantly reinforced by the community of their fellows'.[3]

How such essentially philosophical and social differences translate into literary terms in Africa has been the subject of a number of studies,[4] the upshot of which is an appreciation of the way the so-called 'romantic formula' of western romance fiction has been subtly transformed to answer specific, local, cultural needs. That the formula has proved itself flexible enough also to adapt to changing western perceptions of femininity and 'love' (for example, targeting 'older' women with imprints like Harlequin's *Second Chance at Love*, or providing more explicit sexuality, like *Silhouette Desire,*[5] should not detract from our premise: that knowledge of the formula permits us to identify divergences, and through these we can begin to trace the specific constructions of femininity and desire in a post colonial context. In the African case, there are strong arguments that romance fiction has been appropriated and adapted as a vehicle for the exploration of new possibilities in sexual behaviour and relationships, brought about by the intervention of Christianity and western education in traditional practices. While far less exclusively the property of a female readership than the western variety, romance in Africa also fulfils a function of utopian rewriting for women, a kind of encoded subversion of the status quo, in which love is metonymic of the desire for change.[6]

The proliferation of indigenously published romances in a country like Nigeria points to the eagerness with which writers and readers alike have seized on the romance as a way of interrogating their own social reality. This has not so far been the case in the Caribbean, where publishing is to a far greater extent controlled by the multinationals (notably Heinemann and Longman in the anglophone Caribbean).[7] While the ubiquitous presence of foreign based imprints[8] testifies to the popularity of romance fiction in the anglophone Caribbean, it was only in 1991 that the British publisher, Heinemann, identified the 'gap' which its new series, 'Caribbean Caresses', is designed to fill. The guidelines to prospective authors explicitly claim the highly respectable genealogy of a British imprint which has been in operation since 1908:

> Mills & Boon are tremendously popular throughout the Caribbean, but these lack any real Caribbean setting or connection. Heinemann plans to fill this gap.[9]

Since Mills & Boon has been the bastion of formula romance fiction, we should perhaps pause for a moment over the implication of another British publisher's project, using something so culturally specific to plug the perceived 'gap' in the field of Caribbean cultural production.

The Mills & Boon guidelines tape, 'And Then He Kissed Her...', claims that there is no such thing as a 'formula', then proceeds to prescribe the precise attributes of the ideal hero ('he won't be very short, or very fat, or bald') and heroine (younger than the hero, attractive, relatively 'innocent'), and the narrative structure which constitutes the romance plot. This entails a misunderstanding, obstacles which are eventually overcome and a happy ending with a wedding on the horizon. Explicit sex is absent from the pages of Mills & Boon, as from the romances of another British institution, Dame Barbara Cartland (asked to comment on the desirability of representing safe sex, she is reported as responding 'What's that?' and, on being enlightened: We know it happens, but we don't want to read about it. I never have anything to do with sex whatsoever - in my books).[10]

Dame Barbara's social status, as step grandmother to the Princess of Wales, points towards another implicit assumption of British romance, one which the plummy upper class tones of the Mills & Boon voiceover endorse - that of class. The very notion of the 'lady' is a class construct, one which comes with a trail of implications as to what constitutes 'proper' social and sexual behaviour. As researchers have shown, the romance heroine is typically of a lower social status than the hero, but in marrying him she is transformed, like Cinderella, into a 'lady'. She could not, however, achieve this transformation, unless she already possessed the attributes of 'ladyness' - modesty, propriety, grace under pressure and a good clothes sense. It is precisely this notion of 'ladyness', embodying the Victorian virtues of demureness and submissiveness, which is interrogated in successive texts by Caribbean women writers - the *Fat Black Woman* poems of Grace Nichols, the novels of Erna Brodber (*Jane and Louisa Will Soon Come Home*), Merle Hodge (*Crick Crack Monkey*) and Jamaica Kincaid (*Annie John* and *Lucy*), and a short story like Olive Senior's 'Lily Lily' in *Arrival of the Snakewoman*.[11] The aspiration, implanted in the Caribbean feminine consciousness by colonialism, to 'respectability' and 'ladyhood', is wickedly parodied in Merle Hodge's Auntie Beatrice with her 'high heels and stockings voice'[12] and shown to be a chimera, a siren call which repeatedly wrecks the self esteem of Caribbean women on the rocks of contradiction. For, as Hazel Carby has shown, the 'cult of true womanhood' whereby femininity was judged in the context of the American plantation, was a cult whose votary was, by definition, white. While delicacy and fragility of appearance and constitution denoted the 'true' woman, Carby points out that:

> ...strength and ability to bear fatigue...were positive features to be emphasised in the promotion and selling of a black female field hand at a slave auction.[13]

That the same applied to the Caribbean context is testified to by Evelyn O'Callaghan, who cites an early narrative to the effect that black women were considered 'very ugly things to look upon' by its white female author, even while they might be objects of desire for white men'.[14]

Thus a paradox grew up surrounding the notion of feminine beauty and womanly deportment. Since the qualities of vulnerability and delicacy had been designated white, it followed that the black woman, who had been seen, as Carby points out, to survive the horrors of slavery, could be raped with impunity:

> The white male, in fact, was represented as being merely prey to the rampant sexuality of his female slaves...not regarded as being responsible for his actions...On the contrary, it was the female slave who was held responsible for being a potential, and direct, threat to the conjugal sanctity of the white mistress.[15]

By the same sleight of hand, bell hooks shows how the discourse of racial domination in the US has as its central narrative:

> ...the overwhelming desperate longing black men have to sexually violate the bodies of white women...a story of revenge, rape as the weapon by which black men, the dominated, reverse their circumstance, regain power over white men.[16]

The question Carby asks is how, then, early black woman writers were to represent black 'womanhood', when only the most evil of stereotypes were available to them, and all supposedly positive virtues had been assigned to the white 'lady'. One response, already referred to in Caribbean women's writing in the form of satire or caricature, was to have black women aspire to 'ladyness', or, at least, the qualities of the bourgeois housewife. When it comes to narrative fiction, the same question arises: how is a black hero or heroine to be represented in a discourse which is central to Europe's notion of itself, presided over by the 'lady' of the chivalric ideal?

This indeed is the question that confronted the Trinidadian writer, Valerie Belgrave, when she embarked on her historical romance, *Ti Marie*.[17] The novel declares itself from the outset as a utopian revisioning of Trinidadian history. The cover design consists of a batik painting, by the author herself, of a dark haired, dark skinned woman and a man in eighteenth century dress, embracing beneath a yellow blossomed poui tree. In the background, a stately plantation house, and all around, vivid tropical flowers, complete this natural idyll. In a brief foreword, Valerie Belgrave situates that idyll in eighteenth century Trinidad, 'a haven of liberalism and racial and cultural tolerance' which has bequeathed the 'exceptionally cosmopolitan and racially harmonious nation' which she claims Trinidad is today.[18] The novel, she says, is a 'fairy tale', cast in the form of a historical romance, a genre in which, despite its popularity among Caribbean readers:

> ...we are not familiar with seeing ourselves portrayed...especially not with dignity and commanding respect.[19]

Hence Belgrave's project is quite explicit: her work, both as batik artist and novelist is 'a deliberate attempt to ennoble my country and its people, to promote racial tolerance...by promoting positive images of West Indians', through a medium that is pleasurable and entertaining. Like Heinemann, her own publisher, Belgrave has noticed that 'West Indians love romances but are starved for local ones', and feels that this 'gap' encourages the incursions of cultural imperialism. One effect of this is the naturalisation of 'sympathetic white characters', of whom her hero is one:

> ...not because he is brave or strong or just because he loves his grandmother, but because he becomes politicised into our concerns.[20]

The hero of her historical romance, a 'Georgian beau, a young Corinthian', escapes to the Caribbean from an imbroglio in England involving a fortune hunting lady and a duel. Appalled by his first brush with the plantation system in Barbados, he is persuaded by a friend to go to Trinidad, where:

> ...slavery is much more humane under the Spanish. Lots of free blacks are allowed to be citizens. They practice a liberal slave code too.[21]

The romance that subsequently evolves between the young aristocrat and the beautiful mulatto, Elena, does so against the background of the struggle between contending European powers for possession of Trinidad and the larger movement for liberty in the West Indies, which included the Haitian Revolution. Barry, the hero, and Elena, the heroine, are part of Belgrave's attempt to rewrite the script of both racial and sexual domination. In a short essay, she demonstrates her awareness of the issues raised by Carby et al. with regard to the representation of black sexuality, sketching 'a typical scenario' under slavery involving a white hero and his beautiful black victim, which, she says, 'would neither be truly romantic nor ennobling to black readers'.[22] The curious part of her argument is that, nonetheless, a white hero is necessary because 'recognisable' and a 'prototype' of a particular popular convention. Moreover, he must be treated 'sympathetically', and the only way to do this is by constructing a 'fairy tale' peopled by liberal, abolitionist, 'progressives', or as she puts it, 'beautiful people in a land of compelling beauty'.[23] The entire narrative is one of 'global humanism' in which the only victims are victims of humanism's 'contradictions', and in which the reader is expected to play an active part, 'to take up the gauntlet and continue the struggle in the present'.[24]

In the space of this brief essay, Belgrave addresses issues of convention and formula, reader expectation and authorial function, the effects of stereotyping and the necessity of counteracting a (past) racist reality with her own positive reconstruction. It is clear how she envisages her project, yet at least one critic has taken issue with the novel's racial revisioning, positing that she herself is not able to withstand what he calls 'the metanarrative of race in Trinidad'.[25] In seeking to celebrate racial harmony she has elided racial difference resulting in a 'monstrous distortion' which by aligning itself with the nationalist rhetoric of Afro-Trinidadian hegemony, effectively obscures the East Indian presence and writes it out of history.[26] In the process, Harney's analysis suggests, Belgrave not only 'invents a Trinidad for the Afro-Trinidadian nationalists born of the independence period', but also 'writes a history of gender full of hierarchy and ignorant of class prejudice'.[27] This is conspicuously at odds with Belgrave's own assertion that: 'The absence of marked sex role typing...shows the futuristic orientation' of her characters.[28]

I offer Harney's analysis as a suggestion of one way in which the romance vehicle, even with its utopian impulse and potential for subversion, can be construed as performing quite the opposite function - i.e. embodying conservative values and supporting the status quo. Yet, what Harney characterises as 'the metanarrative of race' is also a fundamental informing principle of the novel's construction of gender, and specifically, the construction of the black woman as romantic heroine. Is Harney's point: that by sidestepping the issue of class, Belgrave effectively reproduces the old plantation hierarchy, whereby the lighter skinned or mixed race woman is treated with a civility and respect not accorded the black slave woman, borne out in the novel?

Writing of how earlier perceptions of white and black femininity have conditioned contemporary stereotypes, Barbara Bush has noted that in the eighteenth century, the period of Belgrave's novel:

> Mulatto women were generally viewed by contemporary observers in a more favourable light than pure African women and the individual slave women whose beauty impressed European men were usually of mixed blood.[29]

By contrast, black women, says Bush, were seen as 'physically strong, exuding a warm animal sensuality, an inferior subspecies of the female sex. While the 'pure African woman did not fit the Graeco-Roman ideal of beauty which prevailed in Western Europe', mulatto mistresses were perceived as simply darker, more exotic versions of the ideal (a case in point is Stedman's 'Joanna', whose relationship is the subject of Beryl Gilroy's novel *Stedman and Joanna: A Love in Bondage*, and whose description, according to Bush, 'fits perfectly, in physical features and behaviour, the contemporary European ideal of a refined, modest woman').[30] What, then, may we expect from a historical romance which sets out to rewrite the stereotypes in a more 'sympathetic' light? The meeting of Barry and Elena is marked by Belgrave with an underlining of the difficulties of representation:

> For centuries there have been poems, books and letters praising the beauty of women with skins as white as the driven snow, eyes as blue as the cloudless

> skies, and lips like rosebuds. History has scant record of the equally dazzling beauty of black women, and metaphors and similes come less readily to mind.[31]

Deploying the cliché language of fairy tale and conventional love poetry, Belgrave gestures towards the defining power of discourse, the way our very capacity for aesthetic appreciation is constructed in language. The description of Elena juxtaposed with this moment is as follows:

> The very olive brown of her flawless skin gave her a special radiance which was rivalled only by the lustre in her large round eyes whose pupils were as black and as bottomless as the night. The nose, which she had obviously inherited from the unknown white father, was straight and turned up slightly at the tip. But it was her lips that stole Barry's heart. Her full lips tilted up at the corners and could not help but smile. When they did so in earnest, her face lit up with a blushing glow that made Barry's heart do a violent somersault.[32]

Belgrave's lamentation of the absence of metaphors and similes draws attention to those that are brought in to fill the 'gap', notably here 'black and bottomless as the night'. Obviously contrapuntal to 'white as the driven snow', this simile is equally a cliché which points towards a stereotype. Barbara Bush states that, in eighteenth century iconography:

> The 'Sable Queen' was one of the more pleasant contemporary images of the black woman. Part of white male mythology, it reflected a common and often near obsessional interest in the 'exotic charms' of African womanhood.[33]

This question of 'exotic charms' is an integral part of Said's analysis of Orientalism, whereby the Other (in this case, the black woman) is the screen onto which the (western) observer projects his own repressed desire. Hence, the obverse of the white lady's chastity is the myth of the black woman's lasciviousness, while the obverse of the familiar and domesticated is the unknown and mysterious. The bottomless blackness of Elena's eyes holds out this promise, in the same way that her half Amerindian mother is described as 'inscrutable'.[34] Since Belgrave has stated both explicitly and in her choice of images, that she is dealing in stereotype, the question of the extent to which this description should be read ironically arises. But why set the stage for a serious challenge to prevailing notions of white beauty only to undermine it with irony? A more likely explanation is that Belgrave, by invoking 'olive skin' and a 'straight nose', is, as Harney says, enmeshed in the metanarrative of race, which decrees that even today a light skinned woman is the appropriate image for the Carib beer poster,[35] or to represent the different islands in the Miss World contest. Elena, in other words, is not a 'black' woman at all, but a mulatto, a fact which would be neither here nor there without Belgrave's conscious insertion of her into the romantic convention. Far from providing a counter discourse to the scopophilia that privileges 'white' features over black, Elena, like Stedman's Joanna, 'fits perfectly in physical features and behaviour, the contemporary European ideal of a refined, modest woman'. Citing Stedman's description of his mistress, Bush shows that she:

> ...was full of native modesty...with cheeks through which glowed, in spite of the darkness of her complexion, a beautiful tinge of vermilion, when gazed upon. Her nose was perfectly well-formed, rather small, her lips a little prominent.[36]

The fact that the features are identical, down to the ladylike 'blushing glow' that lights up Elena's face when she smiles too broadly, leads one irresistibly back to the question of irony. But the contradiction remains: Belgrave, in setting out to counter one stereotype, has unquestioningly invoked another, and one just as implicated in the hierarchy of both eighteenth and twentieth century discourse of race and gender. As Harney points out, the figure of the black woman, in the sense of African slave rather than mixed race daughter of an enlightened white father, is poorly served in the novel in the person of Tessa, Elena's maidservant. Elena, with her 'ladylike' and 'cosmopolitan' attributes, is an appropriate figure to be reverenced as romantic heroine, where low status, black Tessa is not, and their treatment accordingly differs.

My purpose in embarking on this analysis of *Ti Marie* is not to 'trash' the novel, which I think succeeds admirably in what Belgrave herself calls its project of providing 'pure entertainment'[37] - as if entertainment ever can be 'pure'! What I am attempting to do, rather, is to use the novel to demonstrate the slipperiness and instability of the genre to which it lays claim. As Diane Elam says, romance is as much vilified for its conservatism and promotion of patriarchal values as it is celebrated as a subversive vehicle of women's pleasure and utopian fantasies.[38] *Ti Marie* embodies that contradiction. In its recognition of how we as readers are conditioned to take pleasure in texts which may be blatantly ethnocentric (like most western romance fiction), and in its brave struggle, and ultimate failure, to provide a counter discourse, it reiterates the power the metanarrative of romance has over us all. Moreover, it is the first full fledged attempt at a transposition of the romance formula to the Caribbean, and as such, lays the ground for the series that follows: *Caribbean Caresses*.

Heinemann's specifications for the series, issued in 1991, draw attention to the paradoxical popularity of Mills & Boon (and of course the numerous other suppliers of romance fiction from the UK and North America) and its lack of 'any real Caribbean setting or connection'. In the next paragraph, sub-titled 'Setting', we are told that 'this should be Caribbean, escapist...'. The innocent juxtaposition, 'real' and 'escapist', alerts us to the first of the problems of relocating the romantic formula outside its own cultural parameters. A gap exists. This gap is one of realistic representation of a region constructed in the discourse of tourism as 'Paradise', and in romance fiction as exotic backdrop to the intimate involvement of alien protagonists. How is this gap to be filled, when the 'real' Caribbean is required to reinscribe the fantasy of 'escape'? If the heroes and heroines of the north escape the cold and the pressures of work and family by going on Caribbean cruises, what are Caribbean men and women to do? The setting of formulaic western romance in 'exotic' locations has the effect of isolating the protagonists, who meet as disconnected individuals, and of suspending history and social reality.[39] Not only this, but the West Indies has historically been a site of otherness for colonial adventurers, including white female writers, as Evelyn O'Callaghan observes:

> Conventionally a male vehicle, with a quixotic hero setting out to brave the New World and make his fortune, the traveller's tale is of special importance to the West Indies.[40]

She suggests that contemporary women writers such as Jamaica Kincaid and Joan Riley may be seen intertextually, as reversing the 'voyage of discovery', and anticipates that 'such re-writings are likely to continue in accounts of the migration experience by West Indian women'.[41] What we are addressing here, however, is how Caribbean writers are to re-write 'the West Indies' in an ideologically over-determined genre like the romance.

Two points are at issue here: one is the implications of a multinational publisher essentially soliciting (with all its sexual overtones, including voyeurism) for narratives of black/West Indian feminine desire for the purposes of marketing - that 'gap' is also, after all, a 'gap in the market'. The Heinemann specifications enjoin discretion in the treatment of sex because 'we would hope to sell to the upper level of the school market'. This target readership also affects language: writers are told 'keep the language simple...as not all readers will be totally fluent'. The inappropriateness of 'fluency' in a first language context is again naively unquestioned. Heinemann's motives, however, are secondary to the main point at issue, which is, in being invited, as the poster declares, to create 'a world of Caribbean romance', what kind of Caribbean do the writers construct? By affording writers the opportunity and outlet for revisioning the post colonial subject through romance as what bell hooks calls a 'desiring subject(s) who can freely assert sexual agency',[42] Heinemann has inadvertently opened the issue of revisioning the Caribbean as a site, not of the outsider's desire for 'otherness', but as the very home of desire itself.[43]

Since Mills & Boon is the series explicitly identified by Heinemann as their paradigm, the extent to which the 'exotic' features can be illustrated by a glance at some of its titles. These include *Isle of Calypso*, featuring 'the Most Noble Baron Falcon Falzon of Malta', who 'combined the arrogance of a Spanish Grandee, the thieving instincts of a corsair, and the Arab's contemptuous belief that woman's sole purpose in life was to pander to the pleasure of man...'. *Jacintha Point* gives us Laurel sacrificing herself to save her father from 'rotting in a Mexican jail' by marrying 'the forceful Diego Ramirez', whom she hardly knew but could see 'that he had more than his fair share of machismo and the masculine superiority of his race'. *Stars Over Sarawak* is a story of 'two people thrown together in the primitive jungle of Borneo, with its mysteries and its dangers...', while in *Bride of the Rif,* Sara 'found herself whisked off into the Rif mountains of Morocco with Filipe...with such wedding ceremonies as 'the cleaning of the wheat' and being painted with henna'. It is quite clear from the blurbs that the 'exotic' is both geographical and sexual in these tales in which young English 'ladies' find themselves thrown into the arms of dangerous foreigners. In *An Apple in Eden*, where Eve worries about her 'flighty younger sister' who has fallen for a Spaniard, and ponders: 'It was all very well for Lyn to be thrilled by the glamour of it all - but a Spaniard was not an Englishman, and the Spanish idea of marriage and wifely duties was not at all what Lyn had been brought up with', the opposition of home and foreign, familiar and dangerously unknown, English lady and slightly threatening Mediterranean masculinity, is made even more explicit. Of course, as Tania Modleski points out in a discussion of Harlequin romances, the formula demands male brutality as a covert manifestation of the hero's repressed desire for the heroine and the plot turns on the revelation of that desire, and the hero's subsequent transformation into a gentle/man and lover.[44] In this case, the hero's obvious deviation from the kind of behaviour one has been brought up to expect is both a function of and intensified by his foreignness.

To return to the Caribbean, *One Brief Sweet Hour* tells the story of Lauren embarking on a Caribbean holiday which 'was meant to be a once in a lifetime thing - the end of her unhappy past, her unsatisfactory marriage...and, she hoped, the beginning of a new and more satisfactory life'. On board the cruise ship she is distressed to find herself confronted with Dale, an ex-admirer who treats her with true to form brutality. On a stopover in Barbados, Lauren goes on an outing, reassured from the outset that, 'there was nothing sinister or frightening about Bridgetown to a woman exploring it alone'.[45] In the main square, 'a young man with a shining chocolate face', a taxi driver, offers to take her on a tour, which she accepts. They have no trouble in communicating as, 'He spoke English well, if economically, missing out any words he didn't seem to find necessary to his meaning'.[46] This is a sample of their conversation:

At one point Rico asked, 'You married lady, lady?'
'Not now', she said, 'I'm widowed. Are you a married man?'
'No'...he added without embarrassment, 'I got five children and sweetheart gal'.
'Oh', was all Lauren could find to reply.[47]

Rico persuades Lauren to meet his 'piccanins', and she decides 'she could humour him by meeting his brood and his 'sweetheart gal' '. At Rico's house ('built of wood and iron sheeting'), Lauren expertly recognised that his baby is having a fit, and treats it for convulsions. As a result of her humanitarian impulse, she is late back at the boat, cue for Dale to rebuke her with customary brutality, informing Lauren that neither Barbados nor St Just, their next port of call, are free of 'hazards to foolhardy young women who think they know it all. Neither of them is England, with street lamps and telephone booths every few hundred yards'.[48]

The obverse of the paradisical Caribbean of freedom and sensual delight is the Caribbean as site of potential danger and threat to unprotected white/English/ladyhood. Enough has been said to indicate how far the exotic myth is founded on both racial stereotyping and a displacement of desire onto elsewhere and other. And so we return to the question of what kind of Caribbean the Carribean romance writer is going to construct out of such a welter of contradictions. Of the six titles so far published, four are set in Trinidad, one in Jamaica and one in Barbados, but a common thread that unites them is a spirit of national pride. On one level, this is conveyed through description, the use of scenery and architecture to create a suitable romantic setting:

They had driven in from the road along what appeared to be a never ending driveway, on either side of which were majestic royal palms. And then suddenly there was the house, impressive with its country style white washed walls and a rust coloured Spanish tile roof.[49]

While this may owe something to tourist cliché, the difference is that it is being observed by a young Jamaican woman who shares a flat in Kingston with her sister, works in an office in New Kingston and has to negotiate the traffic between the two. In other words, such descriptions are part of an overall context which marks them as glamorous and out of the ordinary. Sensitivity to the natural environment, a feature of most of the heroines, denotes an identification with place which is actually part of the heroine's character. For example, this is how we are introduced to Khadija, heroine of *Hand in Hand*:

> As the sun rose slowly over Tyrico Bay Khadija, dressed in an old grey t-shirt and shorts, ran along the shore. Her waist length black hair streamed behind her as she pounded down the edge of the surf, practising her Spanish grammar as she ran.[50]

Khadija's early morning exercise routine is the occasion for a description of 'her curvy torso clad in a black swimsuit' as she 'waded into the powerful waves', obviously at one with her environment and equal to its challenges. Again, this scene of natural beauty is an intrinsic part of a world which includes the university campus, and coffee bars in Port of Spain. While there is no shortage of the kind of settings obligatory to romance: luxurious, expensive, architect designed houses, hotels, offices, etc., these are counter balanced by a more realistic tendency. The heroine in *Merchant of Dreams,*[51] though she ends up in an exquisite period house in a characterful Bridgetown suburb, starts out as the exploited employee of an advertising agency, only able to afford a hot and poky little flat where she loses her underwear from a shared washing line.

Perhaps the most 'realist' treatment of environment, however, is given in Valerie Belgrave's *Sun Valley Romance,* which opens: 'The sound of a heavily laden truck straining its way up Main Street mingled with the rattle of the sewing machine and the unhappy wail of the toddler in the next room.[52] This single sentence encapsulates the heroine's background and present situation, living in a community which is being ravaged by a ruthless mining concern (the straining truck), dust from whose operations infiltrates houses and lungs alike (the unhappy toddler). The sewing machine is an indication of how Giselle supports herself - assisting her mother in dressmaking, having dropped out of university because her family can no longer find the fees. The fate of Sun Valley village in fact provides a sub plot to the romance between Giselle and her rich admirer, who turns out to be heir to the mining company. When the subsidence caused by quarrying leads to a flood and a child is drowned, Gary makes extensive reparations to the community and convinces Giselle that he had not been responsible. Far from the isolated individuals of the western formula, Belgrave and the other writers have unanimously opted for heroines who are locked into family and community, a significant feature in their construction of a Caribbean 'world'. Ann Bar Snitow observes of *Harlequins* that : 'Old people hardly appear except as benevolent peripheral presences. Young women have no visible parents, no ties to a before'.[53] In this respect, the *Caribbean Caress* authors deviate radically from the formula, for the heroines are surrounded by grandmothers, parents, siblings, uncles, aunts, friends and workmates, many of whom play a crucial role in the progress of the romance. Rena of *Love in Hiding* lives with her grandmother, and mis-perceives Thierry, the neighbour's son, as an adopted big brother.[54] *Hand in Hand* actually takes the form of a family saga in miniature, with elements of mystery, suspense and concealed identity, and a secret to which Andel, the hero, holds the key. In *Sun Valley Romance*, the family plays an important role throughout, for example, the mending of the relationship between Giselle's brother and their stepfather as a result of campaigning against the mining company. There are collective scenes such as village meetings, the panyard, the market and above all, Carnival. Furthermore, it is the grandmother who orchestrates Giselle's eventual reunion with Gary, whose ally she has been all along: 'Oh yes, me and him is good friends. He comes to see me and he sits down here, and I sit in the rocker and we talk'.[55] When Gary and Giselle finally come together it is in the graveyard during Divali, where Giselle is laying flowers on her father's grave, the context one of collective festival spirit and filial remembrance.

This then is one significant way in which the *Caribbean Caress* authors have chosen to interpret their call to construct 'a world of Caribbean romance'. While acquiescing in romance fiction's preoccupation with clothes and furnishings, they have repudiated the dictates of the formula that:

> They reduce the allure of difference, of travel, to a mere travelogue. The couple is alone, there is no society, no context, only surroundings.[56]

Furthermore, the element of 'escapism' prescribed by Heinemann finds a peculiarly Caribbean solution, provided by the diversity of the region, even of individual islands. When an 'exotic' setting is called for, either for a romantic interlude, for a retreat for the heroine or to stage a dramatic event, every locale has its own version. For Erica in *Hand in Hand*, it is first Ocho Rios, a 'fantasy land for love', then the Blue Mountains which she views as 'heaven on earth', and where Jamaican weather intervenes dramatically to cut her off from the elusive Julian long enough for his love to be made manifest. When further problems drive them apart, the final denouement is staged at Erica's parents' village, two and a half hours drive from Kingston, which turns out to be where Julian also has his roots. When, as Julian wryly comments, he needs a 'romantic setting' for his proposal, one is literally right on the doorstep: 'He pulled her into the living room and opened the front door...A full moon crept over the nearby mountains, its white light creating a silver and grey landscape'.[57] For the Trinidadian heroines of *Heartaches and Roses* and *Sun Valley Romance*, the 'exotic' is Tobago, while for Khadija and Andel (*Hand in Hand*), it is the compromise location of their future life - he won't live in Trinidad and she won't live in London.[58] Rena (*Love in Hiding*) flees to her old convent school in Barbados to try and escape Thierry, while the most consciously ironic use of the 'exotic' is made by *Merchant of Dreams*, actually (though not explicitly) set in Barbados.

The whole novel, indeed, whose heroine is an advertising executive, plays with the stereotyped elements of the formula, deconstructing fantasy even as it creates it, through detailed descriptions of the advertising process. Sent to Aruba to do a location shoot, Lorna excitedly anticipates adventure:

> Everybody in the business knew stories about ads shot in exotic locations. In some places they thought that this was an exotic location, if you please. Sure didn't seem so exotic when you lived here.[59]

(Interestingly, *Merchant of Dreams* is the only novel to move out of the anglophone Caribbean. The whole French and Spanish speaking Caribbean offers itself for future exploration, not to speak of Guyana and Surinam!) Contrasting the names of places she wants to visit with those in Barbados, Lorna comments: 'Malmok, Bushiribana, the Hooiberg...they all sounded so exotic, so different from places with names like Hillaby, or Morgan Lewis, or Long Pond'.[60] And she is not disappointed. In Aruba, she creates a spectacular commercial for Atlas beer, which plays on the Paradise paradigm while revealing its falsity:

> It was all pure fantasy of course - anyone who knew anything about Aruba would realise that Bushiribana was on the other side of the island from where they had done the windsurfing sequence. If the happy couple had really had to walk from Palm Beach to the ruins of the gold smelting plant to get to their ice cold bottles of Atlas they would have collapsed from heat exhaustion long before they had got there.[61]

Apart from being the backdrop to the heroine's successful advertising project, Aruba is also, ironically, the place where her own fantasy - of running over a cliff into the arms of the hero - comes true, although being on the hefty side, she knocks him over and they end up rolling in the sand. The title, *Merchant of Dreams*, explicitly draws attention both to the heroine's profession - 'selling dreams to other people', as a friend comments - and to the function of the narrative itself, to make dreams come true. And so, if the heroine is anxious about what she perceives to be her slight tendency to overweight, the hero exhibits the prevailing Barbadian male appreciation for exorbitant female flesh, while more importantly admiring her for her talent and application. Fulfilling one dream by getting the handsome male model, she also realises her dream of leaving the advertising agency and setting up on her own.

This last aspect of deviation from the formula is most conspicuous in Nigerian romance fiction, where self realisation is envisaged, not only as marriage to the ideal man, but much more importantly as the heroine's achievement of something for herself, in terms of professional or business success. It points towards a different conceptualisation of the heroine function, which privileges autonomy and pragmatism. In nearly all cases, *Caribbean Caress* heroines combine emotional fulfilment with other kinds of achievement. Even the most formulaic of them, such as *Heartaches and Roses*, has the heroine rescue the hero's hotel business through her accountancy and organisational skills. There is, however, a marked degree of variation in the representation of the heroine along the continuum from stereotype to reconstruction. To fulfil her function, the romantic heroine will inevitably partake of the stereotype to some extent, but she may also subvert it by subtle deviations. The least deviant in this respect is Betty of *Heartaches and Roses*, who signals her candidacy for wifehood from the outset by befriending the hero's children while on holiday in his hotel. The author's uncritical adherence to romantic cliché makes this novel, paradoxically, the least pleasurable to read. The heroine, recovering from being jilted, falls in love after only one encounter with the hero. The major obstacle to their union - the fact that she has had a hysterectomy - is too flimsy to be convincing, and the ending's categorical endorsement of bourgeois values is less satisfying than it is absurd:

> 'It's beautiful beyond description', she exclaimed in ecstasy. 'But that gorgeous, brilliant diamond ring didn't come from a magic wand, did it?'[62]

Cyril's explanation that it is a family heirloom is the cue for Betty to promise that it will always remain in the family, and for Cyril to whisper, 'You'll be a wonderful wife and mother'. Yet, even this must be seen in the light of her inability to have children, and her earlier betrayal at the hand of the unscrupulous Randy, who used her money to finance another relationship.

Despite, or perhaps because of, its failure to transform or evade the metanarrative of romance, *Heartaches and Roses* highlights a common problem of *Caribbean Caress* authors: how to enable their heroines to retain the qualities of assertiveness, self-motivation and independence characteristic of Caribbean women, while also retaining the attributes of reticence, modesty and sexual innocence until recently considered desirable by the western formula. The heroines' conservatism in sexual matters may perhaps be seen in the light of Barbara Bush's discussion of the pernicious effects of earlier stereotypes, where she says:

> The European assessment of black female sexuality has been seminal in the development of many unfavourable misconceptions about black womanhood in general. It has coloured and influenced both contemporary and modern attitudes to the black woman, not only in the sexual sphere, but also as a worker, mother and wife.[63]

The exact nature of this colouring and influence is more complex than I am able to do justice to here, incorporating the sociology of the family in the Caribbean, attitudes to marriage, the prevalence of female headed households, the 'outside woman' phenomenon and no doubt other considerations, including the impact of tourism. In relation to *Caribbean Caress*, I am speculating that a number of issues may be at play. Firstly, the fact of writing about black sexuality for a foreign based publisher means that a foreign readership is implicit, even if the primary market is in the Caribbean. Secondly, the series has been designated as for a youthful audience, so it inevitably has an implicitly educational function. Thirdly, the very fact that monogamy and the nuclear family are far from the norm may render them all the more desirable as fantasy, where the reality decrees that many women carry the main burden of responsibility for family survival alone. And finally, the writers may well have a considerable investment in counteracting negative stereotypes, including immorality, irresponsibility and black male predatoriness. It is notable that even heroines like Erica in *Fantasy of Love*, who are shown to be highly competent and confident in other areas, live in dread of revealing themselves as overtly sexual or too 'responsive', as in this passage where Julian snatches a kiss by the filing cabinet:

> She knew she was staring at him, still mesmerised. She knew she had responded to his kiss. Had she also pressed her body against his? She couldn't remember. She couldn't bear to think of it if she had.[64]

It is a characteristic of romance fiction that it gives out contradictory messages, and in the repression of natural desire *Caribbean Caress* heroines are no different from the old Mills & Boon or Harlequin. The difference in social context may, however, suggest another way of reading this obligation to pretence - an insistence on commitment and responsibility. There can be no other way of explaining the struggle of *Love in Hiding*'s Rena to control what is quite obviously her exclusive passion for Thierry, which is carried to such extremes as to undermine the credibility of the plot. Since the narrative constructs sex as woman's most precious gift to man, Rena's 'response' to Thierry makes her vulnerable, and several kissing sequences are in fact depicted in terms of male domination which are close to rape. Each time, however, Rena subsequently blames herself for giving way and shrinks in horror at being thought a 'tramp', so that she is prepared to go to the extent of joining her old convent to avoid this.

As with the 'exotic', the most fun in terms of overturning stereotypes is had by *Merchant of Dreams*, whose unconventional heroine lusts after the handsome hunk of a male model she uses in her beer commercials. There is a deliberate inversion of power relations in her position as director of the film shoot, arranging the objectified male body to suit her own concept, yet Lorna too is the victim of prevailing notions of beauty. In competition with the female model, her self confidence deflates, and it is only right at the end, after the hero has explained all, that she takes over again. 'She knew at last she had what she wanted. But right now she wanted more. 'Come let's go', she said'.[65] This forthrightness is rare so far in the construction of the Caribbean romance heroine, and it may be that romance fiction, with its chivalric and bourgeois antecedents, is the wrong place to look for it. Steve Harney and Carolyn Cooper both point to popular culture as the site where radical alternatives to inherited notions of 'ladyness' can be found. Although romance occupies an anomalous space between 'high' and 'low' culture, in what Cooper calls the Slackness/Culture dialectic', it would no doubt be on the side of Culture.[66] Yet, the example of Nigeria shows that romance fiction can become a vehicle for a covert form of rebellion which, through fantasy, rewrites the script of women's desire and middle class social expectations. I suspect that *Caribbean Caresses* may well be doing the same for the Caribbean.

Notes

1. Emmanuel Obiechina, *An African Popular Literature*, Cambridge University Press, Cambridge, 1973, p.70.
2. Diane Elam in *Romancing the Post-Modern*, Routledge, London, 1992, makes the point, with which I wholeheartedly concur, that romance is the most elusive of categories, covering 'a wide range of often widely divergent materials which simply do not seem to fit one generic category very comfortably' (p.4), and transcending the perceived boundary between 'high' and 'low' culture. She argues that every text which signals itself as romance by, presumably, some adherence to recognisable conventions, also exceeds and transforms those conventions, so that 'the ability of romance texts to act upon the genre of which they are said to be a part, occurs in such a way as to defy the very notion of generic conventions...which necessitates a rethinking of genre itself' (p.176).

   This conclusion seems to be well demonstrated by the case of Nigerian (and, by extension, African) romance fiction, as I suggest in the text of this paper. However, with respect to the Caribbean, I am dealing specifically with 'popular' or 'low' form or romance fiction exemplified by brand names like Mills & Boon and based on the well known Romantic formula, while recognising that romance in its wider sense informs much earlier work, from travel narratives to Jean Rhys's paradigmatic *Wide Sargasso Sea*, 1966.
3. Obiechina, 1973, op. cit., p.71.
4. Virginia Coulon, 'Onitsha Goes National: Nigerian Writing in Macmillan's Pacesetter Series', *Research in African Literatures*, 18(3), Fall, 1987, pp. 304-19; Jurgen Martini, 'Sex, Class and Power: The Emergence of a Capitalist Youth Culture in Nigeria', *Journal of African Children's Literature*, 1, 1987, pp.43-59; Wendy Griswold and Misty Bastian, 'Continuities and

Reconstructions in Cross Cultural Literary Transmission: The Case of the Nigerian Romance Novel', *Poetics*, (16), 1987, pp.327-35; Jane Bryce and Kari Dako, 'Textual Deviancy and Cultural Syncretism: Romantic Fiction as a Subversive Strain in Black Women's Writing', *Wasafiri,* 17, Spring, 1993, pp.10-14.

5. See Wendy Griswold and Misty Bastian, 1987, op. cit., p.333
6. For theoretical analyses of the disguised feminist role and function of the western romance genre, see Janice Radway, *Reading the Romance*, 1984; Ann Bar Snitow, *Mass Market Romance*, 1986; Alison Light, *Returning to Manderlay: Romance Fiction, Female Sexuality and Class*, 1984; and J. Radford (ed.), *The Progress of Romance: the Politics of Popular Fiction*, 1986. For a discussion of formulaic literature, see John Cawelti *Adventure, Mystery and Romance,* 1976.
7. Virtually the only locally published romance I have been able to discover is by the pseudonymous Tatanka Yotanka, *Dorothea's Ambition,* Caribbean OPC Consultants, Barbados, 1989. Publication of this novel, a cross between historical romance and sociological commentary, was made possible by commercial sponsorship and the text is framed by advertisements. There is a dedication to Barbadian storyteller Timothy Callender, who 'taught and showed us how to publish and market books. He not only edited, typed and bound his own, but also went out and sold them', till one day, 'in frustration at his thwarted efforts to have his books accepted by the educational institutions of Barbados, he challenged us to beat the pulp romances' (p.v). By responding with a romantic novel which s/he has published and marketed him/herself, the writer acknowledges the crucial role played by the publishing and literary hierarchy in the production and reception of popular fiction. The imbalance in power relations to which it points may well account for the absence of other, 'local' romance fiction, the very 'gap' identified by the British publisher Heinemann.
8. For example, Loveswept, Harlequin, Mills & Boon.
9. In 1971, Mills & Boon merged with the Canadian firm Harlequin, itself established in 1957 and a huge supplier of romance fiction to North America and Europe. *The Sunday Times* , 6 February 1994 reports cataclysmic changes at Mills & Boon with the removal of 'two top executives' after 20 years, in the name of 90s marketability. The split is characterised in the report as a divorce between 'the British approach to romance and the Canadian approach to business', resulting from the British firm's resistance to Harlequin's notoriously aggressive marketing strategies, and pressure to become more 'modern' in its approach to sex. A former editor, quoted as saying: 'The old culture was very beautiful and a lot of people would still like to live, fantasise and write in that world', pinpoints the essential conservatism of a cherished but archaic notion of chivalry. Will *Caribbean Caresses*, born at the moment of the demise of the old Mills & Boon, provide us with the ultimate irony: the displacement of a central tenet of European 'civilization' onto a decentred, post colonial revisioning of romance, the New World as last repository of the fantasies of the Old...?

10. *Guardian Weekly*, 13 February, 1994.
11. Grace Nichols, *Fat Black Woman's Poems,* Virago, 1984; Erna Brodber, *Jane and Louisa Will Soon Come Home*, New Beacon, London, 1980; Merle Hodge, *Crick Crack Monkey*, Heinemann, London, 1970; Jamaica Kincaid, *Annie John*, Farrar, NY, 1985; Jamaica Kincaid, *Lucy,* Picador, London, 1990; Olive Senior *Arrival of the Snake Woman*, Longman, Essex, 1989.
12. Merle Hodge, *Crick Crack Monkey*, Heinemann, UK, 1970, p.2.
13. Hazel Carby, *Reconstructing Womanhood,* OUP, Oxford, 1987, p.25
14. Evelyn O'Callaghan, *Woman Version*, Macmillan, London, 1993, p.25.
15. Hazel Carby, 1987, op. cit., p.27.
16. bell hooks, *Yearning: Race, Gender and Cultural Politics,* Turnaround Press, London, 1991, p.58.
17. Valerie Belgrave, *Ti Marie*, Heinemann, UK, 1988.
18. Ibid, p.vii.
19. Valerie Belgrave,'On Combining Batik Art and Novel Writing' in Selwyn Cudjoe (ed.) *Caribbean Women Writers*, Mass, Calaloux Publications, 1990, p.317.
20. Ibid, p.318.
21. Valerie Belgrave, 1988, op. cit., p.42.
22. Valerie Belgrave 'Thoughts on the Choice of Theme and Approach in Writing *Ti Marie*' in Selwyn Cudjoes, 1990, op. cit., p.325.
23. Ibid, p.326.
24. Ibid, p.327.
25. Steve Harney, 'Men Goh Respect All O' We: Valerie Belgrave's *Ti Marie* and the Invention of Trinidad', *World Literature Written in English*, 30(2), Autumn, 1990, p.28.
26. Ibid, p.111.
27. Ibid, p.116.
28. Valerie Belgrave, 'Thoughts on the Choice of Theme and Approach in Writing *Ti Marie*' in Selwyn Cudjoe, 1990, op. cit., p.327.
29. Barbara Bush, *Slave Women in Caribbean Society 1650-1838,* James Currey, London, 1990, p.15.
30. Ibid, p.17.
31. Valerie Belgrave, 1988, op. cit, p.46.
32. Ibid, p.46.
33. Barbara Bush, 1990, op. cit., p.31.
34. Valerie Belgrave, 1988, op. cit., p.6.
35. Steve Harney, 1990, op. cit., p.110.
36. Barbara Bush, 1990, op. cit., p.17.
37. Valerie Belgrave 'Thoughts on the choice of theme and approach in writing *Ti Marie*' in Selwyn Cudjoes, 1990, op. cit., p.325.
38. Diane Elam, 1992, op. cit., p.20.
39. In 'Mass Market Romance: Pornography for Women is Different' in Mary

Eagleton (ed.), *Feminist Literary Theory*, Blackwell, UK, 1986, Ann Bar Snitow observes:

While the heroine waits for the hero's next move, her time is filled by tourism and by descriptions of consumer items: furniture, clothes and gourmet foods...Several of the books have passages that probably come straight out of guide books, but the particular setting is not the point, only that it is exotic, a place elsewhere (p.135).

40. Evelyn O'Callaghan, *Woman Version*, Macmillan, London, 1993, p.27.
41. Ibid, p.28.
42. bell hooks, 1991, op. cit., p.61.
43. This is a paradoxical concept, which I'm not sure I have expressed clearly, since desire is always a desire for something 'other', an elusive alterity expressed metonymically in romance in terms of gender. If love is the impulse towards self-recreation through identification with another, some kind of transformation is implicit in this process. The contrast I seek to draw is between the Caribbean as a tourist Paradise of sun-drenched beaches, and the Caribbean as the lived reality of men and women contending with all the economic and cultural imperatives of the post colonial situation.
44. Tania, Modleski, *Loving With A Vengeance*, Routledge, London, 1990, pp.39-43.
45. Jane Arbor, *One Brief Sweet Hour*, Mills & Boon, 1980, p.45.
46. Ibid, p.46.
47. Ibid, p.48.
48. Ibid, p.54.
49. Deidre d'Allan, *Fantasy of Love* , Heinemann, London, 1993.
50. Lyn-Anne Ali, *Hand in Hand*, Heinemann, London, 1993.
51. Lucille Colleton, *Merchant of Dreams*, Heinemann, London, 1993.
52. Valerie Belgrave, *Sun Valley Romance,* Heinemann, London, 1993.
53. Ann Bar Snitow, 'Mass Market Romance: Pornography for Women is Different', *Radical History Review*, 20, 1979, pp.141-61.
54. Annette Charles, *Love in Hiding*, Heinemann, London, 1993.
55. Valerie Belgrave, 1993, op. cit., p.130.
56. Ann Bar Snitow, 1979, op. cit., pp.138.
57. Deidre d'Allan, 1993, op. cit., p.139.
58. Dorothy Jolly, *Heartaches and Roses.* Heinemann, 1993.
59. Lucille Colleton, 1993, op. cit., p.80.
60. Ibid, p.89.
61. Ibid, p.114.
62. Dorothy Jolly, 1993, op. cit., p.152.
63. Barbara Bush, 1990, op. cit., p.61.
64. Deidre d'Allan, 1993, op. cit., pp.86-87.
65. Lucille Colleton, 1993, op. cit., p.98.
66. Carolyn Cooper, *Noises in the Blood*, Macmillan, London, 1993, p.43.

Houses and Homes
Elizabeth Jolley's *Mr Scobie's Riddle* and Beryl Gilroy's *Frangipani House*

Mary Condé

Elizabeth Jolley and Beryl Gilroy, both born in the nineteen twenties, both changed countries in the nineteen fifties, Elizabeth Jolley leaving England for Australia and Beryl Gilroy leaving Guyana for England. They both wrote novels in the nineteen eighties set in old people's homes: an unusual choice of setting. Old people are a difficult subject for fiction, partly because old age does not give much scope for action and so is fundamentally bad for plots (unless memory is brought very strongly into play, in which case old people effectively cease to be the subject) and partly because old age is disconcertingly repellent, inspiring reactions of guilt and disgust. We feel that old people ought to be revered and protected, and consistently imagine either that this used to happen in our own culture, or else that it is still happening elsewhere in other cultures. Old age has frightening implications, too, because the only way we can avoid it is by dying in good time. And as Mr Scobie's very easy riddle in *Mr Scobie's Riddle* reminds us, this is very difficult. He asks Matron Price, hoping to put her in a better mood, 'What is it that we all know is going to happen but we don't know when or how?'[1] Matron gives up. When Mr Scobie whispers the answer, she flushes furiously, and punishes him by forcing him to have a shower, although he protests unhappily that he is 'All clean and correct'. Mr Scobie himself dies during the course of Jolley's novel, as do the two men, Mr Hughes and Mr Privett, with whom he is admitted. Their ages, eighty-five in each case, and symptoms, hemiplegia, left side, hypertension, and altered mental state, respectively, are exactly reproduced in the three men who are admitted in their places as the novel closes. This reminds us of the bleak and brisk turnover in all old people's homes, but is also typical of Jolley's narrative in its drawing of our attention to the idiosyncratic methods of the home, St. Christopher and St. Jude, called after the saint of the wayfarer and the saint 'of all hopeless cases, right from the first century', as Mr Scobie observes.[2] All six admissions are noted as occurring at four in the morning, the time Night Sister M. Shady invariably selects for any event in her reports, because, as she explains:

> I am sorry matron about the time 4 a.m. There is no clock here as you know and so when the milk comes I know it is four o'clock as he is punctual and I hear his word when he falls on the broken step out there.[3]

Eighty five is perhaps, by analogy, merely Night Sister M. Shady-speak for 'very old'. Shady, with her triply appropriate name (she works only at night, she colludes with the cheating of the matron's brother at cards, and she is a very shadowy character), appears in the novel only through her garbled notes to Matron Price, and a volley of these notes opens the novel proper, after a deliberately confusing 'Guide To The Perplexed'. Elizabeth Jolley said in an interview that she had originally told Mr Scobie's story in the first person but had decided that 'you can't inflict that kind of pain on a reader'.[4]

Despite the babble of voices which Jolley chooses instead, her novel still remains far more painful than *Frangipani House*. For one thing, Beryl Gilroy does not express, either authorially or through her characters, the same disgust with old bodies expressed by Jolley through Mr Scobie's perceptions: he has a particular horror of fat old women, by whom he is surrounded, and:

> Often he sat for hours trying not to notice their unpleasant smell, the saliva trickling from their partly open mouths and the food spilled on their clothes.[5]

By contrast, the scene, for example, in which Miss Mason in *Frangipani House* dances, and lifts 'up all her nighties to show a dark-brown flabby bottom' is a serene and gentle one.[6]

Another important difference between the novels is that Beryl Gilroy's heroine, Mama King, is only sixty-nine and strong enough not only to engineer her own escape from the home, an escape which Mr Scobie, despite some gallant efforts, miserably fails in attempting, but also to enjoy her wanderings with the beggars until she it attacked by two boys. Mama King's escape also allows for some action in the present, which Elizabeth Jolley is forced to supply through a bizarre web of blackmail and intrigue in *Mr Scobie's Riddle*. Most important of all, whereas Mr Scobie has been cheated out of his own house and land, which is taken over at the end of the novel by a rather dubious commune, a sort of junior version of St. Christopher and St. Jude, Mama King still owns her own house and triumphantly returns to it, a property owning emotional survivor in the tradition of Zora Neale Hurston's Janie and Alice Walker's Celie. The importance of this house as Mama King's own space is underlined both by Mama King's refusal to leave it to go and live in the States with her granddaughter Cindy, and by the inadvertent burning down of her friend Ginchi's house by Carlton, who needs to exist in his own right and not just as 'Miss Ginchi's grandson'.[7] Not only is Mama King left in control of her own house, but she helps Cindy to give birth to the next generation in it, defeating the efforts of the midwife 'Missy New Fangle' to exclude her. She has broken the rule, outlined on the first page, that 'Death comes to lodgers in Frangipani House!'[8] Similarly, in Beryl Gilroy's *Boy -Sandwich* Tyrone's grandparents escape the old people's home in England and return to their island home by what seems the almost magical device of the discovered painting.[9] Such outcomes are inherently unlikely, but Beryl Gilroy's major preoccupation is not to write a fiction which conforms to rules of credibility, any more than it was Hurston's in *Their Eyes Were Watching God* or Walker's in *The Color Purple*, but to celebrate the reassertion of individuality against attempts to render it anonymous, which both Gilroy and Jolley see as the ultimate indignity inflicted on old people. One of the finest touches in *Frangipani House* occurs at its close, in an exchange in which Mama King gracefully but inexorably takes control. In response to Missy New Fangle's demand that the new born babies be labelled, Mama King smiles and nods, saying: 'Yes, label them. Two nice parcel that come from God'.[10]

She acquiesces with the bureaucratic procedure, but endows it with her own meaning. It is no accident that this tiny, crucial tussle is over a shift of viewpoint, for this is what Mama King has been insisting on throughout the novel.

The reader, too, must make adjustments. At first sight, Mama King appears to be the strong, good, hard-working grandmother, manifesting her love and strength through traditional skills, recently celebrated in Nikki Giovanni's anthology *Grand Mothers,*[11] and featuring so frequently in Caribbean women's fiction. Examples are Merle Collins' road-making 'Gran',[12] the grandmothers in Jean Buffong's *Under The Silk Cotton Tree*[13] and Velma Pollard's short story 'Gran',[14] who are both bakers, Granny Ruby in Joan Riley's *Romance*[15] who does exquisite crochet work, and Ma-Mariah in Audre Lorde's *Zami*[16] and Ma Chess in Jamaica Kincaid's *Annie John,*[17] a root woman and a healer. When Mama King is imprisoned in *Frangipani House*, she feels that 'more than anything else, she wanted work',[18] and she visualises work as a faithful friend who has deserted her, confirming her friend Ginchi's verdict that 'Confinement and do-nothing destroy people'.[19] Mama King remembers her 'grandchildren's clothes washed and ironed with love'[20] and relives happily in her imagination:

> ...The squelching of cheap soap and the slithering confidence of the starch, the familiar feel of cotton, crisp as new biscuit.[21]

But this positive imagery is immediately subverted by the descriptions of

Matron 'shouting as if her voice had been starched and left in the sun to harden'[22] and of Mrs Gomez, another inmate, in a fit, 'froth coming from her mouth like soapy water on wash day'.[23] Mama King is forced to recognise that although she has been a good grandmother, she has been a bad mother, because:

> Work had been the culprit that wrecked her life, robbed her of her perspicacity and deprived her children of her love.[24]

Another shift of viewpoint occurs when we discover that Mama King's beloved husband Danny, whom she remembers so fondly, is, as an acquaintance puts it, 'an imaginary man',[25] since he was in reality a cruel brute, a further shift when we discover that Danny, who mysteriously disappeared one night, was effectively murdered by Mama King's loyal friend, Miss Ginchi,[26] and yet another when we discover that Miss Ginchi has a sexual motive of her own.[27] *Frangipani House*, which opens so lucidly with extended personification of the house, 'eloquent, compelling and smug', wearing its skirt of closely-cropped grass, is actually as complex a story as Jolley's deliberately confused and disjointed narrative.

What both novels do is to draw our attention to the connections between the old people's homes and the activities of reading and writing. Elizabeth Jolley's Matron Price draws on a fiction, inherited from England, of a cosy boarding school trio in order to coerce one schoolmate, Miss Hailey, into becoming an inmate of St. Christopher and St. Jude, and another, Mrs Rawlings, into working there without pay. Matron Price affects to be a devout Christian, but drops this pretence quite readily: 'Oh never mind about Jesus just now' she says to one patient. 'He's been dead for years, dear'.[28] Her feelings about her old school, whose real-life bullying and cruelty she probably reproduces fairly accurately, run much deeper, particularly when she herself is drinking deeply of the brandy which, Mrs Gamp-like, she reserves for her 'own personal medicinal use',[29] and the glow which her (essentially false) memories provide enable her to justify herself:

> 'I do do my bit', Matron Price reasoned with herself, 'I mean, I employ people. I employ girls to wash up instead of having machines'.[30]

Miss Hailey, a 'real' fiction writer, although she has had her novel rejected one hundred and forty two times, draws an explicit parallel when she tells Matron Price that:

> We writers...are responsible to our readers just as you...are responsible to your patients.[31]

The patients are the unwilling, but necessary, audience of Matron Price's fantasies of power.

Beryl Gilroy's Matron is also sustained by alcohol and her conviction of altruism:

'God bless you, rum', she says, 'You look like piss and you hot like fire'[32] and she readily persuades herself that Frangipani House was the best eventide home in the world.

But the inmate of Frangipani House who is most contented with her lot is Miss Mason, who is 'fake-happy - Paper-happy!' as one nurse says,[33] since she immerses herself in 'true romances'[34] and is discovered after her death to have written poetry to an imagined lover.[35] The activities of reading and writing are part of the hard work (and hard work is not necessarily a good thing) which has gone into building the old people's homes; incidentally, in both *Mr Scobie's Riddle* and *Frangipani House* inmates have particularly poignant memories of bricks. Despite his year with an African tribe, these activities have also helped Chuck, Cindy's American husband, to erect his theories about the good place elsewhere:

> The old in Africa have a place and a function, they are never cast aside.[36]

As Cindy points out, he has used these ideas only to distance himself from his actual home and family.[37]

The concept of home is a focus for much Caribbean women's fiction and is reflected in the titles of Erna Brodber's *Jane and Louisa Will Soon Come Home,*[38] Joan Cambridge's *Clarise Cumberbatch Want To Go Home,*[39] Vernella Fuller's *Going Back Home,*[40] Velma Pollard's *Homestretch,*[41] and June Henfrey's short-story collection *Coming Home.*[42] A home is suggested only by its absence in *Mr Scobie's Riddle*, just as we never actually hear the answer to the riddle, or the milkman's word when he falls on the broken step, and time there has stopped still at 4 a.m. In *Frangipani House*, Mama King starts the clock ticking again when she confronts the mistakes she has made about her own life and makes the transition from house to house, affirming the strength and resilience of the Caribbean grandmother.

Notes

1. Elizabeth Jolley, *Mr Scobie's Riddle*, Penguin, Harmondsworth, 1983, p.120.
2. Ibid, p.130.
3. Ibid, p.3.
4. The Nights Belong to the Novelist', documentary video directed by Christina Wilcox, 1987.
5. Elizabeth Jolley, 1983, op. cit., p.121.
6. Beryl Gilroy, *Frangipani House*, Heinemann, London, 1986, p.13. It is tempting to see Miss Mason's name as a literary allusion to *Jane Eyre*'s Bertha Mason, like Elean Thomas's mad Mrs Mason in *The Last Room*, Virago, London, 1991, but the name is taken not from literature but life.
7. Gilroy, 1986, op, cit., p.82.

8. Ibid, p.1.
9. This device, Beryl Gilroy assures me, is also taken from life! Beryl Gilroy, *Boy Sandwich*, Longman, Harlow, 1985.
10. Ibid, p.109.
11. Nikki Giovanni (ed.), *Grand Mothers: Poems, Reminiscences and Short Stories About the Keepers of Our Traditions*, Henry Holt, NY, 1994.
12. Merle Collins, 'Gran' in *Rain Darling*, Womens Press, London, 1990.
13. Jean Buffong, *Under The Silk Cotton Tree,* Women's Press, London, 1989.
14. Velma Pollard, 'Gran' in *Considering Woman,* Women's Press, London, 1989.
15. Joan Riley, *Romance*, Women's Press, 1988.
16. Audre Lorde, *Zami: A New Spelling of My Name*, Trumansburg, NY, 1982.
17. Jamaica Kincaid, *Annie John,* Farrar, Straus & Giroux, 1983.
18. Beryl Gilroy, 1986, op, cit., p.19.
19. Ibid, p.48.
20. Ibid, p.52.
21. Ibid, p.53.
22. Ibid, p.54.
23. Ibid, p.56.
24. Ibid, p.80.
25. Ibid, p.34.
26. Ibid, pp.75-76.
27. Ibid, p.78.
28. Jolley, 1983, op, cit., p.54.
29. Ibid, p.4.
30. Ibid, p.153.
31. Ibid, p.151.
32. Beryl Gilroy, 1986, op. cit., p.74.
33. Ibid, p.13.
34. Ibid, p.10.
35. Ibid, p.44.
36. Jolley, 1983, op, cit., p.95.
37. Ibid, p.99.
38. Erna Brodber, *Jane and Louisa Will Soon Come Home*, New Beacon Books, London, 1980.
39. Joan Cambridge, *Clarise Cumberbatch Want To Go Home*, Women's Press, London, 1987.
40. Vernella Fuller, *Going Back Home*, Women's Press, London, 1992.
41. Velma Pollard, *Homestretch*, Longman, Harlow, 1994.
42. June Henfrey, *Coming Home and Other Stories*, Peepal Tree Press, Leeds, 1994.

BEYOND THE DIVIDE OF LANGUAGE

The many languages of the Caribbean have played, historically, a divisive role in maintaining political, social and, we have come to appreciate, literary boundaries informed by earlier colonial ties. In more recent years through debate reintegrating women's literature of the region, it has become clear that while individual traditions: anglophone and francophone, for example, may be linked to relatively small bodies of writing, collectively within the region, the corpus of women's writing is a substantial one. Within the anglophone tradition, for example, we have largely been aware of 'West Indian' literature to the exclusion of much else. The principle holds similarly true for Hispanophone speakers for example and the role of Caribbean women's conferences in highlighting this is to be acknowledged. The erstwhile pattern characterised by insularity has, latterly, been subject to critical change and when Caribbean women's writing is referred to, there is a growing understanding that the body of work includes literature written in a variety of languages.

In Part Three of this volume, four contributors whose essays push back the boundaries even further, allow invaluable insight beyond the divide of language. Spanish writers in Cuba, Surinam poets writing in Dutch and Sranan and Jamaican Creole writers are, in turn the focus of the essays.

Catherine Davies' 'Women Writers in Twentieth Century Cuba: An Eight-Point Survey' indicates the range of published contemporary women writers from the Caribbean's largest island, Cuba. Her overview of twentieth century writing begins by contextualising the Cuban situation to show ways in which both pre-revolutionary Cuba and the later nationalism or 'Cubanidad' impacted upon the literary history of the island. A substantial and detailed literary history is revealed prior to the development of Cuba's feminist movement, 'arguably the most advanced of its kind in Latin America'. Catherine Davies highlights the major women writers of pre-revolutionary Cuba many of whom, middle class Hispano-Cuban writers, it is suggested showed little particular interest in the Caribbean as such.

An examination of women's writing from the first two decades following the Revolution gives indication of the sheer range of writing as well as changes in thematic focus and style as the African heritage of the island becomes influential and black and mulatto women begin to claim a published voice. Catherine Davies shows how, in this period, with Cuba becoming established in a Third World or Caribbean context, Socialist and identity politics become articulated in the poetry of black women published. Critical attention paid to Nancy Morejon published since the sixties is highlighted and the role of lesser known black women writers of the island is outlined.

As for women's writing generally in the region, so too, a 'blossoming' is described within the Cuban context since 1980. Poetry is shown to be the foremost genre of the period and an interest in a range of forms and 'innovative directions' illustrated. Particular attention is paid to black women's erotic literature before questions of genre are addressed which clarify differences in literary production of the pre and post Revolution eras. Catherine Davies's comprehensive survey 'puts the record straight' by indicating both the quality and quantity of women's writing currently published in Cuba.

In 'Patterns of Resistance in Afro-Cuban 'Women's Writing', Nancy Morejon's 'Amo a mi amo', Conrad James's close reading of Nancy Morejon introduces the reader to a particularised articulation of the African-Caribbean woman's sexual exploitation and racial subjugation during the period of slavery. Conrad James shows how Morejon explodes, in her poetic reinscription, 'Amo a mi amo', the myth of preferential treatment leading to sexual acquiescence on the part of African women during slavery and simultaneously constructs 'a model of African female resistance'. Modes of resistance of the African woman, from verbal resistance to plots of revenge are highlighted, until the moment when, 'at the psychic level' she is spiritually free of her master.

Conrad James's interpretation turns on the social imperative of writing upon which Morejon insists, to reconcile the contradiction between the 'overt womanist perspectives' in the text and Morejon's tendency to subvert gender politics. Finally, Conrad James locates the poem in a tradition of the 'doubled or split discourse' with allegorical implications, he suggests, not just for the African-Caribbean situation but also for patriarchy within the Revolution.

Susanne Mühleisen's 'Encoding The Voice: Caribbean Women's Writing and Creole' addresses the question of how Caribbean women have 'constituted a prominent force' in the development of the orality-literacy debate of the region. She places the discussion in both the context of linguistic theory and the sociopolitical domain. Examining the works of three generations of Jamaican women writers: Louise Bennett, Olive Senior and Patricia Powell, Susanne Mühliesen argues that the writers may be 'considered paradigmatic' of the process whereby women, with their special relationship to the oral domain, have initiated, shaped and re-shaped the Caribbean language debate and 'their public status in the post-colonial age'.

The essay moves from a discussion of the special status of Creole to demonstrate ways in which the selected writers with their specific interest in Creole voices and oral culture are not only innovative and empowering but also signify the changing role of Creole in literary discourse.

Petronella Breinburg's 'Surinam Women Writers: Reflections on Language and the Process of Translation' ends this section with its particular focus on language. The essay addresses the relative invisibility of Surinam women writers in the debate about Caribbean women writers. Petronella Breinburg suggests that this neglect has held despite literacy skills acquired by Surinam women during the period of slavery. Women's scribal involvement has, Petronella Breinburg argues, played special parts from 'permission to be absent notes' of the period, through to later involvement in missionary writing and twentieth century literary writing. Petronella Breinburg pays tribute to contemporaneous Surinam women writers and considers some of the difficulties of translation from Sranan, a mothertongue Creole, to varieties of English.

Women Writers in Twentieth Century Cuba: An Eight-Point Survey

Catherine Davies

The aim of this essay is to provide an overview of women's writing in twentieth-century Cuba for the benefit of those who are interested primarily in Caribbean women's literature and who probably do not speak Spanish. In order to cover such a broad agenda in a coherent fashion I have summarised what in my opinion are the most salient features of this literary tradition in eight points.

Contextualisation

Cuba is, of course, the biggest Caribbean island with a population, in 1992, of ten and a half million of which over half are women. It is a Spanish speaking, multicultural society (about a third of the population are black or mixed) whose hybridity (European, North American, Latin American, African) is difficult to fix. It is a postcolonial society, dependent on Spain until 1898, and a quasi-dependency of the United States until 1959.[1] After the Socialist revolution of that year Cuba became a socialist society. The plantation economy of colonial Cuba was broadly similar to that of other parts of the Caribbean; slaves were imported mainly from West Africa (Yorubaland of today's Nigeria) and their cultures survived in religions such as Santeria. But Cuba was a settler society, so while links with the Spanish metropolis continued to be strong, Cubans distinguished themselves from their European inheritance by means of a syncretic culture of their own. Before the revolution, many wealthy Cubans looked to the US as a model of cultural modernity; Havana was an extremely sophisticated and cosmopolitan city. After the Revolution cultural ties with Latin America and Africa were cemented. However, the strongest ideological force in Cuba this century has been nationalism, or 'Cubanidad'. It has led to an homogenous national culture, despite class, racial and gender differences, always defined in opposition to somewhere else (Spain, US). The Cuban context for writers, therefore, presents many similarities but also marked contrasts with other parts of the Caribbean.

As far as women writers are concerned, generally speaking those publishing before the Revolution belonged to the educated white middle classes. After 1959 women writers are drawn from a much wider social spectrum and several black women writers begin to publish regularly. However, the literary expression of female sexuality and desire which the more daring women writers had attempted before the Revolution (in the 1920s) was not encouraged in what was, until recently, a fairly puritanical socialist society.

Reconstructing a Literary History

Cuban Creole women first made their names as writers in the Romantic period. The childhood memories of the Countess Merlin (1789-1852), who spent her first twelve years in Havana before settling in Spain and France were published in Paris in 1831 (and in Spanish in 1833).[2] The most outstanding Cuban woman writer of the nineteenth century was the Romantic poet, novelist and dramatist Gertrudis Gómez de Avellaneda (1814-1873). She left Cuba for Spain in her early twenties and returned to live there between 1859 and 1864. Her much acclaimed anti-slavery novel *Sab* (1841), published eleven years before Beecher Stowe's *Uncle Tom's Cabin* (1852), was considered to be highly subversive. Both *Sab* and a later novel *Dos mujeres* (Two Women) (1842-3) were prohibited in Cuba and seized by customs. *Sab* tells the story of a black slave, Sab, who falls in love with his gentle mistress, Carlota. She, in turn, loves the unscrupulous son of an English merchant who only wants her for her money. Thanks to Sab's crucial intervention Carlota marries her suitor but is very unhappy. Finally, Sab dies of a broken heart and Carlota visits his grave having realised how much he loved her. The novel is romantic and sentimental but unique for its times. In other Cuban anti-slavery novels, written by men, the catastrophic denouement is usually attributed to the white mother who takes on a masculine role; the black male slave is usually feminised and represents the virtuous woman. In this way, one subaltern subject becomes the victim of another. In *Sab*, however (as in Avellaneda's work generally) the mother figure is absent and all blame is placed on the nasty English suitor and his father. Also, although in *Sab* the mulatto slave is whitened (his lack of freedom is clearly analogous to that of the married woman) Avellaneda's novel is significant in that is introduces a third perspective, that of the Indian Martina (Sab's adopted mother). This endows the mulatto with subjectivity and agency because he too can focalise through the (indigenous) other.[3] In her novels, plays and women's magazine, Avellaneda consistently undermines concepts of centralised power and rewrites official versions of history from a subaltern point of view.[4]

There were many other successful women writers in nineteenth-century Cuba: the poets Luisa Pérez de Zambrana (1835-1922) and Juana Borrero (1877-1896) are just two of the better known.[5] Antonio González Curquejo's three volume *Florilegio de escritoras cubanas* (Anthology of Cuban Women Writers) (Havana: 1910-1919) includes the work (poetry and short essays) of over 120 women writing and publishing between 1833 and 1919. Another anthology, *Arpas cubanas* (Cuban Harps), appeared in 1904 containing the poetry of five women out of 29 contributors. Interestingly, many poems in these collections are overtly erotic, but the female sexual desire they articulate is projected onto objective correlatives, for example, a feminised landscape. 'Spring Scene' by Nieves Xenes (1859-1915) describes the virile sun surrounded by his passionate harem, the spring flowers. However, one indoor plant, whose leaves are as soft as a woman' skin, prefers the shade. When the sun visits her, she tingles with pleasure:

> when an uncontrollable, ardent lover
> swept magnificently by love,
> kisses her leaves and stems insatiably
> with fiery desire it's the sun.
> She stretches with voluptuous shivers
> she pauses trembling, and then
> fainting with listless languor
> she droops, with pleasure spent
>
> Nieves Xenes[6]

The Feminist Movement 1915-1940

All the above mentioned women belonged to the white Creole elite. Middle-class Cuban women of these years were, on the whole, educated, politically conscious and extremely patriotic. Many had participated actively in the Independence Wars as 'mambisas' and expected legal and political equality to ensue. But the 1901 Constitution did not give women the vote and from 1917 onwards a strong feminist movement developed, arguably the most advanced of its kind in Latin America. It culminated in the First National Women's Congress of 1923 in which 31 women's associations participated. A Second National Women's Congress was held in 1925, and a Third in 1936. Out of this feminist movement emerged several feminist journalists and writers. The most important were: poet laureate, Dulce María Borrero (1883-1945) who, as well as poetry, published an important book on marriage and divorce in 1914 and became director of Culture in the Ministry of Education in 1935; Mariblanca Sabas Alomá (1901-1985) known as the red feminist; and Ofelia Rodríguez Acosta (1902-1975) who wrote several feminist novels.[7]

The most popular of Rodríguez Acosta's novels, *La vida manda* (Life Demands), 1929, tells the sad story of Gertrudis, an independent and ambitious typist, whose affair with the handsome but deceitful Damian leads to her downfall. Intent on losing her virginity, unaware that her lover is married with a family, she gradually forfeits her hard-gained self-confidence and will-power. Their break-up leads to her almost having an affair with a lesbian, to a nervous breakdown, to having a baby fathered by her ex-fiancé (it later dies), to losing her job, and to shooting herself unsuccessfully so that she ends up blind and deranged. The moral of this tragic melodrama is that free love does not lead to women's emancipation. Economic independence must be matched by a radical rethinking of heterosexual relations and the private sphere. What is surprising about this long novel, given the date of publication, are the erotic bedroom scenes: 'there wasn't a corner of the woman's body his mouth hadn't sucked; under his mouth Gertrudis burned with insatiable, irresistible desire',[8] 'his legs crossed over her, with a precise thrust...The lover's chest covered his loved one's breasts without pressing them down. Their hips, swaying with the rhythm of a love song, kissed voluptuously with a burning, intricate touch'.[9] She smells of the 'scent of a man's body'[10] and when she is away from Damian, feels sexual desire 'with such a soft and demanding call' that unable to satisfy her desire brings her to tears.[11]

Although the narrator distances herself from these scenes by using third-person narrative the novel is nevertheless a courageous and successful attempt to chart female sexual desire from a woman's point of view and, not surprisingly, was much criticised by right-wing women.[12]

By the 1930s and 1940s a number of women writers held important public posts, for example, in education (Mirta Aguirre, 1912-1980, poet, essayist and professor and Camila Henríquez Ureña, 1884-1973) professor and essayist, poet and translator). Of course, unlike the above, not all women writers were feminists. Some had very sad lives. María Luisa Milanés (1893-1919) committed suicide at age of 26 because of an unhappy marriage and wrote despairing, aggressive poetry which was published posthumously. Following nineteenth-century models she likens her condition to a slave's:

I've made my decision, I'll leave, I'll break the bonds
that tie me to life and its pains.
I'll do as Spartacus;
I'll rise up breaking the chains

that made my existence so hopeless,
I look at tomorrow and yesterday and rage;
For better things have I been born
than to be a master's slave!

María Luisa Milanés[13]

Other writers were more fortunate. The wealthy socialite Lydia Cabrera (b.1900) came into contact with the negritude movement while studying fine arts in Paris. She remained in Paris until 1939 and it was there that she published her well-known *Contes nègres de Cuba* (Paris, 1936) followed by *¿Por qué..?.cuentos negros de Cuba* (Why? Black stories from Cuba) (Havana, 1940) and *El monte* (Havana, 1954). These studies of Afro-Cuban religions, rituals, languages and stories were extremely popular in Cuba which was swept by cultural nationalism in the 1930s. In 1960 Cabrera left Cuba for Miami where she published her book on the secret society *Abakuá* (1970) and on the Cuban *orishas* (deities) *Yemayá and Ochún* (1980). She has collected some 69 stories altogether in which she blurs the boundaries between fiction and ethnography by drawing no clear distinction between what she recorded from informants and her own creative material. Her work was extremely important for the documentation of Afro-Cuban culture and its recognition of the aesthetic value of Afro-Cuban traditions.

Major Women Writers in Pre-Revolutionary Cuba

Some of the most important women writers in twentieth-century Cuba and Latin America belong to the pre-revolutionary period. Dulce María Loynaz (b.1902) and Fina García Marruz (b.1923) both grew up in established white, Creole families which cultivated the arts. These Hispano-Cuban writers show little interest in African traditions and in fact refer not to the Caribbean as such but to the *Antilles*.

Dulce María's father had been a General in the Independence Wars and her home was a meeting place for the Cuban literati of the 1930s. She wrote and published poetry in the 1920s and 1930s, often with woman-centred themes (for example, *Song to a Sterile Woman*, 1937) although much of her work was not published until later. Her most intriguing work, the lyrical novel entitled *Jardín* (Garden) was written in the late 1920s and published in 1951. A reworking of the tale of Sleeping Beauty, it tells the story of a lonely girl, Barbara, who is taken from her secluded garden to Europe by her new husband. She expects to encounter civilisation but instead is faced with the ravages and aftermath of the First World War. Escaping from Europe she finds another love and they return to her garden only to be killed by a falling wall. This outstanding novel was unique in its time for its fluid portrayal of female subjectivity, its stream-of-consciousness effects and avant-garde techniques. Dulce María's lifetime work was recognised when she won the Cuban national prize for literature in 1987 and, in 1992 (aged 90), the coveted Spanish Cervantes Prize.[14]

Fina García Marruz was the only woman in the influential 'Orígenes' group founded by José Lezama Lima. Married to another member of the group, Cintio Vitier, García Marruz has always placed herself in the shadows of her more internationally famous colleagues but she has written some of the most beautiful poetry in Cuba this century. Her first collection was published in 1942 and she has continued to publish right into the 1990s. *Las miradas perdidas* (The Lost Gazes), 1951, and *Visitaciones* (Visitations), 1970, are her most important books. Influenced by the Spanish poet Juan Ramón Jiménez and, to a lesser extent, Paul Valery, García Marruz writes lucid, carefully wrought, metaphysical poetry that shines with a transparency bordering on mysticism. She writes about her home and family, her Catholicism, and about Cuba. Her poetry is woman-centred but not overtly feminist. She looks to the poetic traditions of Latin America, Europe, and Spain for her cultural models. A return to the mother and mother tongue is particularly explicit in her long poem 'Spain', a eulogy to the Spanish language. The poem inscribes the encounter between subject and language in both erotic and maternal terms:

...fill me, take me
to I know not what eternity
and I will not run away: rock me, great mothertongue...
When did I, unsure and trembling,
still a girl without a memory
seek your breast of strength,
like a sobbing child buries its head
in the bountiful mother's lap?...

Fina García Marruz[15]

Clearly, both these writers inscribe in their work the kind of ambivalent relationships with Europe (and the Spanish metropolis) that is evidenced in the work of women from other parts of the Caribbean.

Women's Writing in Cuba 1960-1980.

After the 1959 Revolution, women's politics and writing were subsumed into the collective project. As previously mentioned, most of the established writers had belonged to the white middle classes. Some left Cuba (Cabrera, Bernal); others felt alienated by the socialist programme and remained silent for many years (Loynaz); others were forgotten (the majority of the feminists). However, many welcomed the Revolution and continued publishing as far as they were able: Fina García Marruz, Mirta Aguirre, Carilda Oliver Labra (b. 1923), Cleva Solís (b.1926), Dora Alonso (b.1910). Indeed, those who had been exiled under Batista were now able to return (Camila Henríquez Ureña). Nevertheless, the middle-class culture which had given rise to a blossoming tradition of women's writing in the first half of the century was gradually phased out (95 per cent of those who left for Miami in 1959 were middle-class whites). It would take some twenty years for Cuban women's writing to approach its pre-revolutionary heights, either in volume or quality.

In 1959 the government inherited a situation in which a quarter of the population of five million was illiterate. The majority of these were women and blacks. In 1953 twenty three per cent of women over the age of ten were illiterate and only one per cent of women reached university.[16] During the 1960s all efforts were channelled into the literacy and education campaigns. The two main results of this were: the formation of a much wider reading public and a broader catchment area for new writers. The publishing industry was reformed to produce cheap or freely available books to cater for this new, multi-ethnic mass reading public of all ages (from children to grandparents) who were clamouring for suitable material. Schooling was free and compulsory for all children from nursery to University (only about 50 per cent had received schooling before 1959) and these new recruits needed books. Meanwhile, Cuban history and culture were rewritten from a popular, socialist point of view. Many women writers who would have found it difficult to publish before the revolution were now encouraged to write but also to eschew avant-garde works associated with the decadent bourgeoisie. They tended to publish either literature for children (considered particularly important) or 'testimonies' (personal accounts) of their experiences in the literacy campaigns and in the coffee and sugar harvesting brigades. Needless to say, there was little call for or tolerance of erotic literature.

The 1970s were less exuberant years; the cultural climate became more restrictive and censorship was more strictly enforced. But two developments had important consequences for women writers. First, Cuban interest shifted from Latin America to the Caribbean and Africa and this focused attention once more on the African heritage in the island. Second, International Women's Year of 1975 pinpointed gender roles. It was mainly during the 1970s, therefore, that black and mulatto women writers made their mark and that Cuban literature was perceived to be part of a Third world and Caribbean tradition.[17]

Black and Mulatta Women Writers in Cuba

One of the first mulatta[18] poets to make her name in Cuba was Rafaela Chacón Nardi (b.1946) whose mother was born in Martinique. She published her first collection, *Viaje al sueño* (Journey to Dream), as early as 1948. But neither in this nor in her more recent books is there any overt reference to African or Caribbean traditions. In fact, *Viaje al sueño* shows a marked obsession with the colour white: there are poems on the white carnation, the white butterfly, white clouds, white handkerchiefs, white lily, the white page; love is a 'rose without colour'; her mother is 'a flower of white petals'; Cuba is an island 'small and white'; and the stars, white flowers in the sky. Of course, these sonnets - written with great delicacy and flair - draw on the tradition of the French Parnassians and Symbolists who also delighted in the symbolical connotations of the colour white. It would be of interest, however, to read Chacón's early poetry in the light of Frantz Fanon's ideas on the cultural and psychological alienation of black and mulatto writers in a racist society. Even after the Revolution her poetry reveals little concern with black themes. Her only reference to an African heritage in her two recent collections of poetry, *Del silencio y las voces* (Of Silence and Voices), 1978, *Coral del aire* (Choir of The Air), 1982, is a tentative association of her grandmother's voice with a plausibly African or Caribbean Landscape, 'in her native tongue - of sun and nets, of volcanoes / and jungles at dawn'.[19] Much of her poetry is overtly political in tenor articulating socialist rather than identity politics.

Despite the fact that the negritude movement had wide repercussions in Cuba in the 1930s and that both black writers and black aesthetics were assimilated into the Cuban canon from then on (the most famous Cuban poet this century is arguably the mulatto Nicolás Guillén) it is not until after the Revolution that a tradition of black women's writing was established. The writer who has received most critical attention is Nancy Morejón (b.1944) who, as a linguist, has read widely in Caribbean literatures. In 1966 she published her first major collection of poems, *Richard trajo su flauta* (Richard Brought His Flute) which contains poems to her two grandmothers (one black, one mulatta), to her working class parents, to Afro-Cuban gods (*Eleggua*), and to Fidel, Havana and the Revolution. In this book she writes about the black freedom movement in the United States, the Vietnam War and the Russian cosmonauts. And many of the poems are dedicated to contemporary black Cuban writers and to women. Since then she has continued to publish widely. Her 1979 collection, *Parajes de una epoca* (Places of an Age) contains her most famous black poem, 'Mujer negra' (Black Woman), possibly the most translated of all post-revolutionary Cuban poems written by women. *Piedra pulida* (Polished Stone), 1986, includes more intimate poetry and several poems on

African themes: 'Blackman', 'Song for Maroons', 'I Love My Master' and 'Worlds', many of which have been translated into English. Nancy Morejón writes love poetry but the tone is muted rather than erotic. Some poems describe heterosexual love but others inscribe a female love object, for example:

'The Unfaithful Plant'

The plant I loved
the most
juicy in her leaves
seaweed of sun
on the full heads of flowers
never did spread out her lights
towards me.
She only clamoured from where she stood
for the passer-by who
glanced at her aimlessly
not seeing the dearly-loved blaze
of her beauty...
And I am still wondering how to transplant her
since she has no roots
not one single root
wherein to hold so much affection

Nancy Morejón[20]

The critical bibliography on Morejón is growing,[21] and it is interesting to note that she is the only poet of the four mentioned in this section to have an entry in the official *Diccionario de Literatura Cubana* (1984).

The poetry of Georgina Herrera (b.1936) has also been translated into English. The oldest poet in this group, she hailed from a very poor family and is self-educated. Like Morejón, she published poetry in the 1960s but it was not until *Gente y cosas* (People and Things), 1974 and *Granos de sol y luna* (Grains of Sun and Moon), 1977 that she established her name. *Gente y cosas* includes poems mainly about her family and neighbours. Her simple poems to her children, particularly to her daughter are among the most moving. Herrera shows in her 1977 book a marked interest in African history, and in the traditions, rituals, and pantheon of Afro-Cuban religions. She writes poems on Ana de Souza, heroine of colonial Angola, queen Subad of the Ur, Agostinho Neto, on Soviet heroines and her anonymous female neighbours. None of this fine poetry is propagandistic verse; the political themes are always filtered through the perspective of an ordinary Cuban woman, a working mother going about her everyday chores in the home.

Grande es el tiempo (Great is Time), 1989, is a more intimate collection of poems and includes possibly her most famous poem, 'Africa', in which she portrays 'Africa' as a loved-one whom she cares for, 'Africa' (daughter and mother) is a love object with whom she identifies and who gives her a sense of self.[22]

Soleida Ríos (b.1950) first published poetry in 1977 but her two most important collections are *De pronto abril* (Soon April), 1979, and *Entre mundo y juguete* (Between World and Toy), 1987. Ríos writes intimist poetry, searching deep for memories of childhood, or quizzing the impact of love. In her later collection several poems focus on sexual relationships, the female body and early memories:

[...] Another has entered my body
(we wanted to create ourselves, recreate ourselves
two naked angels falling
that ocean
that tree)
and, so you see,
I'm still thinking of you [Bolero of the Other]

Those who praised my shame
see me here.
Those who demanded above all
my bra beneath my blouse
see me here - without him - with these feet
not very long nor well-heeled
but happy in their wounds [Locks]

Painful word I never lived,
I have not seen
its step did not see the footprints
of my feet
unless enclosed in memory.
I am thankful
because crossing it from wall to wall
is the wet skirt of my mother...

[House] Soleida Riós[23]

In her later work, *El libro roto* (The Broken Book, in press) Ríos writes short pieces of dream-like poetic prose. Clearly, she is more concerned with female subjectivity, desire and the subconscious than in the African or Caribbean cultural and literary traditions.

The work of Excilia Saldaña (b. 1946) is more explicitly Afrocentric.

Saldaña first published in 1967 and thence dedicated herself to children's literature. She shows particular interest in the African cultural legacy in Cuba and in her own African roots. In 1987 she published a book of five *patakin* (Yoruba traditions) in *Kele Kele* (Suave, suave/Softly, softly) with a short history of slavery, an introduction to the Afro-Cuban orishas and a glossary of Afro-Cuban terms, plants, rites etc. It is in her autobiographical poetry, however, that Saldaña makes the most powerful connections between female subjectivity and an African, Caribbean heritage. She was born into a black, Catholic, Creole family which did not welcome the revolution. Consequently she left home and rejected Catholicism. According to her own account her father attempted to have an incestuous relationship with her when she was a girl which left deep psychological wounds. Throughout her youth it was her mulatta grandmother who stood by her and it is to the grandmother that she dedicates most of her work. This long and dramatic story is recounted in her poetry: 'Monólogo de la esposa' ('Monologue of the Wife'[24] and *Mi nombre. Antilegia familiar* (My Name. Antielegy for the Family).[25] One of Saldaña's main themes is the re-encounter with the mulatta body as the site of female identity. She writes about the black female body without prudery and inserts it in the Caribbean context of a plantation economy:

Through the mulatto shades of cane syrup
I see a body:
I take cruel delight
in the unwritten cane-fields of the pubis
in the crest of a head
in the cane-cut arm pits
in the brief sugar-press breasts
in the thick legs
in the bronze round-bottomed boiler of a navel
in the centrifugal force of the eyes
in the refined teeth

Excilia Saldaña[26]

She writes of puberty and menstruation, sexual relationships and birth:

And the fruit of the girl explodes in blood and cotton
splashes the whole house as she walks
waters the rose,
nourishes the dove...
the first seed announces the Spring

Excilia Saldaña[27]

Some of her most endearing poems to her grandmother have been published in a children's book (beautifully illustrated and produced in Berlin) entitled *La Noche* (The Night), 1989. Here the grandmother is represented by the mysteries, magic and dark beauty of the night.

A potential black women's literary tradition has thus been briefly outlined, but in Cuba identity politics is not really an issue and black writers these days seem to show little interest in black themes. In contradistinction, white (or non-black) women have written not only about African history and politics, as one might expect, but have also assumed black cultural identities. Minerva Salado (b. 1944), for example, adopts a black persona in her long poem 'Song of the Acana Tree', *Palabra en el espejo* (Word in the Mirror), 1987. The different sections of this poem recount the epic story of the Middle Passage and describe the major Afro-Cuban deities (*Eleggua, Changó, Oyá* etc.). They are also lyrical expressions of love for Africa and of solidarity with other black peoples. In the following extract Salado adopts the persona of a slave woman recently brought to Cuba; she knows the island is her future home but she longs for the African motherland:

'Song of the Acana Tree, III'

Island,
beside the serene hollow of your mantle
I'll cherish your mysteries with my hands
And my children, deep within me,
Will see the light shine like honey.
But my land is another, her tree enflames me
Across the sea-spray and the dire
My skin is the flowing of her branches
And her fruit calling from home fires
My heart breaks like a fragile sea-shell
Longing for her voice

Minerva Salado[28]

Poems written by white women which inscribe African-Caribbean traditions can be found in several collections and indicate one of the more interesting developments of post-revolutionary poetry in Cuba.[29]

Women's Writing Since 1980

Since 1980 there has been a blossoming of women's writing in Cuba. The country is criss-crossed with workshops (*talleres*) where writers read out and discuss their work. Women of all ages, colours, and backgrounds were publishing throughout the 1980s until about 1992 when the present crisis meant the paper ran out and publishing virtually ceased. Crafted, home-made plaquettes (unbound booklets) produced in short runs by the 'talleres' is a courageous but short-term answer to the problem of the shortages of printing materials.

It is impossible in this short space to cover in any depth women's writing of this decade. The 'boom' has been mainly (but not exclusively) in poetry which, generally speaking, has become less socially and family oriented, less political, less puritanical and, conversely, more intimate, subjective, erotic and philosophical. Some poets have tended to favour the hermetic or metaphysical mode (Lina de Feria, Reina María Rodríquez), others the irreverent and 'pop' (Marilyn Bobes, Chely Lima, Zoe Valdés), yet others the oneiric (Soleida Ríos). Whereas free verse was the favoured poetic form after 1959, there is now a return to the sonnet (Damaris Calderón) and to poetic prose (Soleida Ríos, Reina María Rodríquez). There is also a return to the literary mothers and fathers of pre-revolutionary Cuba, in particular to the mystical hermeticism of José Lezama Lima. Older women writers, whose work had been virtually ignored during the 1960s and 1970s, were encouraged to publish anew (Dulce María Loynaz, Fina García Marruz, Carilda Oliver Labra, Loló de la Torriente) while poems which had remained out of print for many years were recollected in anthologies. Unfortunately, the economic crisis stopped this process in full flow.

Of all the innovative directions taken by post-revolutionary women poets, perhaps the most significant have been their incursions into erotic poetry. The lyrical articulation of female subjectivity and sexual desire tends to be of two interrelated types: the expression of the female subject's encounter with her own body and desires, and the expression of her response to or appreciation of the male body. The tone can vary from the ironic and jocular to the deadly serious. As we have seen, it would be a mistake to suggest that eroticism is new to Cuban women's writing. Far from it; Cuban women have published erotic literature throughout the century. What is new is black women's erotic literature (see Saldaña above), a tone of open frankness and, above all, the self-portrayal of women as active (even aggressive) agents of the sexual encounter.

The poet who has contributed most to the long tradition of female-authored erotic poetry in Cuba is Carilda Oliver Labra (b. 1924) who published throughout the 1940s (*Al sur de mi garganta* [To the south of my throat], 1949, won the National Literature Prize). Her poems have been reprinted recently in *Sonetos* (1990) and *Antología poética* (1992). The sonnet, 'I'm disarranged, love I'm disarranged', was written in 1946:

I'm disarranged, love, I'm disarranged
when I enter your mouth, I'm delayed;
and simply for no reason, no reason at all,
with the tip of my breast I touch you again...

Carilda Oliver Labra[30]

and 'I'm telling you now to forget it all' in 1955:

I'm telling you now to forget it all
that breast of cream and tenderness
that breast pointing up in a way
that for you was firm land always

that obedient but burning thigh
from millenarium snakes it came
that thigh of flesh and 'I shall die'
in solitary afternoons reclaimed...

Carilda Oliver Labra[31]

This more lyrical approach can be contrasted to the daring and, for some, outrageous poetry of the much younger Chely Lima (b.1957). Many of the poems in *Terriblemente iluminados* (Terribly Illuminated), 1988, describe bedroom scenes between the poet and her husband. In 'The Other Version of a Poem by a Contemporary' she describes the kind of men she likes and ends with a political jibe:

And almost, in conclusion,
I like men madly
- that's to say
in perhaps a highly censurable way -
And to finish
mouths
buttocks
eyes
penises
and hands apart,
I love the few, the delicious ones, who
love me

Chely Lima[32]

'Psalm', from the same book, is a eulogy to her lover's body and a rewriting of Catholic discourse:

Blessed be the form and colour of your eyes
when in orgasm they no longer die.
Blessed be your mouth
because it has quenched my thirst with its fig-tree, calm...[33]

In 'Carnal Survey' she describes in detail her lover's body as she kisses it full-length: throat, cheek, back, waist, buttocks, chest, legs, thighs, the 'secret routes' under the 'pubic grass' where 'the fish sleeps in the palm of my hand/closed up in its ancient amphibian rings'...[34] Her 1992 plaquette, *Rock sucio* (Dirty Rock) is more varied in theme but still as ironically frank. She wants:

A man who says to me take me and do what you will.
A man who takes his clothes off looking me in the eyes.
[...] A man who lets me come and takes me in like a holy communion wafer...[35]

Soledad Cruz Guerra (b.1952) writes in 'Public declaration of love':

I love this man I ride,
who I mount without reins
saddles, bridles,
not even stirrups when I jump.
He doubts and tries to defend himself [...][36]

More restrained is the quiet poetry of Cira Andrés (b.1954) whose two poems to her own body reveal a new awareness not so much of sexuality but of the materiality of the embodied self. In 'The Body', her thirty-five year old body still keeps:

The memory of a happy beast
slipping
slipping
beautiful
burning in the mid-day fire

humbled in the putrid night

Cira Andrés[37]

and again in the poem 'Nude':

Body of mine...
I present you to the cameras

to the light, to the eyes of whoever wants to see you
I shed you off, I laugh at you
because you cannot take me further
than the moment where I am now ...
Strangers and thieves enter in you
I watch them with repugnance and pleasure...[38]

Reina María Rodríguez (b.1952), recognised as one of the leading poets in Cuba today, writes complex, intimate poetry and poetic prose. In her recently published book *En la arena de padua* (On Padua Sand), 1992, the poem 'He wipes his spectacles with my skirts' is a rare and subtle excursion into erotic poetry:

Under my skirts my legs are dark.
He wipes his spectacles with my skirts.
I crumple the leaves on a tree
apparently distant.
Under my skirts are his hands
stroking the cloth as he tries to polish the glass
he is wiping my legs
he has no idea what he's doing
as if my legs would never one day
devour him.
He lost his head
for a moment.
My skirts. His eyes. The glass.
But once more he lowered his glance
I wanted to be a tree
to be anything
to disappear
apparently distant

Reina María Rodríguez[39]

Zoe Valdés (b. 1959) also prefers more hermetic poetry. She does not privilege the erotic particularly, but is similarly frank in her descriptions of the female body and female reproduction. The following poem, 'Abortion', is from *Todo para una sombra* (All for a Shadow), 1986:

Although I'm not pregnant
a baby is dying in me.
No one can love it as I do,

not you, the moment of greed forgotten.
While it develops
its gaze crosses tissue and blood
and in the mirror it has told me its colour
is one I couldn't define.
You arrive in order to save it
and if you stroke me it shivers with joy.
My breasts fill and something odourless and soft
drops down.
They say that witches cry from their breasts
and that their hair turns to silver with so much magic.
The child is casting a space in my body.
I'm telling you.
What a shame my empty bosom
my uterus bleeding every full moon
and your semen falling over the precipice

Zoe Valdés[40]

Questions of Genre

The genre most preferred by Cuban women throughout the century is without doubt poetry. As we have seen, several important novels were published in the pre-revolutionary period but after the Revolution few full-length novels of literary value appeared. There are, however, some good collections of short fiction. Dora Alonso, María Elena Llana, Mirta Yáñez, and Olga Fernández are the most outstanding short story writers and a recently published anthology, *Los últimos serán los primeros* (The Last Will Be the First) edited by Salvador Redonet, 1993, includes stories by twelve young women born in the 1960s and 1970s.

The writer and journalist Dora Alonso (b.1910) is the most important and productive prose fiction writer of the last forty years.[41] Her novel, *Tierra inerme* (Defenceless Land), 1961, is a tale of an unhappy romance set in the beautiful but threatening landscape of the rural Cuba of her childhood. The harsh conditions of the countryside are recounted from the perspective of the young white mistress of the estate. Alonso returned to this setting in several of her short stories where she describes the misery of the black peasants, particularly the women, and her love and respect for them, but because she often focuses the theme of social injustice through the eyes of a child (in *Pololani*, 1966, for example) these stories have been perceived - erroneously in my view - as children's literature. Most of the stories she wrote in the 1940s foreground conflict and violence. After 1959 they become increasingly woman-centred focusing on the dignity of poor, black women and the problems encountered by elderly women and women with unfaithful husbands. Many stories, for example, those in her 1989 collection *Juega la dama* (The Lady Plays), are fables, usually involving an oppressed female animal, with a marked didactic intention.

Mirta Yáñez (b.1947) has published one novel and three collections of short stories. The novel, *La hora de los mameyes* (The Hour of the Mammy Apples), 1983, and the early short stories in *Todos los negros tomamos café* (All We Negroes Drink Coffee), 1976, are based on her experiences in the coffee harvesting campaigns. In the latter she incorporates snippets of oral tales she hears in the countryside and thumbnail sketches of local characters, for example, the Haitian Yulian. But it is in her later book *El diablo son las cosas* (What the Devil...!), 1986, that she writes with style and flair. The title story tells of a lonely woman who desperately tries to get rid of a mouse in her house. When she finally traps and kills it she can't face the loneliness and is broken hearted. 'Opera prima' is the story of a young Cuban gymnast who, when in Moscow in the depths of winter, decides to give up her career. Totally ignorant of her own sexuality and facing her first period with utter confusion, she is nursed through the crisis by a group of burly Russian women (the hotel staff) who help her celebrate her new womanhood with bottles of vodka. Generally, though, Yáñez writes about everyday life in Havana; her chatty, colloquial style full of light-hearted humour, whatever the theme, makes her fiction a delight to read.[42]

Conclusion: Research on Women's Writing in Cuba

Women's writing in Cuba is desperately under-researched both in Cuba and abroad. The rich work of the pre-revolutionary years was virtually ignored by the post-revolutionary establishment which disapproved of middle class feminism; only recently has the work of older Cuban women been rescued from oblivion. Sadly, the recuperation was in full swing when Cuba entered the 'Special Period' of the austere 1990s. Post-revolutionary women writers have faced the same problems as their male counterparts, that is, problems and delays in publication and difficulties in the distribution of their work to the world markets. This has much to do with the inefficiency of the Cuban state publishing industry but also with the thirty-five year US trade embargo to which Cuba has been subjected. Cuban women writers are better known in Berlin and Moscow than in London. Since the 1980s it has been easier to find information on Cuban women writers living outside Cuba because of exile or emigration, than information on those living and working in Cuba. Cuban women writers, therefore, have been marginalised on two counts: in Cuba (because they are women) and in the West (because they are socialist).

Current bibliographies on Cuban literature are, on the whole, incomplete. They give the false impression that there are few (or no) women writers publishing in Cuba today. Part of my purpose here is to put the record straight. One of the best sources is *Writers of the Caribbean and Central America* (Fenwick, M.J., Garland, 1992). Less useful is David William Foster's *Cuban Literature: A Research Guide* (Garland, 1985) which includes three twentieth-century women (Alonso, Loynaz, Cabrera). Julio Martínez's Dictionary of *20th Century Cuban Literature* (Greenwood Press, 1990) includes seventeen women's names, but not, for example, Nancy Morejón. Hopefully, cross-cultural studies comparing Cuban and women's writing from other parts of the Caribbean will point to new, exciting areas of literary research.

Notes

1. The Platt Amendment of 1902 allowed the US to intervene unconditionally in Cuban internal affairs whenever US interests were threatened. US troops occupied Cuba on two occasions. The Amendment was revoked in 1934 after the downfall of the dictator Machado by the same revolutionary government which gave women the vote. The Batista Dictatorship 1952-1959 again privileged US interests.
2. *Mes douze premières années*, Paris, 1831. This is possibly the first account of childhood memories in Spanish American literature. See Sylvia Molloy, *At Face Value: Autobiographical Writing in Spanish America*, CUP, 1991, pp.85-96.
3. See Evelyn Picon Garfield, *Poder y sexualidad en la obra de Gertrudis Gómez de Avellaneda*, Barcelona, 1994.
4. A good English translation of *Sab* and Avellaneda's epistolary autobiography have been published recently: *Sab and Autobiography*, translated by Nina M. Scott, University of Texas Press, Austin, 1993. See also Hugh A. Harter, *Gertrudis Gómez de Avellaneda*, Twayne, Boston, 1981. The relevant chapter in Susan Kirkpatrick's seminal work *Las Romanticas. Women Writers and Subjectivity in Spain 1833-1850* , University of California Press, Berkely and London, 1989, is essential reading for an appreciation of Avellaneda's poetry.
5. For more details of these and other nineteenth-century women poets see the introduction to Monica Randall, *Breaking the Silences* , Vancouver, 1982.
6. Nieves Xenes in *Arpas cubanas*, 1904, p.410
7. See K. Lynn Stoner, *From The House To The Streets. The Cuban Woman's Movement For Legal Reform 1898-1940* , Duke UP, 1991.
8. Rodríguez Acosta, *La vida manda*, 1929, p.75.
9. Ibid, p.118.
10. Ibid, p.69.
11. Ibid, p.71.

12. See Nina R. Menéndez, *No Woman Is An Island: Cuban Women's Fiction in the 1920s and 1930s*, PhD dissertation, Stanford University, 1993.
13. María Luisa Milanés, *La poesía moderna*, 1926, p.378.
14. See Verity Smith, 'Dwarfed By Snow White: Feminist Revisions of Fairy Tale Discourse In the Narrative Of María Luisa Bombal And Dulce María Loynaz' in L. Condé and S.M. Hart (eds.) *Feminist Readings on Spanish and Latin American Literature*, Edwin Mellen Press, Lewiston, 1991; Miriam Díaz Diocaretz, 'I Will Be a Scandal in Your Boat': Women Poets And The Tradition' in S. Basnett, S. (ed.) *Knives and Angels*, Zed Books, 1990.
15. Fina García Marruz, *Visitaciones*, 1970
16. Niurka Pérez Rojas, *Características sociodemográficas de la familia cubana 1953-1970,* Editorial de Ciencias Sociales, 1979, p.51.
17. See Monica Randall, *Breaking The Silences*, 1982, op. cit., for English translations of a selection of Cuban women's poetry from Loynaz onwards.
18. Both the older spelling 'mulatta' and the recent 'mulatto' are used in this paper.
19. Rafaela Chacón Nardi, *Del silencio y las voces*, 1978, pp.30-31.
20. Nancy Morejón. See also note 21.
21. Translations of poems by Nancy Morejón: 'Mujer negra/Black Woman'; 'La cena/Dinner'; 'Para escapar herido/To escape wounded' in *Poems from Cuba*, selected and translated by J.R. Pereira, The University of the West Indies, Mona, Jamaica, 1977. 'A un muchacho/To a boy'; 'Hay el calor/There is the warmth'; 'Masacre/Massacre' in M. Crow (ed.) *Woman Who Has Sprouted Wings: Poems by Contemporary Latin American Women Poets*, Latin American Literary Review Press, Pittsburg, 1984. 'Black Woman'; 'Barely Hero'; 'A Rose'; 'Impressions'; 'Farewell'; 'The Ocujal mine' in M. Agosin and C. Franzen (eds.) *The Renewal of the Vision. Voices of Latin American Women Poets 1940-1980*, Spectacular Diseases, London, 1987; 'Black Woman'; 'Confession' in A. Hopkinson (ed.) *Lovers and Comrades. Women's Resistance Poetry from Central America*, The Women's Press, London, 1989.

    See also M. Busby (ed.), *Daughters of Africa*, Jonathan Cape, London, 1992; Captain-Hidalgo, Yvonne, *Nancy Morejón* (1944); 'Cuba' in D. Marting (ed.) *Spanish-American Women Writers. A Bio-Bibliographical Source Book*, Greenwood Press, Westport 1990; *Ours the Earth: Poems by Nancy Morejón*, translated by J.R. Pereira, Institute of Caribbean Studies, University of the West Indies, Mona, 1990; Where *The Island Sleeps Like a Wing. Selected Poetry of Nancy Morejón* in K. Weaver (ed.) Black Scholar Press, San Francisco, 1985; Elaine Savory Fido, 'A Womanist Vision of the Caribbean: An Interview with Nancy Morejón' in C.B. Fido and E.S. Fido (eds.) *Out of the Kumbla, Caribbean Women and Literature*, Africa World Press, New jersey, 1982; Miriam de Costa Willis, 'The Caribbean as Idea and Image in the Poetry of Nancy Morejón', *Journal of Caribbean Studies*, 7(2-3), 1990, pp.233-43; Diane

Marting, 'The Representation of Female Sexuality in Nancy Morejón's 'Amor. cuidad atribuida', *Afro-Hispanic Review*, 7(1-3), 1988, pp.36-38.

22. For a more detailed discussion of the work of Morejón and Herrera see Catherine Davies, 'Writing the African Subject: The Work Of Two Cuban Women Poets', *Women, A Cultural Review*, 4(1), Spring, 1993, pp.32-48. Also see Conrad James' essay in this volume.
23. Soleida Ríos, *Entre mundo y juguete* (Between World and Toy), 1987, Bolero of the other, p.59; Locks, p.16; House, p.7.
24. Excilia Saldaña, *Monólogo de la esposa* (Monologue of the Wife), Casa de las Americas, 1985, p.152.
25. Excilia Saldaña, *Mi nombre. Antilegia familiar* (My name. Antielegy for the Family), 1991. See also *Autobiografía* (Autobiography) in Randall, 1982, op. cit.
26. Ibid, p.15.
27. Ibid, p.14.
28. Minerva Salado, 1987, op. cit., p.51.
29. See Lina de Feria (b.1945), *A mansalva de los años*, 1990; Maria Elena Cruz (b.1953), '¿Legado?', *Letras cubanas*, 1(4), abril-junio, 1987, 00.101-2; Elsa Claro (b. 1943) *Agua y fuego*, 1980, foreword by N. Guillen, 'Angola'.
30. Carilda Oliver Labra, *Antología poetica*, 1992, p.78. See Lina de Feria (b.1945), *A mansalva de los anos,* 1990; María Elena Cruz (b. 1953), 'Legado?', *Letras cubanas*, I(4), abril-junio, 1987, pp.101-102; Elsa Claro (b. 1943), *Agua y fuego*, 1980, 'Foreword' by N. Guillén, 'Angola I'.
31. *Antologia*, p.79.
32. Chely Lima, *Terriblemente iluminados* (Terribly Illuminated), 1988, p.24.
33. Ibid, p.107.
34. Ibid, pp.108-109.
35. Chely Lima, 'Enunciation', *Rock sucio* (Dirty Rock), 1992 p.17.
36. Soledad Cruz Guerra, *Documentos de la otra* (Documents of the Other), 1991, p.32.
37. Cira Andrés, *Sobre el brocado de los ojos* (On the Brocade of Eyes, plaquette), 1991, p.11.
38. Cira Andrés, *Plural* [Mexico], July 1991.
39. Reina María Rodríguez, *En la arena de padua*, 1992, p.69.
40. For more translations of Zoe Valdés' poetry see *Travesía. Journal of Latin American Cultural Studies*, Kings College London, 2, 1992.
41. See Seymour Menton *Prose Fiction of the Cuban Revolution*, Texas UP, Austin, 1975, pp.34-35); Catherine Davies. 'Beastly Women and Underdogs. The Short Fiction of Dora Alonso' in *Women Writers in Twentieth-Century Spain and Spanish America*, Edwin Mellen Press, Lewiston, 1992, pp.55-69.
42. See *Her True-True Name,* Heinemann, London, 1989 and *Green Cane and Juicy Flotsam,* Rutgers University Press, New Brunswick, NJ, 1991, for translations of some of Yáñez's stories.

Patterns of Resistance in Afro-Cuban Women's Writing: Nancy Morejón's 'Amo a mi amo'

Conrad James

Nancy Morejón, who has to date published thirteen collections of poetry is, undoubtedly, the most widely anthologised and translated Cuban female poet of her generation.[1] Her ouevre begins with *mutismos* (Silences) in which we observe a hermetic poeticising of anguish, alienation and psychic disorientation but develops, in later collections, into a more complex exploration of the relationship between the individual and the wider social processes mediating his or her existence.[2] In this respect her work is emblematic of much of the literature of Post-Revolutionary Cuba.

Morejón rejects being categorised as a 'woman poet' and has emphasised that she does not believe that 'women's poetry or a woman's novel as such exists'.[3] Nonethelesss issues of womanhood are a central concern in the poet's work and the treatment of the image of woman in her poetry often crystalises the dialectical relationship between the intimate and the social which characterises her work. The persona of the poem 'Mirar adentro' ('Looking Within')[4] (1986) for example, situates her personal suffering within a diachronic context which evokes female ancestral memory. Similarly in 'Madre' (Mother) (1986) the poet's mother is praised for her undying faith and spiritual strength while the poem recalls the social marginalisation of blacks in colonial Cuba. The poem I discuss in this paper, 'Amo a mi amo' (I Love My Master), foregrounds the psychological dimensions of this dialectic between the social and the intimate and simultaneously problematises questions of national history from a womanist perspective.[5] 'Amo a mi amo' from the 1986 collection *Piedra pulida* (On Polished Stone) is an extremely powerful reinscription of the experience of the African woman enslaved in the new world. Despite her experiences of racial and sexual exploitation the woman is buttressed by a transgressive psychic disposition and this is used by the poet to construct a model of African female resistance.

For Morejón, poetry must have a social imperative. In an interview with the Puerto Rican critic Emilio Bejel she stresses that 'esa forma de creación debe ser útil a la sociedad' (this form of creativity ought to be of use to society) and the sphere in which she expects the utility of her poetry to be felt extends beyond Cuban society to include 'la de otros mundos: Caribeños, Latino Americanos, Africanos, Asiáticos (that of other worlds: Caribbean, Latin American, African, Asiatic).[6] Morejón's poetic talent is complemented by her skill as an essayist and cultural critic and the question of the purpose of poetry is one that she has grappled with, in one way or another, in several of her essays.[7] Commenting on the work of outstanding male Caribbean poets in one such essay Morejón makes the following observation:

> Many writers have taken the language of the oppressor and have converted it into a weapon against the artificial values of that society while others use it merely to sensationalise the tropical landscape or to evoke a nostalgic past.[8]

Apart from reinforcing her conviction of the explicitly socio-political role which she thinks literature ought to serve, these comments give us an insight into the role of history in her own work. Far from being a simply decorative presence it is a trope used to further specific ideological concerns. The reconstruction of the slave past in 'Amo a mi amo' is a case in point.

'Amo a mi amo' writes the emotional trajectory of an African slave woman from the point at which she is ostensibly dedicated and attached to her master *cum* lover to the point where she hates him passionately. This development runs parallel to one in which she grows from insularity and political myopia to solidarity via socio-political consciousness.

Two historical moments are important in any analysis of 'Amo a mi amo'; the moment of its inscription in Post-Revolutionary Cuba and the moment of slavery which it recreates. I offer, later, a tentative suggestion of how the attitudes expressed in the poem might be related to the revolutionary context. The subject's self-representation, however, raises several issues concerning the character of the African woman's response to enslavement.

The use of a first person discourse coincides with an obvious ideological agenda of abrogating colonialist literary traditions. It contests the Euro-centric tendency of a one-dimensional presentation of the African slave woman which perpetuates the myth of her as being a submissive, docile character.[9] By allowing the slave woman to use her own voice to represent herself she transforms her from passive object to subject of history and simultaneously gives her a greater degree of complexity than is granted in colonialist-oriented traditions. The content of the slave woman's revelations is shocking and serves Morejón in protesting against the evils of slavery and the superficial representation of it in apologist discursive traditions.

At first the slave woman's proclamation of romantic love for her master belies any notion of psychic disorientation occasioned by slavery. This impression would seem to coincide with colonialist historiography in which accommodation, if not total acquiescence, is deemed to be the African woman's characteristic response to slavery. The subject here does not present her everyday rendezvous with her master as a function of her exploitation. Instead they are inscribed as labours of love. In the opening lines, for example, there is no semblance of coercion: 'Amo a mi amo/recojo leño para encender su fuego cotidiano' (I love my master/I gather brushwood to light his daily fires).[10] The doubly marginalising character of the status quo, in which African/woman is placed in subservient roles to European/ man, would therefore seem to be accepted.

However, this position is subtly undercut at several points in the first stanza itself even as the subject attests to her love for the master. What this stanza highlights is a constant struggle between a surface passivity which is encoded in romantic myth and constant internal conflict and discontent. The relationship between master/lover and slave/concubine represents a clash of cultures in which what is African is, of necessity, repressed. The African woman's devotion to her master and lover heals his physical wounds and this occasions his singing which is compared to the beauty of the work of the fifteenth-century Spanish lyric poet Manrique (line 18). But the point at which he is healed is the point at which the woman experiences her greatest sense of psychological anxiety: 'Yo quería haber oído una marímbula sonar', (I longed to hear a marimbula sound (line 19). The woman is inundated with the outpouring of European culture and therefore yearns for a form of cultural expression which is more Afro-centric in character.

The crisis of non-communication is another index of the clash of cultures which is used to underline the enslaved woman's unease in the relationship with her white master/lover. Thus the proclamation of erotic love for his mouth is counteracted by the emphasis that the language which he speaks is incomprehensible to her as is hers to him: 'Amo su boca roja, fina,/desde donde van saliendo palabras/que no alcanzo a decifrar/todavía. Mi lengua para él ya no es la suya (I love his fine red mouth/that speaks words I can't understand/for the language I speak to him/still isn't his own (line 20-23).

In addition, though the first stanza expresses love for the master, the terms in which he is described further sabotage the construction of romantic myth. His feet have pillaged foreign lands and he has been involved in plundering wars. The subtext therefore vilifies the master and underlines the fundamentally antagonistic character of the relationship between master and slave, woman and man.

Both European man and African woman are associated with animal imagery in the text. The woman describes herself, for example, as being mansa cual un cordero' (gentle as a lamb) (line 4). Despite its connotation of docility, this might be read as a more positive image in the context of the poem working in tandem with other images to present the woman as a therapeutic force. On the other hand it is the slave master who is invested with the barbarity which pro-slavery ideological texts transmit as the forte of the African: 'Mi amo muerde y subyuga (my master bites and subjugates) (line 8).[11] In contradistinction to the woman's kindness, therefore, he is constructed as the epitome of harshness and cruelty.

The metaphor with which the second stanza begins 'y la seda del tiempo hecha trizas' (and the silk of time is in threads) indicates the rupture which takes place in this semi-romantic situation when the African woman's consciousness is raised concerning her lover's acts of cruelty towards fellow enslaved Africans. Initial subliminal conflict now develops into conscious resistance against the Master/lover. Not only does she express solidarity at the physical level with the brutalised Africans but this new consciousness also leads her to question the material depravity which she suffers as a result of her enslavement. Here things which were originally glossed over as being done out of love are recognised for what they are, functions of her sexual exploitation and racial subjugation.

The enslaved African woman's voice is used at one point to comfort her enslaver. However, nascent womanist consciousness leads her to use her voice to react against her oppression. The word 'maldigo' (I curse) is thus isolated between stanzas two and three as a way of emphasising the significance of this linguistic aspect of the woman's resistance to her s exploitation and the oppression of her counterparts.

The poet's use of language in 'Amo a mi amo' is geared toward underscoring the violence of slavery as an institution as well as toward highlighting the modes of resistance employed by the African woman against her enslavement. The use of reflexive verb forms throughout the poem identify acts of the dominant culture as oppressive. This is present in its most subtle form in lines six and seven of the poem: 'Amo a sus manos que *me depositaron* sobre un lecho de hierbas (my emphasis) (I love his hands/that placed me on a bed of grass). The rapaciousness of the situation is foregrounded here by the use of the reflexive.

In the second stanza of the poem it is the foisting of European religion upon the African woman which is called into question:

...supe
que mi amor
da latigazos en las calderas del ingenio
como si fueron un infierno, el de aquel Señor Dios
de quien me hablaba sin cesar (25-29).

(I learned how my lover
doled out whip-blows

in the vatroom of the sugar-mill,
as if they were a hell that of the Lord God
they harped upon so much).

The constant preaching of christianity is identified as an act with which the woman is disgusted. She is told about God *ad nauseum*. In her rejection of this religion she distances herself from it and this is conveyed through the use of the demonstrative 'aquel' (that) to refer to its most important icon, God. What is more interesting though is the link that is established between the God of christianity and physical suffering. It is his antagonist, Satan who is more closely associated with the eternal suffering of hell in western religious thought. God, on the other hand, is linked to the reward of everlasting life in a mythic paradise. Here, by juxtaposing images of whipping with the figure of God, the poem recalls the twin use of physical violence and christian indoctrination as tools of enslavement. The woman must therefore invert christian paradigms in order to exorcise herself of the effects of oppression and so God is therefore aligned to 'el inferno' (hell).

The specific focus of the third stanza is the exploding of the myth disseminated through colonialist historiography that the preferential treatment from which women often benefited during slavery made them acquiescent to its atrocities. Here the speaker has clearly been the recipient of 'preferential' treatment. As a house slave she has received muslin robes and laces. However, it is the harshness of the language used in this stanza which demonstrates that far from making her less outraged at the acts of violence perpetrated against other Africans these gifts are viewed by the woman as yet another set of impositions which exacerbate the oppressiveness of her condition. Her verbal resistance is complete as it attacks every aspect of her life as slave:

esta bata de muselina que me ha impuesto
estos encajes vanos que despiadado me endilgó;
estos quehaceres para mi en el atardecer sin girasoles;
esta lengua abigarradamente hostil que no mastico;
estos senos de piedra que no pueden siquiera amamantarlo;
este vientre rajado por su látigo inmemorial;
este maldito corazón (line 38-44).

(this muslin robe he has draped over my shoulders;
these vain laces he has pitilessly made me wear;
my household tasks in the afternoon where
no sunflowers grow;
this language so stubbornly hostile I can't spit it out

these stone breasts that can't give him suck,
this belly slashed by his age-old whip;
this dammed heart).

The horrendous plots of revenge which are expressed in the pen-ultimate stanza of the poem are pre-figured when the woman redefines her love for her master. It is now like ' la maleza que cubre la dotación/única posesión inexpungable mía (line 35-36) (the creeping weeds that overrun the private food plot of the slaves/the only thing I can really call my own'. Womanist consciousness, in addition to heightened social awareness, are therefore brought to bear on the perception of the nature of her personal relationship with her lover. Thus the initially subdued conflict explodes into open confrontation between African woman and European man.

Sardonic strategies sustain the poem. There is no difference between the overt responses of the subject at the stage represented in stanza one and that represented at the end of the poem. She carries out all her duties, including her acts of love, in the same fashion. However at the psychic level, she has ceased to be controlled by the master. She is now spiritually free. The master/slave relationship is inverted at this stage and it is he who is powerless at this point since he can have no access to the radical transformation in the woman's mental disposition.

The relationship between perceived innocence and transgression is figured in the terms in which the slave woman envisions her revenge on her lover turned adversary. He is presented at the end of the poem as the innocent animal being flayed with a knife. The lamb has, therefore, been able to dominate the biting and subjugating animal. Thus there is a curious contention between power and powerlessness in 'Amo a mi amo'. Even at the initial stages represented in the poem the woman could be read as being in a situation of power. After all, she is in control of lighting his daily fires and nurses him back to physical health. The equivocal response to this domination which we see at the end of the poem is therefore just an extension of this kind of power. It is precisely this disposition which provided the more active forms of resistance for which up until recently the male slave was almost exclusively valorised in history as well as imaginative literature.[12]

One way of reconciling the overt womanist perspectives in 'Amo a mi amo' with the aims of the Cuban Revolution would be to consider it as being essentially allegorical. Such a reading would see the woman and her experiences as poignant metaphors for the Cuban nation and the Caribbean in general, which have been ravaged by colonialist exploitative practices. What could only have been achieved mentally in the specific situation constructed in the poem has been achieved materially by the Revolution and continues to be consolidated as the process of Revolution wages war against colonialism and neo-colonialism in whatever form they occur. The plausibility of such an argument is clearly endorsed upon consideration of Morejón's tendency to subordinate gender politics in favour of nationalist politics as exemplified in her famous poem 'Mujer negra' (Black Woman).[13]

But a more subversive strategy of reading, one that is characterised by a sense of irony, could identify another possibility of signification in the text. Linda Hutcheon's observations on the way the trope of irony is utilised in post-colonial and post-modernist discourse might help to clarify this idea. Hutcheon highlights 'the use of the trope of irony as a doubled or split discourse which has the potential to subvert from within'. She suggests that 'as a double talking forked tongue mode of address, irony becomes a popular rhetorical strategy for working within discourses and contesting them at the same time'.[14]

Reading the poem along these lines it is possible to further problematise the political vision expressed in 'Amo a mi amo'. Could the poet be struggling to find a location for the expression of personal anxieties without seeming subversive to the general Revolutionary cause? Here the use of history, women's history, clearly serves as a means for the poet to establish a black female subjectivity in the overall framework of Post-Revolutionary discourse. Whereas the Revolution is the context from which the subject derives empowerment, finds voice, it seems to me that 'Amo a mi amo might be read as an occasion in which there is a subtle challenge posed to what is deemed permissible for that voice to express. In addition to its reaction against the racial and gender abuse of plantation society, the poem might also be seen as an attempt to unsettle the vestiges of patriarchy within the Revolution.

APPENDIX

'I Love My Master'

I love my master.
I gather brushwood to start his daily fire.
I love his blue eyes.
Gentle as a lamb,
I pour drops of honey for his ears.
I love his hands
that threw me on a bed of grasses.
My master bites and subjugates.
He tells me secret tales while
I fan all his body,
running with wounds and bullet pierced

from days in the sun and plundering wars,
I love his pirate's feet
that have pillaged foreign lands.
I rub them with the softest powders
I could find, one morning,
coming from the tobacco fields.

He strummed his ornate guitar and
melodious couplets soared
as from Manrique's throat.
I longed to hear a marimbula sound.
I love his fine red mouth
that speaks words I can't understand
for the language I speak to him
still isn't his own.

And the silk of time is in threads.
Overhearing the old black overseers
I learned how my lover
doled out whip-blows
in the vatroom of the sugar-mill,
as if it were a hell, that of the Lord God
they harped upon so much.

What's he going to say to me?
Why do I live in this hole not fit for a bat?
Why do I wait on him hand and foot ?
Where does he go in his lavish coach
drawn by horses that are luckier than me?
My love for him is like the creeping weeds
that overrun the private food-plots of the slaves,
the only thing I can really call my own.

I curse

this muslin robe he has draped over my shoulders:
these vain laces that he has pitilessly made me wear
my household tasks in the afternoon where
no sunflowers grow;
this language so stubbornly hostile I can't spit it out
these stone breasts that can't give him suck,
this belly slashed by his age-old whip;
this dammed heart.

I love my master but every night
when I cross the blossoming path to the canefield
I see myself knife in hand,
flaying him like an innocent animal.

Bewitching drum beats
now drown his cries, his sufferings,
The bells of the sugar-mill call...

Nancy Morejón

Notes

1. The popularity of Morejón's work outside of Cuba has tended to obscure the fact that there are several other black women and certainly numerous other women who are publishing in Cuba today. For an extremely useful bibliographical guide to contemporary Cuban women's publications see Catherine Davies 'Women Writers in Cuba 1975-1994. A Bibliographical Note', *Bulletin of Latin American Research,* 14(2).
2. On this issue see Lourdes Martínez-Echazábal 'Oposiciones Binarias en *Octubre impresinible* y *Cuaderno de Granada*', *Cimarrón*, 1(3), Spring, 1988.
3. See Mary Crow *Woman Who Has Sprouted Wings* , Latin American Literary Review Press, Pittsburg, 1987, p.111.
4. For 'Mirar adentro', 'Madre' and 'Amo a mi amo' see Nancy Morejón *Piedra Pulida* (On Polished Stone), Letras Cubanas, La Habana, 1986.
5. Alice Walker uses the term 'Womanist' to denote a black feminist or feminist of colour. In explaining the term's derivation she highlights the qualities of audacity and courage and posits these as major characteristics of a womanist disposition. See Alice Walker *In Search of Our Mother's Gardens,* Women's Press, London, 1984. This is a term which Morejón herself has identified with despite her scepticism of labels. See 'A Woman Vision of the Caribbean', Interview with Elaine Savory Fido in Carole Boyce-Davies and Elaine Fido (eds.) *Out of the Kumbla*, Africa World Press, Trenton, NJ, 1990, pp.265-69.
6. See Emilio Bejel *Escribir en Cuba,* Universidad de Puerto Rico, Río Piedras, 1991, p.238.
7. A noted scholar of the poetry of Nicolás Guillén with whom she worked closely, Morejón's critical works include *Recopilación de textos sobre Nicolás Guillén*, Ediciones Unión, La Habana, 1974; and *Nación y mestizaje en Nicolás Guillén*, Ediciones Unión, La Habana, 1982. She has also published *Fundación de la imagen,* Letras Cubanas, La Habana, 1988.
8. See Nancy Morejón 'Poesía del Caribe', *Revolución y cultura 82*, June, 1979, p.56.
9. For a detailed, even if problematic discussion of colonialist images of the slave woman see Barbara Bush, *Slave Women in Caribbean Society*, James Curry, London, 1990.

10. All translations of excerpts from the poem in the text of this essay as well as the appendix are from Kathleen Weaver *Where the Island Sleeps Like a Wing*, Black Scholar Press, San Francisco, 1985. Other excellent translations of Morejón's poetry are available in Margaret Randall, *Breaking The Silences Twentieth Century Poetry by Cuban Women,* Pulp Press, Vancouver, 1982; Mary Crow, 1987, op. cit.; and Joe Pereira, *Ours the Earth: Poems from Cuba.*
11. There are, of course, many examples of excellent scholarship on colonialist images of the African. I find Abdul Jan Mohammed's treatment of the subject in his 1986 essay, however, extremely succinct and insightful. See Abdul Jan Mohammed 'The Economy of the Manichean Allegory: The Function of Racial Difference in Colonialist Literature' in *'Race' Writing and Difference*, Chicago University Press, Chicago, 1986, pp.78-106.
12. Thankfully, revisionist-oriented historians and creative writers from the Caribbean have, in the last few decades, dedicated their talents to redressing this situation. Verene Shepherd's *Engendering History* is one of the most recent examples of this tendency. See Verene Shepherd et al. (eds.), *Engendering History: Caribbean Women in Historical Perspective*, James Curry, London, 1995.
13. For an excellent discussion of 'Mujer negra' which points up the gender/nation tensions see Claudette Rose Green-Williams 'Rewriting the History of the History of the Afro-Cuban Woman: Nancy Morejón's 'Mujer negra', *Afro-Hispanic Review,* VIII(5), September, 1989.
14. Linda Hutcheon, 'Circling the Downspout of Empire', *Ariel,* 22, 4 October 1989, pp.17-27.

Encoding the Voice: Caribbean Women's Writing and Creole[1]

Susanne Mühleisen

One of the notions which has traditionally been associated with Caribbean literature is the divide between the oral and the literate traditions. When in 1986 one of the first comprehensive anthologies of Caribbean writing, *The Penguin Book of Caribbean Verse in English*, was published the editor classified the different poems along these lines.[2] Even though this has not remained entirely undisputed, the categorisation of orality and literacy is still prevalent in many discussions of Caribbean writing - and for good reason, too, as even a glimpse at the history, sociology and politics of the region would suggest. As a result of colonisation and external cultural domination, at least since the times of Caribbean plantation societies, the literate-oral divide demarcates the lines of power relationships. As a number of historio-linguistic studies have comprehensively demonstrated, language in general and written language in particular have served as a foremost tool of imperial conquests, most notably by way of reshaping the relationships in the semiotic field and suppressing the continuities of communication that prevail in oral societies, in favour of the manipulatable constructions of written signs.[3] Without writing, one might summarise these analyses, empire cannot function.

It is important to note, however, that even under imperial rule, the written medium of a European language was never unchallenged but had, in fact, to contend and defend itself against a number of non-European languages which it tried to dominate. In the case of the Caribbean, these were - after the genocide of the indigenous population - a number of non-European languages such as Bhojpuri but most importantly the linguistic products of the violent contact situation between the European language and West African languages during plantation slavery. Creoles with different European lexifiers (English, French, Dutch, Spanish) are the mother tongues of the majority of the inhabitants in the region whereas the European standard language functions as official language[4] and generally maintains 'public' functions. The language structure of the Caribbean has thus, for a long time in history, constituted a hierarchical situation: at least one European language of power trying to maintain control over the other language groups. Power establishment and maintenance has always been shaped by parameters which, following Walter J. Ong's influential analysis,[5] we may characterise as written language, literate language and textualised language, i.e. the status of codification, the interplay between oral and literate thought and communication as well as the cultural ties of the language to an archive of textual monuments. The oral languages that form low varieties of the diglossia, by contrast, must continuously challenge the position of semiotic power by trying to establish alternative ways and means of communicative processes. It is here that oral elements like proverbs, jokes, tales, songs, rumour and gossip have become functional as sites of popular resistance.[6] Their revolutionary potential notwithstanding, oral traditions as combative concepts (in their role in slave rebellions and plantations communications, for instance) have ultimately affirmed the divide between oral and literate.

Even in cultural terms, such as in the anthology cited above, the dichotomy continues to work. Orality vs. literacy here bears the connotations of 'popular culture' vs. 'high culture', European traditions vs. African/ Caribbean traditions and, in the Caribbean context, Creole vs. Standard language forms. It is only one reflection of a diglossic language situation in the 'anglophone Caribbean' that the high prestige domain of literature, writing and literacy has traditionally been associated with the high prestige language, Standard English whereas the 'low variety', Creole, the first language of a large proportion of the population has been associated with other functions. The power which is connected with writing and literacy is evident since access to high prestige domains, including writing, can only be achieved via the learned language. Education in the second language hence becomes a linguistic requirement for political participation and until recently, the divide between the oral Creole and the literary English was still largely perceived as a social divide.

It is crucial, however, to realise that it is also women who are most frequently associated with the oral, which may, on the one hand, point to their strong ties in the oral culture as preservers and perpetuators of indigenous traditions through folk tales, legends, riddles and songs - many contemporary writers claim to still benefit from the stories that their mothers and grandmothers told them. But it may, on the other hand, also point to the traditional exclusion of women from the domains of public power, especially under colonial rule which granted women no official space at all for any affirmative participation in the political processes. While the recognition is gradually gaining ground that Caribbean women have in fact, for most of their history, been 'working miracles' (as Olive Senior, in the first comprehensive study of their situation, calls it), in terms of active affiliation to the ranks of power, their social status has long been marked by double colonisation, that is, by the combined impact of the patriarchal as well as colonial (or neo-colonial) forces. If education and access to the Standard language was hard to come by for the majority of Caribbean persons, women clearly had an even greater barrier to overcome. The oral culture, their domain, would also seem to function as a political restriction.

This conclusion, however, is unwarranted because it proceeds on too static a notion of culture. However strong and powerful the oral-literate divide may be, we must not underestimate the actual interrelations of the two domains, nor underrate the possibility of changing their parameters of power. This paper will not only emphasise the fact familiar to all readers of Caribbean literature that Creole has indeed long entered the written text but will also examine how Caribbean women in particular have constituted a prominent force in overcoming the historical divides of language. On the basis of textual analyses of three Jamaican authors I intend to argue that they may be considered paradigmatic for a process in which women have been initiating, shaping and reshaping the debate on Caribbean language and their public status in the post-colonial age. The foregoing should have made clear that, although my immediate concern is literary texts, the ultimate significance of the linguistic strategies under discussion must be seen in the political domain. By focusing on textual samples from Louise Bennett, Olive Senior and Patricia Powell, whose writings represent three different generations over a period of roughly fifty years, I will not only discuss their work in terms of the social commentary that it might offer, but mainly in the social acts that they perform in their language patterns. Caribbean women who write Creole voices, rooted in an oral culture but breaking out of its confines, engage in a process of empowerment and change the social order.

Before I proceed to substantiate these claims, a few remarks on the special status of Caribbean Creole and the attitudes which have traditionally been associated with it are necessary. There is, of course, nothing intrinsic in Creole languages which makes them less suitable for standardisation or for the official medium of communication - two important status markers - and, in fact Creole languages have experienced a change in status elsewhere: French Creole in Haiti, for instance, or Tok Pisin in Papua New Guinea both have the status of an official language in their respective countries.[7] There are, however, a number of points which form an obstacle to any successful attempts of standardisation. One is the relative lexical vicinity to the European language and therefore the high rate of, at least, one-sided intelligibility, from Creole to the European language. The great degree of variation in Creole languages has certainly contributed to a long-standing non-recognition of Creoles as autonomous systems. And furthermore, in the case of English-related Creoles, the role of English as a language of international communication and the high status connected with it has made the choice of English as an official language a particularly desirable one.[8]

The biggest obstacle, though, is not the relationship between the languages but the different values connected with them which arose out of the tension of the colonial situation. Negative attitudes towards Creole have not only been held by outsiders but also by the speakers themselves. The painful memory of the condition out of which the language developed seems to have prevented any unbiased dealing with the language situation for a long time. In the introduction to his collection of poetry *Slave Song*, Guyanese-British writer and academic David Dabydeen recalls this memory to characterise the language as vulgar and 'angry, crude and energetic' and he sees the 'brokenness' which he attributes to the language as 'no doubt reflecting the brokenness and suffering of its original users'.[9] The essay in its entirety is more complex, also reflecting positive potentials and values of the language but in this short passage, most of the negative qualities which for a long time have been attributed to Creole are brought to the point.

It is therefore small wonder that writers who transgressed the functional boundaries of the languages at first had to fight for recognition. Louise Bennett may well serve as a case in point. When she started to perform her poetry on stage in the late 1930s, her art was not considered serious and, when she even started to publish her poems in newspapers and later in books, her writing was often neither recognised as art nor, indeed, as writing at all because it was conducted in 'dialect' (a term which she herself used frequently to refer to the language and whose implications will be considered below). In retrospect, however, her first poetry collection in print must be seen as a milestone in the move between the oral and the written Creole form. At that time, there were not many models of writing in Creole she could draw upon.[10] Bennett herself did not perceive the lack of standardisation of Creole as a problem but rather as a creative challenge, declaring that 'if the Jamaican dialect were to become a standard language in her life-time, she would 'still write in the free expression of the people (...) a manner of speaking unhampered by the rules of (Standard English) grammar, a free expression - a dialect'.[11] This, of course, obscures the fact that Creole does have grammatical rules despite the lack of prescriptive rules Standard English has. However, her affirmative use of Creole in her work certainly contributed a lot to change at least some of the negative attitudes associated with it. In her poem 'Bans O' Killing' she explicitly states her view that the 'Jamaican dialect' is simply one dialect of English, on equal footing with other dialects:

Meck me get it straight Mass Charlie
For me noh quite undastan,
Yuh gwine kill all English dialect
Or jus Jamaica one?
Ef yuh dah-equal up wid English
Language, den wha meck
Yuh gwine go feel inferior, wen
It come to dialect?

and she also comments on the fact that the standardisation of English is a fairly recent phenomenon:

Dat dem start fe try tun language
From de fourteen century,
Five hundred years gawn an dem got
More dialect dan we!
...
Yuh wi haffe get de Oxford book
O' English verse, an tear
Out Chaucer, Burns, Lady Grizelle
An plenty o' Shakespeare!

Louise Bennett[12]

Despite the matter-of-factness of Bennett's writing in Creole it is by no means self-evident how the language is presented in writing. The linguistic situation above carries a number of implications on the choices the author has to make in this respect: The degree of variation, the fact that there is a continuum between basilectal (deep Creole) forms and acrolectal forms (which are closer to the Standard language) makes it necessary to first of all select the level of Creoleness, as well as the degree of regional markers and, perhaps most crucially, the form of orthographic representation - between a largely phonemic representation and the conventions of Standard English orthography.[13] If the author alternates between Standard English and Creole forms, the different proportions and functions of this alternation have to be considered, in addition. Because of this 'freedom of choice', the decisions a writer makes will always carry some political or ideological weight. They can thus be seen in the tension between strategies of abrogation, the 'denial of the privilege of 'English' (which) involves a rejection of the metropolitan power over the means of communication' on the one hand and strategies of appropriation, the 'reconstitution of the language of the centre, the process of capturing and remoulding the language to new usages' on the other hand.[14] It is precisely because Creole is not standardised that it can never be seen completely independently from the European language with which it is in historical and linguistic relation. Whatever form is chosen it is therefore meaningful, reflecting the attitudes of the author and the socio-historic context out of which the work is created. In the case of Creole this goes beyond a matter of style: when it comes to the negotiation between English and Creole, form is content.

In this light, what choices does Louise Bennett opt for and what meaning would they seem to carry? The poetic personae she created, and above all the legendary 'Miss Lou', are mostly lower-class urban women who, in dramatic monologue or dialogue, comment on political and social issues and events. The social positions her personae occupy are clearly constructed in the language choices, a mesolectal (medium level) Creole. Bennett's option is therefore used to create what is perceived as an authentic voice of the people and stands in line with the functional and social divide of language in Jamaican society of the time. Be it a train strike, war-time politics, the New Constitution or Independence Day, be it the physical (post-war) migration to Britain and the rhetorical migration 'Back to Africa', all of that is subject to Miss Lou's involved and yet detached observations and comments. In the following excerpt from the poem 'Problem' an English documentary film on 'Jamaican problems' is commented on critically:

Lawd massa, yuh too cromoogin!
Tap gwan like yuh never know!
For de people tell yuh broad sey
Is a 'Problem' dem a-show!

Ef yuh expec' fe se 'Progress'
Wen de sinting name 'Problem',
Dat a fe yuh ignorance an
Yuh kean blame de people dem!

...

For de ole ooman kean hide weh
An no matta wat yuh do
Dem won' se her eena parlour
But dem se her eena yuh!

Yuh noh se is time we stop fool up
Weself, stop 'save we face'.
Stop negleck we problem dem so till
Dem tun eena disgrace.

Louise Bennett[15]

There are but few lexical differences in this passage, perhaps the most prominent one being *croomoogin* (= Standard English *deceitful*, line 1). The level of Creoleness is perhaps best indicated in the grammatical forms, e.g. preverbal progressive markers *a* and *dah* (e.g. line 4 a-show), the pronominal system - which also includes a second pers. plural *oonu*, the pluralisation with free morpheme *dem* (e.g. line 8), the use of the subordinate conjunction *sey (line* 3) and other grammatical features, concerning e.g. the predicate system of Creoles, serial verbs, etc. Phonological differences between Standard English (SE) and Creole in general, and between SE and Jamaican Creole (JC) in particular are expressed in a semi-phonemic orthographic system. Examples for this are:

- The realisation of what is in SE /ð/ and /θ/ as d (*dem*) and t (as in sin*ting* = SE something).
- The final consonant cluster reduction in *expec'* (line 5) and *negleck* (line 15). A difference in orthographic realisation despite a similarity in the nature of the process like the above can often be found - obviously, since there are no prescriptive spelling conventions. This can, however, sometimes be misleading and can increase the problems of the reader (who is usually still illiterate in Creole). The difference in graphic marking is also striking in another aspect: while the first example implies a 'lack of something' in contrast with Standard English, the second example seems to suggest an alternative.
- The dropping of initial sounds, like in the case of an (st) sound: *tap* for SE *stop* (Note, however, that this is again dealt with differently in line 2 and line 15). Another example would be, e.g. SE *woman* becoming JC *ooman*.
- Some differences between the SE and Creole in vowel quality and length are (again inconsistently) marked, e.g. via double spelling of the vowel symbol in *ooman* (line 9) or *eena* (line 11 and 12), insertion of the letter 'w' as in *Lawd* (line 1) and *gwan* (line 2) to mark a long a. The extremely inconsistent and archaic spelling system in SE which is about as far removed from a letter/sound correspondence as one can get in alphabetic writing[16] makes it extremely difficult in Creole to find a compromise between the two extremes (phonemic orthography and orthography based on SE) since the marking of distinctions will have to result in different, again inconsistent forms: short e is represented in e.g. *sey* or *weh*, short o in *no* or *noh*, short i in *se*, *we*, etc.
- Some spelling differences from the SE conventions have no phonological reasons but merely highlight the general differences and can be seen as the author's attempt to increase the distance between the systems, e.g. marked in *yuh* (but: *too*, both line 1), in the initial consonant symbol in *k*ean (line 8, but: *c*roomoogin), or the dropping of the letter 'h' in *wen* (line 6), *wat* (line 10, but: w*h*ite, 4th stanza of the poem, not cited)

If the reader can overcome these inconsistencies quite easily in poetry - after all, poems are usually short texts, ordered in stanzas and the reader is used to paying more attention to language in poetry than in other forms of literature - they may cause more problems in longer prose texts. After all, the decoding of written texts is a complex process involving not only the identification of the lexical units but also the identification of morphological relationships (e.g. in Bennett's writing: expec' but expectin') and the linking of certain key words to their environment through morphological and syntactic particles.[17] Despite the advantages it offers as a strategy of abrogation, the use of a quasi-phonemic writing system is therefore not as straightforward and unproblematic as it may seem at first glance.

The socio-psychological effects of Louise Bennett's pioneering work in writing Creole, however, cannot be underestimated: many younger generation writers, and especially poets, refer to her as their literary ancestor. In a recent interview,[18] Jamaican performance poet and writer Jean 'Binta' Breeze also made this point when she was asked how she made her spelling choices:

> ...I've always read Jamaican fluently, I mean I grew up reading Louise Bennett from the page and that would certainly have been my exposure to Jamaican on the page. So I would think, a lot of my spelling would come from how Louise spells.

But Louise Bennett's writing has not only become a source of inspiration to creative writers but also a resource to linguists and lexicographers: Frederic G. Cassidy and Robert B. LePage, who in 1967 set up a *Dictionary of Jamaican English*, by now a classic which has certainly influenced later projects of codification of other specific Creoles, cite her work as a source of information. By the 1960s academics had taken an increasing interest in Creole languages and the study of Creoles began to establish itself as a separate field in linguistics - Cassidy,[19] for instance devised a phonemic orthographic system for Jamaican Creole and Beryl Bailey[20] described the grammatical features of JC. Even though the actual codification of the language in a dictionary may have had little immediate effect on the consciousness of the average language user - after all, the phonemic system used by Cassidy was not intended for popular usage but fulfilled mainly scholarly functions - the psychological significance should not be underrated. That the status-raising efforts of lexicographers are often met with little response by the public is not necessarily unique to the case of Jamaican Creole, as Walter Ong points out:

> When a present-day linguist laboriously works out a more or less adequate way to transcribe a previously unwritten language, few if any of the speakers

of the language normally learn to write it. The script figures in linguistic journals but not in the language speakers' lives. Often the speakers of the language are even incredulous about its writability, believing that only certain languages, not including their own, can be written.[21]

One could say, though, that this increased interest in Creole stands in one line with a general cultural reorientation and it is, of course, no coincidence that this formal linguistic autonomy was documented around the time of political independence of most of the anglophone Caribbean countries. Also in a non-academic context, Creole forms became more prominent in the post-war period: most of the major internationally successful novelists from the Caribbean, like V.S. Naipaul, George Lamming and, above all, Samuel Selvon, used Creole extensively in their works.

That the authors's linguistic choices in their work are not entirely their own but are indeed linked to a wider social discourse on language must also be seen in the light of the 'gatekeeper' function of publishers. After all, literature needs to be published and the selection process of what language forms are acceptable for the audience - Caribbean and international - lies ultimately in the hands of the publishing company.[22] How public acceptance and awareness changed in the 1960s is illustrated when Anne Walmsley writes that, when in 1961 she first turned in a selection of Caribbean writing she wanted to publish as an anthology to the Publication Branch of the Jamaican Ministry of Education, they rejected it on the grounds that '...the use of the vernacular creates a problem, as it is not the policy of the Branch to produce books containing dialect'.[23] The anthology, *The Sun's Eye* was, however, accepted and published by Longman in 1968.

The strong dependence on a readership outside of the Caribbean as well as the change in publishing practices were also remarked on by Jamaican writer Olive Senior:

> ...we are entirely dependent on metropolitan publishers and all that it entails - though obviously so are the writers in exile. It does mean though that the perceived marketability outside your own country of what you write is what determines publication. Nowadays metropolitan publishers are more accepting of the language in which we write; my publisher never suggested any changes at all to *Summer Lightning* but in earlier days it meant that writers had to make concessions, compromises to suit foreign tastes.[24]

Given that, on the one hand, the language use and in particular the use of Creole forms in literature is subject to the acceptance of the wider society and, on the other hand, the prestigious 'institution' literature can provide a forum to further the acceptance of previously stigmatised language forms, then this has important implications for the study of language attitudes towards Creole languages. It means that literary texts can serve both as an indicator of language attitudes and as a catalyst of attitude change. It is in this way that texts function interactively and have an effect on socio-semantic change: they can be seen as the battlegrounds on which the struggles between social forces are fought in order to establish new codes.

This makes it especially interesting to look at what forms and functions Creole employs in texts which are further removed from the notion of 'orality'. Prose and particularly the novel offer interesting insights for this kind of analysis for a number of reasons. Unlike drama, poetry or even short stories, novels are not meant to be reproduced orally. This can be attributed mainly to the length of this particular form but, partly, also to the highly individualistic ideology out of which it first arose in eighteenth century Europe. More than any other genre, the novel is commonly associated with a literate culture, a notion which may account for the high literary prestige it traditionally holds. However, despite this alleged distance of the novel to orality it has been shown for literary narratives in general that they are subject to aesthetic and structural constraints similar to those of oral narratives.[25] This is particularly important for the linguistic choices the author makes, and especially relevant when the narrative is set in a diglossic and bilingual speech community like in the Caribbean where language choice is a highly sensitive issue. Since many linguistic patterns follow automatically from the purpose, context and medium of communication, the 'choice' does not necessarily have to be a conscious one. That these can be employed on various levels of communication in the narrative becomes important for the function the code is given, as we shall see in the analysis of prose texts.

It is notable that Caribbean women writers for a long time have featured much more prominently in poetry than in prose (or drama). While their male counterparts had reached a strong international presence at least by the 1950s, there were hardly any female African-Caribbean prose writers and novelists before the 1980s[26] - even though today women are displaying the most versatility and are open to transgressing genre boundaries: many write poems and prose with equal facility. Senior, for instance, notes in her interview with Rowell[27] that she doesn't always decide beforehand what form her ideas will take. It is, however, not surprising that most authors who finally did come out with prose started writing as a second career and had held a 'proper job' before, as linguists, sociologists, journalists or teachers. This pattern for the generation of women who were born in the 1940s has to be seen in the light of the socio-economic conditions and the societal attitude towards writing by women as a full job. This becomes explicit when Olive Senior recounts that:

In 1972 when I was writing my first book - a commissioned work on the 1972 general election - a middle class lady asked me what I was doing with myself. I told her I was writing a book. She said 'A book?' and roared with laughter. After that book was published to good critical and public reception, an old school mate saw me and asked me what I was doing with myself. I said 'Writing'. She dismissed that instantly. 'Writing?' she said, as if I had said whoring. 'So when are you going to settle down and have children?'.[28]

In her prize-winning first collection of short stories, *Summer Lightning* (1986), Olive Senior explores life in rural Jamaica, mostly of the 1940s and 1950s, the time of the author's own childhood. Her stories are without any false romanticism about country life and 'old time things'; the characters are often caught in the tension of their ambition towards a 'better life', between traditional life and new values. Her writing is concerned with socio-political issues, but mainly below the surface, and Senior herself once commented in an interview that women writers tend towards 'personalising socio-political issues'.[29]

Olive Senior's sensitive exploration of the different facets of rural Jamaican life is reflected in her use of Creole. In fictional dialogue her characters' social position is carefully encoded in their language use, which is represented with great versatility. Thus language in the fictional dialogue serves to characterise the protagonists; their background, values and attitudes are inscribed in their form of speech, a long- standing strategy in the narrative to create authentic and credible characters not only in the Caribbean context but also in other non-standard language contexts. An example of this can be found in the story 'Real Old Time T'ing' where language differences between Patricia, a younger woman who has climbed up the social ladder and now returns to her father's rural village to buy antiques, and Miss Myrtella, a woman in the village, are a constructive device in the conversation:

So after a time it probably reach even thick skin Patricia brain that Miss M not saying yea or nay to any of her offer. So finally she say to Miss Myrtella:

'What a beautiful little decanter. How much you want for it? My friends will be so envious when they come to my house and see it'.

Miss Myrtella never say a word but she take the decanter out of Patricia hand and put it back on the what-not where it belong.

'Ho Miss Patricia. That was my very mother hown. Is her grand mother did give er and she give me. So you see his very hold. Oi om so hafraid you break hit. Hit his my greatest treasure'.

But Miss Myrtella there is nobody in these country parts to admire it. I will make you a good offer.[30]

The distance between Patricia and Miss Myrtella is created mainly by highlighting phonological markers like the word-initial dropping and adding of /h/ before vowels, a prominent feature of Jamaican Creole. The most interesting voice in this story is, however, that of the third person narrator, which is also created using Creole features and is thus closer to Miss Myrtella and the people from the village than to Patricia. The narrator is clearly taking sides: not only through the language choice but also by other means, e.g. the description of Patricia as 'thick skin', and in fact, the narrator is not a detached one but - even though not a character on the plot level - an involved narrator, a story-telling figure who addresses the reader directly and frequently appears in the first person form.

The point is, however, that the narrator occupies a crucial position in the complex web of discourse relations in the narrative - between author and reader, narrator and implied reader and between the characters. These discourse relations can by no means be seen as non-hierarchical ones: especially in novels where the narrator is not at the same time a character on the level of plot but has an omniscient point of view, the position of the narrative voice is one of power and authority. The narrator thus functions as a mediator between the characters in the plot and the reader. The relationship between a narrator using the standard form and the characters using a non-standard form can achieve different effects: on the one hand, it can affirm the outsider position of the narrator, the standard can be used as an explanatory voice, approximating the implied reader's (assumed) language, or it can even be used to create a silent compact of irony between reader and narrator, exploiting the non-standard-speaking character roles for comical effects.[31] In the handbook *Style in Fiction*, the role of non-standard language in the narrative is seen that way:

One of the factors to be reckoned with is the distancing and stigmatising effect of non-standard forms of language including deviant spellings. The very fact of using such forms of language implies that the character deviates from the author's own standard language. Hence non-standard speech is typically associated with objects of comedy and satire: characters whom we see from the outside only.[32]

It may be this association between the third person narrative voice and the author's norms and standards which makes it extremely difficult to employ non-standardised and Creole forms on that level. While it can be more often found in short stories such as the one mentioned above where, however, either a 'story teller' is employed for the narrator's part or, as, for instance in Senior's stories 'Ascot' or 'Ballad', the story is told through the eyes of a child, examples of this are rarely found in the novel, at the earliest perhaps in the writing of Samuel Selvon and, later, in Earl Lovelace's novels and, more recently, in the work of Patricia Powell.

Born in Jamaica in 1966, Powell emigrated to the United States in 1982. After her well received first novel *Me Dying Trial*, which was completed in 1988 and then published by Heinemann in 1993, she has followed up with another novel. *A Small Gathering of Bones*[33] centres around the homosexual relationship between Dale and Nevin and a strange disease which has befallen Dale's friend Ian. The narrative voice here is a detached chronicler of the events which start in February 1978:

> When Ian Kaysen first come down with the offensive dry cough, Dale did have to tell him one Saturday morning, as him watch Ian stumble into the kitchen rubbing his chest, back hunched over: 'Ian Kaysen, I don't mean to interfere in your personal prerogatives, but that rattle in that back of your throat not any little play-play cold. You going to have to do something about that coughing. Maybe your resistance is low. Eat more fruit and vegetables. Quit the blasted cigarette smoking!' Dale cry out, voice a little bit on edge, as him raise off the couch where him spend the night, and follow the long slender fellow into the kitchen. 'Sleep in your own bed when night come down! Stop hackle-hackle your body!'[34]

The Creole forms Patricia Powell employs both on the level of dialogue and on the narrative level are marked mainly grammatically (mainly verb forms, reduplication, pronouns), less lexically (e.g. eye water for tears) but hardly orthographically. She thus sacrifices the graphic emphasis of linguistic autonomy of JC to readability for those literate in English. The crucial point, however, is her approximation of the omniscient narrative voice to Creole: by placing Creole forms on the level of authorial discourse, it is itself given a form of authority. The 'distancing and stigmatising effect of using non-standard forms of language' is not given in Powell's text because the implication that 'the character deviates from the norm of the author's own standard language' and '...hence from the central standards of judgement in a novel'[35] does not apply here. By using Creole on this rather powerful level of communication - a reliable, sincere and omniscient narrative voice - Creole is not only credited with authority but also established as an unmarked form of communication. Its functions here are neither predominantly expressive - as a means of creating authenticity - nor ironic but, I would argue, it does not have a separate function anymore.

The above analyses have served to demonstrate that, while there are no definite commonly accepted models of writing in Creole in sight (nor proposed in this paper), Caribbean writers have long transgressed the boundaries of the oral/literate and the Creole/Standard English divisions, thus making the 'language of orality' not only a written language but also an (unofficial) literary and increasingly textualised language. The examples of the works of three Jamaican women writers of different generations show that the form and function of their Creole use in the text is certainly connected to the socio-historical context of their works but also forms a powerful and constructive force in the wider social discourse on Creole. Part of this process is also reflected in the re-naming of the language over the last fifty years: *vernacular* or *dialect*, a term Louise Bennett frequently used, seems to accept the close connection to Standard English as the higher norm; *patois*, a term derived from the French word for 'rural', originally used to refer to low, rural varieties of the Standard but is today also used affirmatively; *Creole* which is used in linguistics to refer to a type of language that developed out of a specific language contact situation and which asserts a certain independence from the lexifying language; *nation language*, a term introduced by Edward Kamau Brathwaite[36] to stress the political impact, and finally *Jamaican* (or Trinidadian, Guyanese, etc.) where no connection to the lexifier is drawn.

The textualisation of Creole is also interesting in the light of the decreasing importance of the written language versus spoken language through the newer media: it is not only in the written text but also in other prestigious discourse types like audiovisual media where the domination of Standard English is being challenged. The fact that spoken language is taking over those public spheres which were formerly dominated by writing may be part of a general restructuring of the boundaries between formal and informal, high and low prestige domains. Jean 'Binta' Breeze's comment also seems to suggest this:

> You see, it's an assumption that power is with the book and not with the tapes and not with the videos that the language that's coming out of us, that's reaching the most people is already Jamaican. It's the book trying to catch up with popular culture.[37]

The divide might thus well be narrowed from the other side, shifting towards orality.

Notes

1. I would like to thank Tobias Döring for his invaluable comments and discussions on this paper.
2. See Paula Burnett (ed.), *The Penguin Book of Caribbean Verse in English*, Penguin, Harmondsworth, 1986.

3. See for example, Tzvetan Todorov, *The Conquest of America: The Question of the Other,* translated Richard Howard, Harper and Row, New York, 1982.
4. While this sharp division still applies for the 'anglophone' Caribbean, Creoles with other lexifiers have experienced a change in status, e.g. in Haiti where a French-lexicon Creole has become the official language of the country.
5. Walter J. Ong, 'Orality, Literacy and Medieval Textualization', *New Literary History*, 16, 1984, pp.1-11.
6. See for example, J.D. Scott, *Domination and the Arts of Resistance. Hidden Transcripts*, Yale University Press, New Haven and London, 1990.
7. See Marlis Hellinger, 'Function and Status Change of Pidgin and Creole Languages' in U. Ammon and M. Hellinger (eds.) *Status Change of Languages,* Mouton de Gruyter, Berlin, 1991, pp.264-81.
8. It is notable that the standardisation of Creole languages whose lexifiers are languages other than English (e.g. French- or Dutch-related Creoles) has met with less resistance than is the case with English-related Creoles. The lack of international communicability is often put forward as a chief argument against the standardisation of Creole (ignoring the fact that this applies to many standardised languages).
9. David Dabydeen, *Slave Song*, Dangaroo, Oxford, 1984, p.13.
10. Starting from the 1920s a number of Caribbean novelists (e.g. Alfred Mendes, Trinidad) had begun to make use of Creole in the fictional dialogue, mainly to create 'authentic voices' in their writing.
11. See Rex Nettleford, 'Introduction' in Louise Bennett, *Jamaica Labrish*, Sangster's Book Stores, Kingston, 1966, p.9.
12. Louise Bennett, op. cit., 1966, p.218-19.
13. For a thorough discussion on this, cf. Hellinger, 1986.
14. See Bill Ashcroft, Gareth Griffiths and Helen Tiffin, *The Empire Writes Back. Theory and Practice in Post-Colonial Literatures*, Routledge, London, 1989, p.38.
15. Louise Bennett, 1966, op. cit., pp.43-44.
16. Arguments for keeping this spelling system are that 1. it disambiguates some homophones, e.g. write, right, rite (note, however that there are also homographs, eg. tear (n.) and tear (v.))and that 2. it reveals the morphological relationship between some words such as sign and signify (this, however, applies only for a minority of 'silent letters' in English orthography). The majority of silent letters, e.g. in listen or knight are simply kept for historical reasons.
17. Marlis Hellinger, 'On Writing English-Related Creoles in the Caribbean' in M. Görlach and Holms, J. (eds.) *Focus on the Caribbean*, John Benjamin, Amsterdam, 1986, p.65.
18. Jean 'Binta' Breeze in interview with Tobias Döring at the Berlin festival 'Dub and Beyond', June, 1995.

19. Frederic G. Cassidy and Robert B. LePage, *Dictionary of Jamaican English*, 1967, Cambridge University Press, Cambridge.
20. See Beryl. L. Bailey, *Jamaican Creole Syntax*, Cambridge University Press, Cambridge, 1966
21. Walter J. Ong, 'Orality, Literacy and Medieval Textualization', *New Literary History*, 16, 1984, p.5.
22. Note that Louise Bennett's works were all published in Kingston, Jamaica, where her fame in the media, radio and the daily paper *The Gleaner* made her language choices acceptable.
23. See Anne Walmsley, 'From 'Nature' to 'Roots': School Anthologies and a Caribbean Canon', *Wasafiri*, 11, 1990, pp.4-7.
24. See Charles H. Rowell, 'An Interview with Olive Senior', *Callaloo*, 11, 1988, pp.480-90.
25. Cf., for instance, Pratt, 1977, pp.38-78, who discusses aesthetic and structural similarities between natural and literary discourse on the basis of William Labov's work on oral narratives.
26. Exceptions are e.g. Sylvia Wynter's *The Hills of Hebron*, Jonathan Cape, London, 1962 and Merle Hodge's *Crick Crack Monkey* , Heinemann, London, 1970.
27. Rowell, 1988, op. cit.
28. Ibid, p.481.
29. Ibid, p.485.
30. See Olive Senior, *Summer Lightning and Other Stories*, Longman, Harlow, 1986, pp.61-62.
31. The latter is often achieved in Naipaul's early narratives as in *Miguel Street* where Creole becomes the code of failure and an obstacle for achievement of the Caribbean societies.
32. Geoffrey N. Leech and Michael H. Short, *Style in Fiction. A Linguistic Introduction to English Fictional Prose*, Longman, London, 1981.
33. Patricia Powell, *A Small Gathering of Bones*, Heinemann, Oxford, 1994.
34. Ibid, p.1.
35. Leech and Short, 1981, op. cit., p.170
36. See Edward Kamau Brathwaite, 'The Development of Nation Language in Anglophone Caribbean Poetry - An Electronic Lecture' in E.K. Brathwaite, *History of the Voice*, New Beacon Books, London and Port of Spain, 1981.
37. Tobias Döring, Interview with Jean 'Binta' Breeze, Berlin, 1995, unpublished manuscript.

Surinam Women Writers and Issues of Translation

Petronella Breinburg

Surinam women writers have until recent years not received the attention they so deserve. They were, like their counterparts from the English and Hispanic Caribbean, largely left out in the study or promotion of Caribbean literature: that is except in the case of Jean Rhys, a white Creole.[1]

This neglect of the words of Surinam women is in spite of the evidence that the women of African descent had, during slavery, learnt to read and write, especially in the case of the house slaves who looked after their masters' children.

The slaves, who were specially selected by missionaries to spread the word of Christianity to the slave population, were also taught to read and write. They were encouraged to translate biblical passages and sermons into the local vernacular, mainly Sranan-tongue, at that time referred to as *Neger-Engels* (Negro English), and also into Sarmacan or Nduka in order to win over the Maroons, at that time called *Boss Negers* (Bush Negroes).

These Surinam women have been known to fake 'permission to be absent' notes which they gave to their men folk. There followed in time some writing by women who often worked for the missionaries in Sranan, in order to take biblical tracts to the masses. From the early twentieth century, came more modern writing.

In the meantime Surinam had changed hands from one colonial power to another, which contributed to its varied linguistic background. In addition, African slaves followed by Asian indentures, each brought their own cultural language, making Surinam a multi-cultural, multi-lingual and multi-faith territory as indicated in the writing. In this short paper, which represents work in progress, I have attempted a brief overview to highlight the works of Surinam women, whether writing from home or self-elected exile abroad and whether they write in Dutch, Sranan or Sarnami.

Surinam women are from a variety of racial, cultural, religious and linguistic backgrounds. These factors are very evident in the writing. The cultural and racial mixes represent the aftermath of colonialism because, though prior to European invasion the indigenous population also came from varied racial and cultural backgrounds, it was not until colonialism that there emerged such a blaze of cultures and all that these entail.

The arrival of Columbus in the Americas was soon followed by a mass of Europeans to the colonies, including Surinam. To Surinam's population, for instance, the indigenous group, were added the Spanish, the French, the British, the Dutch, then later waves of British, and finally Dutch.[2] Each waves of time the country changed power, the language and cultural norms were expected to change also.

The colonial powers brought Africans to the Caribbean as slaves, I stress 'Africans as slaves' rather than 'African slaves', since the Africans may not have been slaves in their own country. The Africans brought a variety of cultures, languages and dialects. Though forced to adopt the cultures and values of the group in power, that is the whites, Africans retained some of their own cultures which influenced their development. Later came the Asians, from India and what is now Pakistan and Indonesia, including the island of Java, all bringing their cultures and languages.

Yiddish speakers from Central Europe through to Brazil, also came. Soon Surinam became a 'free-for-all'. People poured in from all directions, including other Dutch colonies where Papiomentu was already developing as a Hispanic Creole.

Generally speaking, because the Dutch attitude to language was contrary to that of the British, while people from the English-speaking Caribbean tend to be monolingual (as are most English people), Surinam people are bilingual (as are most Dutch people). Surinamese are often trilingual in Sranan, Dutch and Sarnami-Hindustani. In addition other languages and dialects survive such as Malay, Surinam-Javanese (from the Indonesian peoples), Haka Chinese (from those of Chinese descent), Aukan, Mdjuka and Sramakan (from those of African descent), and Trio, Karaib and Arowakan (from the indigenous population who survived the European onslaught).

Surinam women, survivors of such a culturally mixed people, have rarely had their voices heard. One cannot really call them voiceless because they were and are speaking and writing, though seldom noticed, even currently. When Caribbean writers are studied, it is usually men, black and white, and of late, the white writer, Jean Rhys, who are very popular with students in higher education.

The Surinam woman writer has an added disadvantage, often she writes in Dutch, and who reads Dutch anyway? But if those writing in Dutch are restricted to a Dutch-speaking audience, which is very small when compared with writing for an English or French-speaking world, the women writing in Sranan are even more restricted. To begin with, only Surinam people read Sranan and what is more, outside Surinam, even within the English-speaking Caribbean, Sranan has a low status and is seen as *Taki-taki* gibberish.

To recap: the very first black women writers of Surinam were those Africans in slavery who had learnt to write while still house slaves, often in homes with children. The women, as historians tell, soon began to fake notes for their men folk, in order to give them a little time off from their plantation life. Slaves, and later indentured Asians, had to have notes from their masters or plantation overseers to venture outside the plantation. Such notes were needed even if they were only going for a brief visit. It was then, that the person who could write, and had access to the handwriting of their masters, came into their own. No doubt men faked notes, but women such as Topsy,[3] a black girl in an old school book, sticks her tongue out in front of a mirror, making a fool of herself, but while seeming stupid, was learning to read and write, even it if was just to be able to read *The Bible*.

Another early example of writing from Surinam women is that written during the early twentieth century. One can look, for example, at the work of Johanna in 1910, a poem written in Sranan.[4]

It must be noted that writing in Sranan tends to be in the form of poetry, seldom novels, which are usually written in Dutch. The content of Johanna's poem tells us a great deal about the harsh lives of black people under colonialism and its effect on the emotions of those people.

There are many women, now writing in Surinam and abroad, especially in the Netherlands. It is difficult to select from the long list which is emerging. Some are of Asian background, others African and some of Chinese or Indonesian background.

The earlier published writers began by recreating and recording in writing the tales told by elders, in one of ten languages or dialects of those elders. For example, *Some Creations,*[5] and *Legends of Surinam*[6] are stories first told in Sranan, then recreated and written in English. A later collection, told by relatives and village elders, is full of stories told by older women, spoken in Arawakan, and scripted in Dutch by Michiel van Kempen.[7] Sometimes the story is by a woman but written down by a man. But there are also stories told by an older male of the village though scripted by a woman, such as in the case of the leriman (preacher), told by a man in Sranan and scripted by Trudi Guda.[8]

The stories, recreated from the oral tradition, tend to retain the original oral telling style. In the case of the leriman's story, the song is crucial. Even across the translated narrative, the reader feels that he/she is hearing a song springing up from the pages.

When the narrative is being told, whether in poetry or prose, even when it is not a folk tale or myth being recreated, the lyrical style is still evident in much of the writing of Surinam women. One example of this is 'Mi Dren'

'Mi Dren'*

Yere mi sten,
lek wan grio e bari
abaka den bigi krepiston
Mi ati e nak te dede fu frede
M'e suk wan kibri olo
pe lobi de,
M'e frey lek wan sonfowru
mindri tranga winti
abra den moro hey bergi
Sula e yere mi sten
Mi skin e degedege

Johanna Schouten[9]

In general, anyone involved in translation agrees that the translating of poetry can be a nightmare. The poem 'Mi Dren' offers a good example of the difficulties. Written in Sranan, it is then translated into English.[10]

A great deal is lost through translation. The degree of loss depends a great deal on the culture and linguistic background of the translator as opposed to that of the original writer. Even when the work is translated by the original writer, there may be difficulties, depending on how well the writer knows both the languages and whether s/he has a feeling for the predominant cultural aspects in both languages.

Taking the second line of the poem, 'lek wan grio e bari' the official translation is 'like a grio calling'. To me, of Sranan mother tongue, the original version is much stronger in creating feelings as far as the reader is concerned, when compared to the English version, 'the grio *calling*' or the original 'like a grio *screaming*'.

Bari in Sranan is nearer to 'screaming or shouting' than it is to 'calling', whilst 'calling' in English would be nearer to 'kari' in Sranan. Similarly, in line five, 'Me suk wan kibri olo', in the English version it is, 'I am looking for a hole to hide'. To a reader familiar with the feelings of both languages, that second line conjures up a stronger imagery in the original. The term 'searching' in English, would have been nearer to 'suk' (short for sukoe) of the original. Also metaphorically speaking, a 'kibri ole' would be better translated into 'hiding place'. Taking the third line of the original: there, the term 'den' in the Sranan means more than one, which gives the reader a vision of lots of large boulders , while in the English translation, there is only one boulder, e.g. 'a' boulder.

When poets use a great deal of idiomatic expression, the translator is faced with having to choose between using equivalent idioms or direct translations.

Often, the equivalent has a slightly different meaning. As an example, in 'Zelfbeeld', the poet used a phrase; 'laat los' (let loose), but 'let loose' in English can mean 'letting our dog loose after a robber'. What the poet meant by 'letting loose' (laat los), is that she is setting herself free of the burden of constantly having her paths to progressive thoughts blocked. Rhythm is another problem and this is based on the number of syllables a poet may use in a particular line, which is what gives the poem what is often commonly referred to as the 'beat'. Take for instance a Sranan phrase at random, 'mi gwe' (I am going).

'Mi' is short for 'mie de gowe', but a poet is more likely to use the shorter version, if for no reason other than the 'beat'. 'Gwe' is monosyllabic, while 'going' has two syllables. Once a series of these monosyllabic words or shorter versions of three or four words are used, creating a monosyllabic effect, translation into another language places the translator in the difficult position of having to find a way of retaining the rhythm of the original poem. In the case of a language such as Sranan, which uses a great deal of shortened forms in speech and literary work, as opposed to Dutch which often joins a series of words into one long word consisting of many syllables, translation into English either from Dutch or Sranan, though desirable, must take into account that a great deal of the original meaning will be lost. Yet, many Surinam women continue to write in Sranan.

When asked when and why she writes in Sranan as opposed to writing in Dutch, Celestine Raalte, poet and dramatist of Afro-Surinam origin now residing in the Netherlands, stated that for a white audience she writes in Dutch but Sranan is the language in which she feels.[11] In Sranan rhyme she can use particular metaphors and personifications which would transmit her emotion to better effect than if she wrote or performed in Dutch. She has written bilingual collections such as *Awanda,*[12] however, she prefers to perform in Sranan.

Awanda,[13] is a collection of poetry and the title is in honour of an African woman during the slave period who, against the rules of the plantation rulers, told folk stories to the children and gave them hope. She told them about their own culture in Africa, about great African Kings, folk stories the children would never hear from the missionaries who taught them. She told the children about the history of Africa, their home, homeland of their forefathers. Part of that collection is the famous 'Zwarte Roos' (Black Rose), which is a love poem, not of one person, but in praise of the black male of African descent in general. She claims that 'the poem is about love for ourselves, love for our men, love for our children'.

Her poetry, in Dutch, is not without merit and received recognition from a wide readership, both in the Netherlands and abroad. There is, for instance, the highly acclaimed, 'Zelfbeeld' (Self Image). Here again, we note the lyrical style in the form of several stanzas, with short refrains in between making it more like a song which has to be listened to rather than a poem to read aloud. The poem opens with the lines which describe the curse of slavery, then goes on to describe how even during the period of freedom, she had chosen to be a slave, strapped hand and foot.

'Zelfbeeld'**

Mijn slavenvloek een
vastgeroest in mikn gedachten
woede en hartzeer verperden
mijn weg tot nuchter denken

In een tijd van vrijheid
had ik sellf gekozen slaaf te zijn
handen en voeten
met stevig touw
vast gehouden.

(The poem ends with a final and striking resolution that she would now rid herself from the slavery curse)

ik laat los mijn slavenvloek
ik weet dat ik mijn zwarten ras zal ont moeten
in de warme koestgering die ik heb voor
mijzelf.

Celestine Raalte [14]

It would be impossible to analyse and write a study of the work of Surinam women writers in just one paper. One other poet who has to be mentioned in this short paper is Gladys Waterberg[15] who writes spontaneously in English and Sranan. Her poetry is often described as feminist poetry, a label she tends to reject. She simply writes about women's feelings and struggles. Her work often talks of unity between women which is necessary. She urges women to use the strength which they have.

There follows two extracts one in English (Sery) and one in Sranan (Meki Wi Sori Wi Egi Krakti):

'Sery'

Mother of our struggle
our righteous struggle
brought us all together
one day
to remember
your words
don't tell lies...
brace yourself
for victory day.

'Meki Wi Sori Wi Eygi Krakti'***

Sisa me'k mek' wi opo luku now
wan fasi fa sranan kan bow
Sisa me'k me'k wi opo lusu wi skin
bika wa ooktu na doti pikin
Tumsi langa wi de wakti
kon me'k mek wi sori wi eygi krakti
Gladys Waterburg [16]

Writing in Sranan is now being traced as far back as 1717,[17] but most of the published writing has been by men. Many of them were chosen to spread the word of Christianity to the masses, especially the Africans who had freed themselves from slavery and attempted to set up a replica of Africa along the various river banks and in the deepest interior of Surinam. Women told stories, chanted verse and used idiomatic expression, but these were seldom recorded in writing. A change came during the twentieth century when Surinam women began to insist that their work be given the same respect as was given to male writers. Younger women are now collecting stories, expressions and song from older women, and recording these in written form.

Impossible, as it is, to deal with all that is being produced by Surinam women writers: poetry, prose and drama, this short paper should be seen as 'work in progress'; it is not only a celebration of the work of Surinam writers going back to the women who faked notes to get their menfolk a short break away from the horrors of the plantation, but also a tribute to the women who have created and are still recreating and scripting the folklore from the various racial and cultural groups. Although we appreciate the oral tradition, it is also important that the stories of our ancestors live on, even when we ourselves become ancestors of a later generation. It is important that Surinam women have their voices heard and noted, whether they write in the language of the former colonial rulers, or the language they themselves have created.

Translations

'Mi Dren' (My Dream)*

Hear my voice,
like a grio calling
behind a boulder large,
My heart beats deadlike with fear.
I'm looking for a hole to hide
where love is to be found.
I fly like a sun bird
amidst strong blasts
far above the highest peaks.
Rapids hear my voice,
My body trembles.

'Zelfbeeld' (Self Image)**

My slave curse
firmly fixed in my thoughts
anger and heartache spread across
my path to soberer thinking

In the period of freedom
I had chosen to be a slave
hand and foot
firmly strapped
with strong ropes.

I let go of my slave curse
I know that I shall meet my black race
In the warm and positive image
which I have of myself.

'Meki Wi Sori Wi Egyi Krakti' (Let Us Show Our Strength)***

Sister let's start looking now
for a way how Sranan can build
Sister let's open up our skin
because we too are children of the earth
too long we are waiting
Come let's show our own strength.

Notes

1. Within the anglophone tradition.
2. Jan Voorhoeve and Ursy Litchveld, *Creole Drum*, trans. Vernie A. February, Yale University Press, New Haven, 1975.
3. This refers to school readers used over 50 years ago in the Caribbean.
4. See Voorhoeve and Litchteld, 1975, op. cit.
5. Petronella Breinburg, 'Some Creation' in Faustin Charles (ed.), *Under the Storytellers Spell*, Viking Kestrel, London, 1989.
6. Petronella Breinburg, *Legends of Surinam*, New Beacon, London, 1971.
7. Michiel van Kempen, *Sirito: 50 Surinaamse Vertellingen*, Kennedy Stichting, Paramaribo, 1993.
8. Trudi Guda in Michiel van Kempen, Ibid.
9. Johanna Schouten 1910 in Voorhoeven and Lichtveld, 1975, op. cit.. In translation *(see page 8).
10. Ramabai Espinet, *Creation Fire*, Sister Vision Press, Canada, 1990.
11. *Surinaams Nieuws*, 16 December, Amsterdam, 1993.
12. Taken from the *Surinaams Nieuws report,* Ibid.
13. Ibid.
14. Translation ** p.82
15. See for example, Espinet 1990, op. cit., pp.335-36.
16. Translation *** p.93
17. See Voorhoeve and Litchveld, 1975, op. cit.

OUT OF A DIVERSE CARIBBEAN WOMANHOOD

The final section, 'Out Of A Diverse Caribbean Womanhood' redefines some of the issues concerning the shaping of the literary production of women in and from the region and the reception of their writing. The diversity of the literature has been illustrated in earlier discussion throughout the book and we turn now from generic and linguistic diversity to cultural or contextual dimensions not yet addressed.

Beryl Gilroy's brief essay on *Frangipani House* touches upon several issues, not the least being the culture of poverty and 'psychosocial dependency within the culture of poverty'. Beryl Gilroy points to wage labour at the centre of this culture which shapes the experience of women such as the protagonist, Mama King, in *Frangipani House*. Like other cultural contexts, poverty, it is suggested, articulates gender roles revisioned by Caribbean women writers. Beryl Gilroy indicates, also, how Mama King is the 'resourceful' rather than 'strong' African Caribbean woman as well as a 'cultural feminist able to use the semiotics of the culture for her own ends'. Discussing black women's survival of oppression, the focus shifts to the issue of men in that context who exist as 'echoes and mutations in the voices of the women' and Beryl Gilroy offers challenging reasons for their absence.

Beryl Gilroy's critical writing raises important questions at the forefront of the debate. By presenting her reading of her own work she offers an interesting challenge to critics concerning the reading or interpretation of her writing.

In 'One Of The Most Beautiful Islands In The World And One Of The Unluckiest: Jean Rhys and Dominican National Identity', Thorunn Lonsdale examines Dominican national identity for meanings to Jean Rhys's sense of rejection by both the Caribbean and Britain and 'her creatively significant' period in Paris. The essay considers Jean Rhys's portrayal of the 'fragmented past' of Dominica as well as her depiction of an 'antagonistic relationship' with England.

The essay suggests that for the writer there is an 'absence' of national identity which itself contributes to the strength of her oeuvre and Thorunn Lonsdale suggests ways in which Rhys's work reveals her attempt to understand the nature of identity. Finally, Rhys's place and influence as a Caribbean writer is addressed.

'Audacity and Outcome - Rewriting African Caribbean Womanhood' addresses the question of how African Caribbean womanhood is being rewritten by contemporaneous writers from the region. The essay draws on specific short stories by Maryse Conde and Merle Collins. It places the discussion in the context of the recent proliferation of Caribbean women's published writing and feminist theory and considers recent developments and directions in Caribbean women's writing.

The essay argues that 'audacity' has not only led to unprecedented literary production but that 'oraliterature' and 'feminist metafiction' from African Caribbean women of the region are powerful signs of an emerging literature 'articulated within and against two influential traditions, the oral and the scribal'.

Finally, Kenneth Ramchand's 'Coming Out of Repression: Lakshmi Persaud's *Butterfly in the Wind*' brings into the discussion hitherto absent voices, those of Indo-Caribbean women. The starting point of the essay is the 'silence' out of which has come the first full length work by a woman of Indian origin from the Caribbean. Kenneth Ramchand explores Lakshmi Persaud's novel indicating possible readings, firstly as 'fictionalised autobiography', but more profoundly as a novel about growing up as a Hindu girl in an Indian community in post-1940's Trinidad.

The essay highlights the context of changing values and the 'collapse of tradition and conservatism' which informs the setting for the young Kamla's world as well as the part played by female oppression within that world. Kamla's inner voice is a particular focus of the discussion and Kenneth Ramchand indicates in the essay ways in which Kamla's inner voice functions so as to critique not only the suppressive role of colonial education but also the traditional education and 'shaping to which the Hindu female especially is subject'.

Frangipani House

Beryl Gilroy

Frangipani House[1] is a story of flight - flight from the effects of racism and colonialism and economic sedimentation. It is a story of psychosocial dependency within the culture of poverty. It is also a study of culture and identity. Waged labour (work), or lack of it, is at the centre of this culture, and through work, major or even macabre scenes in the drama of living are enacted; gender roles articulated; and memory; graphic, variable, insubstantial and mutable, reconstructs the past with all its vagaries and re-interprets the present as a series of lost identities.

Frangipani House chronicles diachronic change, that is change over time. Mama King the heroine is defined by and defines herself through work. After her husband's disappearance she struggles to support her family. Her daughters emigrate and with this comes an immense three sided role change. The daughters are shown as failed wives, absent mothers and economic father substitutes.

To fulfil these roles, life becomes a treadmill for all involved. The young women earn. The old woman spends. The children are served. Providing for the children who experience surrogate mothering from their grandmother, facilitates and sustains a comparison with work. The daughters, though distant, love and trust their mother to rear their children, and yet, suddenly the children must also emigrate. They have become viable, able to survive, able to objectify the mothers' struggle to exist in a foreign land.

There are several barren areas of loss and existential longings in Mama King's life. She falls ill and her children, out of love for her, provide the best care for her. The best care is clinical but deadening. She is surrounded by too much of the same and is in a labyrinth from which she must escape. Her resolution grows as her body begins a dialogue of discontent and rejection with the environment she hates. She expresses herself in a series of virulent ravings against the Matron and Frangipani House.

Old age does not deaden creativity. Mama King proves this. Mama King, by having reconstituted herself so many times, is a survivor, a survivor of neglect, hunger and the brutalities of life. She is the resourceful, rather than the 'strong', African Caribbean woman. She is, in fact, a cultural feminist able to use the semiotics of the culture for her own ends.

I refute the stereotype of the 'strong black woman', since, in my opinion, the route to the loss of those qualities that make men different from us does not consist of strength, but resourcefulness and creativity by which black women survive oppression.

The African Caribbean man, for the greater part, wanders into manhood. There are no rites of passage for him. These have been taken away. The economic route is also blocked. In the women's reminiscences we are able to reconstruct the reasons why the men have walked away. The men endured tortuous gender encounters and survived by using behaviours they found compensatory. This emerges from the women's talk. The women need to be recognised, succoured, nurtured and, in their evening years, infantilised.

Mama King and her friends use memory as a tool and she becomes authentic as she recalls her serial motherhood nursed by solitary struggle. Of course the men have gone. They are echoes and mutations in the voices of women. The men walked away for the same reasons as their progenitors. They walked away from:

- ...over observation as they seek the daily crust;
- racism and rejection;
- under employment;
- status inconsistency;
- day to day sedimentation;
- minimalisation in society and family;
- attributions that destroy character structure;
- inability to dredge up unlearned skills;
- spirit thievery and emotional larceny.

The young boy Carlton, reared by women, wonders what is a 'good man'.

Mama King does not do this. She is too old and wise. She creates one - man as desired - unknown to all but her. Her language moves with poignance along the road to conviction. Her reality is clear. She responds to her inner need to be free. But this need for freedom clashes with her daughters' wishes for her. Cyclette is egalitatarian and pragmatic. She is prepared to let Mama King's life take its course, but Token, the rigid, funless older woman, decides, as she perceives her end in the life of her mother, to take a new path. She expresses her need for individuation. She can no longer be the universal 'breast'. She needs for herself what she must give to others. She walks away, leaving her daughter to provide another turn of serial mothering for Mama King who is ready to offer her breasts, shrunken and withered they may be. Her love, her centre of care has always been and will always be for others.

Note

1. Beryl Gilroy, *Frangipani House*, Heinemann, 1986.

'One of the Most Beautiful Islands in the World and One of the Unluckiest'[1]: Jean Rhys and Dominican National Identity

Thorunn Lonsdale

In his travel book, *The Sunlit Caribbean*, Alec Waugh calls Dominica 'one of the most beautiful islands in the world and one of the unluckiest'. In *The Sugar Islands,* writing of Dominica and its connection to Jean Rhys, he says:

> I could see how Dominica had coloured her temperament and outlook. It was a clue to her, just as she was a clue to it. People who could not fit into life elsewhere found what they were looking for in Dominica.[2]

An examination of Dominican national identity affords 'a clue' to Jean Rhys's sense of rejection both by the Caribbean and Britain, and to her creatively significant time as an expatriate in Paris: '... between you I often wonder who I am and where is my country and where do I belong and why was I ever born at all'[3] says Antoinette to her husband in *Wide Sargasso Sea* as she laments the situating labels of 'white cockroach',[4] allotted by the descendants of slaves, and 'white nigger',[5] which the 'English women'[6] had been heard to use about her and other white Creoles. In this episode Antoinette could be speaking for Jean Rhys in as much as she captures the ambiguities relevant both to Rhys and Rhys's birthplace, Dominica.[7]

In Dominica, locating the elements of national identity is a complex undertaking. This mountainous island has its colonial cultural roots in not one, but three metropolitan powers: Spain, France and Britain. In addition to this mixed European heritage, the cultural influences of a transplanted African population and pre-Columban Carib settlers have also left their impression. This enormously diverse history must be accounted for in the task faced by Dominica - as in many decolonised societies - the task of nation-building.

Another vital component in the job of nation building is development and here Dominica's beautiful but unfortunate nature is revealed. In a region where tourist-led development has become the norm, Dominica has eschewed the 'sun, sea and sand' approach in favour of eco-tourism.[8] The cynical observer might remark that since Dominica is not endowed with the beach resources of other Caribbean islands, it is making a virtue out of necessity. Herein lies an ambiguity: not only is eco-tourism inherently contradictory, it is unlikely that Dominica's virtuous necessity, its beautiful and dramatic mountains, will ever compete with the sandy beaches of other islands. Located at the heart of the hurricane belt, virtually reliant on a mono-crop culture (bananas), Dominica will always be 'at the lower end of the prosperity stakes'.[9] Exceptional beauty is not enough.

As with Dominica, so with Rhys. Born in Dominica, Rhys always felt estranged from the sources of that culture. As a white creole descendant of a planter family, she felt out of step with the numerically superior descendants of slaves and with the English culture from which she traced her origins. Jean Rhys's writing expresses her own sense of dislocation and perhaps behind her work is her attempt to understand the nature of identity: especially that of undefined identity.[10] Like Dominica, Rhys had no firm foundations of national tradition to draw upon, nor a vision of national identity to inspire her work; she was left to explore the absence of national identity. Ironically, it is this very absence that is one of the greatest strengths of Rhys's oeuvre. But, like Dominica, Rhys was commercially unfortunate in that her idiosyncratic talent was not valued, at least not until very late in the day. It was not until 1966 with the publication of *Wide Sargasso Sea* that she received due acclaim. By 1993, fourteen years after Rhys's death 'Jean Rhys's work, particularly *Wide Sargasso Sea,* was among the top eight best sellers of Penguin books (15-20,000 copies sold per year)'.[11] Thus, Jean Rhys lived life at the periphery: she drank, she was poor, she was artistically unrecognised, and she never achieved a comfortable sense of personal identity. Her writing describes the uncertainty of the search for identity by the unformed, rootless individual as surely as it does, metaphorically, of the unformed island nation.

In Rhys's most celebrated novel, *Wide Sargasso Sea*, the newly married young Englishman, visits an unnamed island which is clearly associated with Dominica:

> ...looked at the sad leaning coconut palms, the fishing boats drawn up on the shingly beach, the uneven row of whitewashed huts, and asked the name of the village.
> 'Massacre'.
> 'And who was massacred here? Slaves?'
> 'Oh no'. She sounded shocked. 'Not Slaves. Something must have happened a long time ago. Nobody remembers now'.[12]

'She sounded shocked' establishes one of the underlying tensions of the novel, namely the interrogation of the dynamic between former slaves and their creole counterparts. The word 'shocked' also suggests that Antoinette found the idea of massacring slaves incomprehensible which is consistent with Rhys's portrayal of the relationship between former slaves and their plantation owners. In his study 'The Locked Heart' Peter Hulme says that

> Antoinette, like Rhys, would have known very well that the 'massacre' here was the killing in 1674 of Indian Warner, the half Carib son of one of the foremost English colonists in the West Indies, Sir Thomas Warner.[13]

Hulme's indication that no-one living in Dominica could fail to know the relevance of the Massacre's name draws attention to a gap in memory.

In Rhys's short story 'Temps Perdi', the first person narrator wants to visit the Carib reservation because: 'All my life I had been curious about these people because of a book I once read, pictures I once saw'[14] and in her short story 'Heat' the narrator reads an account of the volcanic eruption of a neighbouring island that she had witnessed as a child: 'I read all this, and then I thought but it wasn't like that, it wasn't like that at all'.[15] Through her narrators it is evident that not only was Rhys aware of the relevance of the Caribs, but that she was also aware of the distinction between documented material and personal experience. Rhys's preoccupation with the importance of the written word and actual experience is apparent in her short story 'The Day They Burned The Books'. Mrs. Sawyer, the mixed race wife of an Englishman, burns and sells her dead husband's library collection because its contents represent the heritage which determined the racial divisions and tensions that permeated the marriage. In *Voyage in the Dark* the protagonist is reading Zola's *Nana* about which her chorus girl roommate, Maudie, says, 'Besides, all books are like that - just somebody stuffing you up'.[16] One might question whether Jean Rhys is merely 'stuffing...up' the reader by her removal of an explanation of 'Massacre' or whether through this negation she is offering a more accurate rendition of the colonial experience, hence the history of the island. In other words, the Caribs were never important to the European colonisers, therefore, 'Nobody remembers now' and the position of former slaves or their ancestors tends to be emphasised.

Ernest Renan in his 1882 ground-breaking lecture, 'What is a Nation', suggested that 'the essence of a nation is that all individuals have many things in common, and also that they have forgotten many things'.[17] And while the appellation Nation may not be correct for Dominica, in the stricter sense of the word, the concept of forgetfulness, which Benedict Anderson takes further in *Imagined Communities,* is important. Antoinette's negation of a significant part of Dominica's history[18] may be read as a necessary 'forgetfulness' thus a portrayal by Rhys of a Dominica that had forgotten the Caribs. For the progeny of former slave owners to 'remember' the Caribs, hence their ancestors' dispossession of earlier settlers, would not be consistent with the conquest, especially since most historical reportage would suggest that the warring for the islands was between the various European settlers with little to no regard for any 'savage' earlier inhabitants who just got in the way. Equally, for the islands' 'inheritors', namely the former slaves, a curious dilemma arises if the Caribs, a severely diminished population, are construed as the legitimate inheritors of the island.

In her portrayals of Dominica, none of these issues elude Jean Rhys; she makes reference to the Caribs in *Voyage in the Dark* as a people who 'are now practically exterminated'.[19] In 'Temps Perdi' when the narrator reaches the Carib Quarter, an area called 'Salybia', the 'negro policeman' details some local disturbances and offhandedly reports that only 'Two-three Caribs were killed' which the narrator re-emphasises and comments 'It might have been an Englishman talking'.[20] This constitutes further evidence that Dominicans, namely the offspring of former slaves, do not 'remember' their past subjugation in their treatment of other oppressed people. Another reading is that the policeman was so much a part of the establishment that he was oblivious to the Caribs as legitimate 'citizens'. The Trinidadian writer, Amryl Johnson in *Sequins for a Ragged Hem* confirms that Guadeloupeans look down on Dominican 'French Creole' as less sophisticated than their own 'true' French which is, of course, nearer to the spoken language of France.[21]

The policeman also refers the visitors to the home of 'a beautiful Carib girl' and the narrator instantly recognises that the girl is not a Carib but of mixed race. The introduction of the girl into 'Temps Perdi' also re-affirms the author's concern with misrepresentative historical documentation. The narrator of events in 'Temps Perdi' takes some photographs of the young girl followed by the local guide, Charlie:

> ...(who) asked if he might take the rest. We heard his condescending voice: 'Will you turn your side face? Will you please turn your full face? Don't smile for this one'.

At this point in the text there is the parenthetical comment ('These people are quite savage - quite uncivilised')[22] which takes up earlier mention in the story of common assumptions of the Caribs as 'wild' and 'savage'. Rhys uses this episode to expose that not only was the girl not Carib, but that she was also being told to respond to photographs in a manner consistent with received ideas about the Carib's character. Benedict Anderson's comment about the technical developments which help to create and sustain underlying assumptions about communities, whilst referring to the embodiment and construction of nation, is pertinent to the concerns evinced in Rhys's work about accepted ideas:

> The photograph, fine child of the age of mechanical reproduction, is only the most peremptory of a huge modern accumulation of documentary evidence which simultaneously records a certain apparent continuity and emphasises its loss from memory. Out of this estrangement comes a conception of personhood, identity...which, because it can not be 'remembered,' must be narrated.[23]

Through her fictional renditions of a complicated national heritage and her awareness of misrepresentation, Jean Rhys portrays the fragmented past of her island of birth and its confused relationship with its former colonial power. Equally, when she focuses on English connections she depicts an antagonistic relationship. In *Wide Sargasso Sea,* when the post emancipation whites arrive, '...to make money as they all do. Some of the big estates are going cheap, and one unfortunate's loss is always a clever man's gain',[24] significantly, it is the black cook, Christophine, who equates them with former slave owners and demonstrates a preference for the 'old ones'. 'New ones worse than old ones -more cunning that's all'[25] and 'Old Mr. Luttrell spit in their face if he see how they look at you. Trouble walk into this house this day'.[26] Former slaves owners are portrayed sympathetically by Rhys and she depicts them in a compromised situation after the abolition of slavery. It had been Mr Luttrell 'who grew tired of waiting'[27] for the 'compensation the English promised when the Emancipation Act was passed'[28] and 'one calm evening he shot his dog, swam out to sea and was gone for always'.[29]

Christophine's assessment of the 'new whites' as trouble corresponds to the later depiction of the new arrivals as opportunists and people who do not understand local attitudes and temperaments. Annette's comment to her new husband, Mr. Mason, 'You don't like, or even recognise, the good in them...and you won't believe in the other side',[30] elicits the response 'They're too damn lazy to be dangerous'.[31] Equally, to Aunt Cora, of whom he disapproved, 'an ex-slave-owner who had escaped misery, a flier in the face of Providence',[32] he says: 'Live here most of your life and know nothing about the people. It's astonishing. They are children - they wouldn't hurt a fly'.[33]

Mr. Mason's attitude is consistent with ideas that were prevalent with the slave owning classes pre-emancipation. In his eighteenth century *The History of the Island of Dominica,* Thomas Atwood states that very few slaves:

> ...on their arrival in the islands have the least appearance of having been civilised, or possessed of any endowments but such as are merely natural. For

the generality of them, on their first introduction, appear as wild as the brute beasts; are indolent and stupid to a degree...[34]

And he goes on to say: 'Every thing appears to them as entirely new, as to the infant just come to a moderate degree of vision...'.[35] An analysis which today is incomprehensible when it is remembered that these people had been forcibly removed from their homeland, endured a treacherous journey and had been confronted by an entirely new and hostile environment.

Coral Ann Howells, acknowledges that '...Rhys belongs to the period of Empire...' and suggests that '... her subversive critique of Englishmen and imperialism (focused by her recognition of difference after arrival in England) should more appropriately be described as a post-colonial impulse'.[36] In *Wide Sargasso Sea* after Mr. Mason arrives Antoinette thinks:

Now it had started up again and worse than before, my mother knows but she can't make him believe it, I wish I could tell him that out here is not at all like English people think it is.[37]

This depiction of difference between colonial English and English is fundamental to Rhys and the contention that her work emanates from a 'post-colonial' impulse. It is perhaps an impulse more grounded in the differences between the English and their treatment of colonials than in a sympathy with other races. Rhys's own antipathy for the English may have developed after her arrival in England, but in her short story 'The Day They Burned The Books' the colonial child narrator admires her friend Willie's denouncement of strawberries and daffodils and thinks:

...my relations with the few 'real' English boys and girls I had met were awkward. I had discovered that if I called myself English they would snub me haughtily: 'You're not English; you're a horrid colonial': 'Well, I don't much want to be English,' I would say 'It's much more fun to be French or Spanish or something like that and as a matter of fact I am a bit'. Then I was too killingly funny, quite ridiculous. Not only a horrid colonial but also ridiculous. Heads I win, tails you lose - that was the English.

This passage also offers substantiation of the confusion faced by the colonial child in relation to identity.[38]

Rarely is the Caribbean absent from Rhys work and even in the three novels that make no direct mention of the islands, the protagonists' attitudes to Englishness belie their author's perspective. In *Good Morning Midnight,* Sasha Jensen remembers losing her job as a receptionist in a Paris fashion house after a visit from the English 'boss':

> What's he like? Oh, he's the real English type, le businessman....I thought: 'Oh, my God, I know what these people mean when they say the real English type'...He arrives. Bowler hat, majestic trousers, Oh-my-God expression, ha, ha eyes - I know him at once.[39]

Sasha is depicted as having a clear understanding of what the French, mean when they say 'the real English type' and then the character's physical appearance is seen to match her expectations 'Bowler hat, majestic trousers', all of which conform to depictions in Rhys's work of the double-standard or hypocritical nature of the English. Sasha remembers being chided by the English 'boss': ' 'Just a hopeless, helpless little fool, aren't you?' he says. Jovial, Bantering? On the surface, yes. Underneath? No, I don't think so'.[40]

In *After Leaving Mr. Mackenzie,* the Englishman, Mr. Horsfield, overhears a Frenchman 'holding forth about Anglo-Saxons, and the phrase, 'cette hypocrisie froid' came back and back into what he was saying'.[41] And in the train on her journey back to England Julia and her companions are described: 'The people sitting opposite to her - obviously a married couple - were also English and they were reading the English papers. To all intents and purposes she was already in England. She felt strange and subdued'.[42] Cold hypocrisy and subdued feelings are representative of Rhys's portrayals of England and the English. Anna's first impressions of England in *Voyage in the Dark* are consistent with Rhys's own: 'I had read about England ever since I could remember -smaller meaner everything is never mind'.[43]

In *Quartet,* national identity is an important element in the depiction of characters who are often defined on this basis.

When Marya first meets Heidler he asks her 'But you are English - or aren't you?'[44] and his hesitation confirms the character's own marginal status because she does not choose to live up to type. Whereas Heidler's English wife, Lois, epitomises her background and is 'country with a careful dash of Chelsea'.[45] The 'careful' representing the usual Rhysian contempt for the English. In her work, Rhys consistently indicates that conformity and appearance are fundamental to the English with their 'majestic trousers' and 'hypocrisie froid' and without it they are like Marya, who is thought to be 'a strange animal or at any rate a strayed animal - one not quite of the fold'.[46] Nationality and cultural distinctions are foregrounded in *Quartet* - in which the English are always referred to as Anglo-Saxons - as is the marginalised status of the protagonist Marya, a status common to all Rhysian heroines. This depiction of marginalisation provides further evidence of Rhys's concern with rootlessness and identity.

It might also be suggested that because of this dislike for the English, Rhys found living in Paris more stimulating and enjoyed a highly creative period, irrespective of extreme financial hardship. It was after her move to France, a country where for once she was indisputedly foreign, that Jean Rhys published her first short story, 'Vienne', set in yet another international capital, in Ford's *Transatlantic Review* and her literary career began.

Finally, when speculating that Rhys's concern with identity is linked to her own ambivalent national identifications, it is appropriate to consider Rhys's place and influence as a writer. Rhys sits comfortably alongside other Caribbean women writers and her influence is evident. The opening lines of *Voyage in the Dark*: 'It was as if a curtain had fallen, hiding everything I had ever known. It was almost like being born again' - are evoked in Merle Collins's poem 'Seduction':

And my sister, she said
The longer you linger
in this seductive dying
the more silent, you'll see
You'll become.

Merle Collins[47]

Grenadian writer and poet, Merle Collins may use death imagery to symbolise alienation and Rhys re-birth, but both work to suggest alienation in respect of reactions to England and home. Laura Niesen de Abruna, writing of Rhys's *Voyage in the Dark,* and Jamaica Kincaid's *Annie John* says: 'Both novels concern a young woman's struggle to achieve an identity based in the West Indian cultural experience'.[48]

Rhys's fellow writer from Dominica, Phyllis Shand Allfrey, for whom *Voyage in the Dark* was clearly a very important novel said: 'It was the simplicity and beauty of the prose that I loved. But it was a horrible book really for a young girl to read'.[49] Allfrey then went on to write *The Orchid House* which is equally 'horrible' in its subversion of a romantic vision. The St. Lucian poet, Derek Walcott's poem 'Jean Rhys' associates Jean Rhys with an age past, but does not discredit the validity of her work as representative of a Caribbean heritage.

Indisputably, Jean Rhys must be included as an important contributor to the literary heritage of the Caribbean and her influence on younger writers must be acknowledged. However, as Walcott rightly points out, the heritage from which Jean Rhys emerges, literary or otherwise is that of Empire, a time:

when the gas lanterns' hiss on the verandah
drew the aunts out like moths
doomed to be pressed in a book, to fall
into the brown oblivion of an album,

embroiderers of silence
for whom the arches of the Thames
Parliaments's needles
and the petit-point reflections of London Bridge
fade on the hammock cushions from the sun.

Derek Walcott[50]

It is perhaps precisely because Jean Rhys's background was that of Empire and because she was aware that received ideas about either Dominica or England could be questioned that she chose to highlight these issues in her work.

Notes

1. Alec Waugh, *The Sunlit Caribbean*, Evans Brothers, London, 1948 (reprint 1953), p.134.
2. Alec Waugh, *The Sugar Islands*, Cassell and Co. Ltd, London, 1958, p.286.
3. Jean Rhys, *Wide Sargasso Sea*, Andre Deutsch Limited, London, 1966, p.102.
4. Ibid.
5. Ibid.
6. Ibid.
7. Coral Ann Howells considers these issues in her excellent work on Jean Rhys and uses many of the same quotations.
8. 'The island is not competing in the 'sun, sea and sand' bracket, but has its own attractions - which are atypical for the Caribbean region: nature above all, with a bit of history and a dash of no hurry, no worry life style (the whole island boasts only a single set of traffic lights)', *The Courier*, 140, July-August, 1993, p.17.
9. Ibid, p.12.
10. Coral Ann Howells explores this issue in her book, *Jean Rhys,* Harvester Wheatsheaf, Hemel Hempstead, Hertfordshire, 1991.
11. 'Etcetera' in Nora Gaines (ed.), *Jean Rhys Review*, 6(2), p.27.
12. Jean Rhys, 1966, op. cit., pp.65-66.
13. Hulme, Peter, 'The Locked Heart: The Creole Family Romance of Wide Sargasso Sea - An Historical and Biographical Analysis' in Nora Gaines (ed.), *Jean Rhys Review*, 6(1), p.27. But note: It is incidentally this very Indian Warner who inspired his descendant, Marina Warner's, Indigo. Also, Hulme's interest is in the connection of event *In Wide Sargasso Sea* and Jean Rhys's family history.
14. Jean Rhys, 'Temps Perdi' in *Jean Rhys: The Collected Short Stories*, W.W. Norton and Company, London, 1987, p.268.
15. Ibid, p.297.

16. Jean Rhys, *Voyage in the Dark*, Penguin, Harmondsworth, 1987 (first published by Constable, 1934), p.9. Also relevant is Benedict Anderson's and Peter Hulme's considerations of the importance of the written word and its relationship to contemporary understandings of nation and history.
17. Ernest Renan, 'What is a Nation?' in Homi K. Bhabha (ed.), *Nation and Narration,* Routledge, London, 1991, 1990, p.11.
18. The assumption here is that the island in *Wide Sargasso Sea* is based on Dominica because of numerous references, such as Massacre.
19. Jean Rhys, *Voyage in the Dark*, op. cit., p.91.
20. Jean Rhys, 'Temps Perdi', op. cit., p.272.
21. Amryl Johnson, *Sequins for a Ragged Hem*, Virago, London, 1988, p.221 (travel book).
22. Jean Rhys, 'Temps Perdi', op. cit., p.273.
23. Benedict Anderson, *Imagined Communities: Reflections on the Origins and Spread of Nationalism*, Verso, London, 1992, 1983, p.204.
24. Jean Rhys, *Wide Sargasso Sea*, op. cit., p.30.
25. Ibid, p.26.
26. Ibid, p.26.
27. Ibid, p.17.
28. Ibid.
29. Ibid.
30. Ibid, p.32.
31. Ibid.
32. Ibid. p.30.
33. Ibid. p.35.
34. Thomas Atwood, *The History of the Island of Dominica*, Frank Cass, London, 1971, (first ed. 1791), pp. 265-66.
35. Ibid. p.266
36. Coral Ann Howells, 1991, op. cit., p.20.
37. Jean Rhys, *Wide Sargasso Sea*, op. cit., p.34.
38. Again, see Coral Ann Howells, 1991, op. cit., p.141.
39. Jean Rhys, *Good Morning, Midnight*, Penguin, Harmondsworth, 1969 (first published by Constable, 1939), p.17.
40. Ibid, p.24.
41. Jean Rhys, *After Leaving Mr. Mackenzie*, Penguin, Harmondsworth, 1987, 1971 (first published by Jonathan Cape, 1930), p.30.
42. Ibid, p.47.
43. Jean Rhys, *Voyage in the Dark*, op. cit., p.15.
44. Jean Rhys, *Quartet,* Penguin, Harmondsworth, 1988, 1977 (first published Chatto and Windus, 1928), p.12.
45. Ibid.

46. Ibid.
47. Merle Collins, 'Seduction' in *Rotten Pomerack*, Virago, London, 1992, p.14.
48. Laura Niesen de Abruna, 'Family Connections: Mother and Mother Country in the Fiction of Jean Rhys and Jamaica Kincaid' in Nasts Susheila (ed.), *Motherlands: Black Women's Writing from Africa, the Caribbean and South Asia*, The Women's Press, London, 1991, p.260.
49. Mary Chamberlain (ed.) *Conversations*, Virago, London, 1988, p.227.
50. Derek Walcott, 'Jean Rhys' in *Collected Poems: 1948-1984*, The Noonday Press, Farrar, Straus and Giroux, New York, 1986, 1962, p.427.

Audacity and Outcome: Writing African-Caribbean Womanhood

Joan Anim-Addo

In Maryse Condé's short story 'Three Women In Manhattan',[1] Claude, domestic help to two other black women and herself a central character reflects on the writing success of her African American contemporary and current co-employer Elinor. Claude assesses, in comparison, her own efforts at writing thus:

> To write! To put her hips, her sex, her heart, into motion in order to give birth to a world inscribed in her obscurity. To think that she'd had such *audacity*! In her garret in Pointe-à-Pitre, on evenings when the household slept, she used to scribble in spiral notebooks. An uncontrollable force within her.[2]

'Audacity', (my italics) derived from the Latin audere to dare, the term Claude equates with her own act of writing and which she attributes to her 'scribble in spiral notebooks' is a useful figurative term for the fiction writing of African Caribbean women because of the group's (literary) history until recently characterised by silence.[3] Very little in either Claude's upbringing or socioeconomic status has prepared her for the powerful urge she feels to write, to inscribe the self. Instead Claude has known a life of service to others; she has known the drudgery of having to 'wash, scrub, iron, water the plants'.[4] Claude has also known silence; she has known the lack of an audience for the 'clumsy scrawlings'[5] born of her particular consciousness, itself shaped by 'humble origins'.[6]

This essay addresses the question of how African Caribbean womanhood is being rewritten by contemporaneous writers from the region. Referring to selected stories from the collection *Green Cane and Juicy Flotsam*[7] and that of *Rain Darling* by Merle Collins,[8] I place the discussion in the context of the recent proliferation of Caribbean women's published writing and feminist theory. I argue that audacity has not only led to unprecedented literary production but that a critical outcome is literature articulated within and against two influential traditions, the oral and the scribal, as recent developments and directions illustrate.

Merle Collins in the opening essay in this volume alludes to the literary history of the anglophone African Caribbean woman writer, the fairly recent breaking of silence and the constraints which circumscribes 'freedom of expression' which writing involves.[9] Political and socioeconomic circumstances are similarly implicated for the larger group, African-Caribbean women, as indeed for Maryse Condé's Claude. In 'Three Women In Manhattan', Maryse Condé points to the precarious conditions under which black women's writing is produced or not; published or not. Claude, whom the reader understands as someone who 'would give birth to her world' is destined to do so in difficult socio-economic circumstances. She lives in 'the dump',[10] has limited knowledge of the language of publication, has had to migrate before appreciating the possibilities of publication and has gained qualifications irrelevant to the occupations available to her. Claude's one apparent asset appears to be her 'handiness', that is, aptitude in the service to others. There is , too, in 'Three Women In Manhattan' the Haitian Vera, Claude's co-employer, who spends a lifetime writing but with no publication success. Vera's collection of manuscripts, 'all unpublished, all returned by editors' bear witness to her denial of a published voice.[11]

Deborah E. McDowell arguing for a 'contextual' approach to black feminist criticism which 'exposes the conditions under which the literature is produced, published and reviewed',[12] highlights the significance of just such details revealed in 'Three Women In Manhattan' about the material conditions of literary production for black women. Claude's situation - like Vera's - illustrates difficulties in the material conditions which though less restrictive than in the past, directly impact upon the literary history of African Caribbean women. The history has gaps which may surprise. Merle Collins for example draws attention to the hundred and fifty seven year gap between Mary Prince's publication and the first group of Caribbean women writers coming together in conference.[13] Another gap, equally telling of the lack of publication opportunities, is that between, for example the publication of the full length nineteenth century works by Mary Prince and Mary Seacole, 1831 and 1857 respectively, and that of Sylvia Wynter's novel, *The Hills of Hebron* in 1962.[14]

'Feminist metafiction', the term used by Gayle Greene to describe 'self conscious' fiction which points to 'women writers' relation to 'the tradition', that is, literary tradition, also describes the texts I am interested in exploring here.[15] The story 'Three Women In Manhattan' is feminist metafiction, in the way in which its protagonists are writers and critique the circumstances of literary production for black women. Gayle Greene refers briefly to black writers in her work in order to explain their exclusion from the body of the text.[16] In this discussion African Caribbean women writers and their relation to 'the tradition' are central to the discussion. For the purposes of this essay, 'tradition' in so far as it relates to the African Caribbean woman writer is a 'doubled' tradition one that is continuous with orature, as well as, in the African Caribbean context, with the more recent tradition relating to scribal literary practice.

In 1970, a key point in the literary history of anglophone African-Caribbean women, Merle Hodge's seminal text *Crick Crack Monkey* was published.[17] *Crick Crack Monkey*, only the second long fictional narrative to be published by an Anglophone African Caribbean woman writer depicts the young black female protagonist, Tee as eager to attend school specifically to become literate. The girl narrator states: 'I looked forward to the day when I could pass my hand swiftly from side to side on a blank piece of paper leaving meaningful marks in its wake.[18] *Crick Crack Monkey* foregrounds black female subjectivity almost exclusively for the first time in anglophone African Caribbean literary history. Tee's desire therefore, 'to leave meaningful marks' or inscribe the self is a powerful sign in this early text. The black female protagonist's intention is all the more significant for having been so clearly stated by a young subject in the first text of its kind to privilege African Caribbean female experience.

Kenneth Ramchand claims that Caribbean women have been publishing short stories and poetry for most of the twentieth century.[19] I would like to suggest here patterns - principally through 'feminist metafiction' and 'oraliterature' - in the current development of Caribbean women's writing and highlight features of African-Caribbean women's contribution to this development.

Increased Access to Publication

Access to Caribbean-wide women's writing for anglophone readers is a recent phenomenon. To illustrate, in *The Faber Book of Contemporary Caribbean Short Stories*, published in 1990, five women writers appear, compared with nineteen male contributors.[20] Furthermore, publication seemed to be not only gender related but also location related, for the writers in the selection were from the English speaking West Indies as well as being predominantly male. Yet only five years later, Kenneth Ramchand proposes: 'The most exciting new voices in West Indian literature in the last ten years, and the dominant figures have been women'.[21] What, one might ask, explains this change in perception?

Her True-True Name,[22] edited by Pamela Mordecai and Betty Wilson, published in 1989, a year before the Faber collection, not only reflected Kenneth Ramchand's view, but interrupted and changed patterns of access to publication by women of the region. The anthology represented the writing of some thirty-one Caribbean women. The editors drew from a wider Caribbean and signalled within the Anglophone world, the arrival on the literary scene of a diverse body of writing from Caribbean women. *Her True-True Name* included, apart from the writing of Anglophone women, contributions from Cuba, Haiti, Puerto Rico, the Dominican Republic and

Guadeloupe. This wide angle on the Caribbean, an exciting and major step in the literary history of women of the region, bears directly upon my use of the term 'access'. Access is used here to refer to both the women writer's access to publication and the reader's access to that which is available through publication.

Broadly speaking, four groups of women became involved in building the nations of the Caribbean. Firstly and at times, apparently forgotten, the Amerindian women, native peoples of the Caribbean region and secondly, the African women whose history is one of enslavement and enforced transportation to the region. European women settlers, who historically enjoyed a more privileged lifestyle than other groups mentioned, comprise the third group. Fourthly, there were Asian women, amongst the latest group to arrive as wives and daughters of indentured labourers brought into the region as a work force to supplant the Africans at the end of slavery.

The Amerindian woman, whose position is rendered more complex by the virtual eradication of the indigenous population by early European settlers,[23] is also given voice in the literature though not always by Amerindian heritage women. For example, in *The Colour of Forgetting* her most recent novel, Merle Collins invokes the memory of the Amerindian past in the fictional setting, Paz.[24] In this text, one of the central characters, Carib bears both ancestral name and collective memory of people and region. Merle Collins asserts in a recent interview 'Carib is the soul of the novel'.[25]

The fact of earliest publication for white women amongst the larger group claiming a Caribbean identity is itself related to the eloquent articulation of factors of race, class and gender power relations within the region. Borrowing from Hazel Carby's work, the cultural production of black women indicated in the literary history of the region reflected 'societies 'structured in dominance' by class, by race, and by gender'.[26] Racial ideology, therefore, may be identified as a 'crucial mechanism in the maintenance of power'[27] as reflected in the literary history and literature of Caribbean women writers.

It is outside the scope of this essay to assess the impact of white Caribbean women writers, or Creoles, upon black women writers of the region. In the Anglophone tradition, Jean Rhys, an important literary figure first published in 1927[28] is claimed by both a Caribbean and a British tradition. Extensively anthologised as a Caribbean writer, Jean Rhys's short story *The Day They Burned The Books*[29] is also included in the collection *Green Cane and Juicy Flotsam* alongside Maryse Condé's 'Three Women In Manhattan'. Mrs Sawyer, the black woman depicted in Jean Rhys's story, seen through the eyes of her drunken white husband, Mr Sawyer, is alternatively 'the nigger showing off' or 'gloomy half-caste' who 'don't smell right'.[30] Like Claude's situation mentioned earlier, in Condé's story, there is a measure of entrapment in Mrs. Sawyer's socioeconomic circumstances. Unlike Claude, Mrs. Sawyer marks the end of her disempowerment by burning, after his death, the books which her husband has collected. Maryse Condé's Claude also burnt books - the notebooks containing her early writing - but would feel strongly again the urge to write renewed in her relationship with Vera, the exiled Haitian. In Claude's case, hope is later ignited. The desire to write 'was already moving within her'.[31]

Condés metaphor, writing as maternity, lends to the African Caribbean woman's literary creative act, at once an 'everyday use' in Alice Walker's sense, though one that is pregnant with irony.[32] Claude is the black woman, the 'Third World' woman of 'obscurity' and without privileges. Her maternity is a dangerous sign which, appropriated by Western rhetoric, signals world crisis and over-population threat. Nonetheless, the dispossessed, alienated, young black woman's body is, as in Kristeva's view 'at the centre of the signifying process', and Condé's metaphor speaks with a doubled voice.[33] For Claude, as for many similarly placed black women, the creative (literary) act, though seemingly natural in the context of a literate world, is an audacious, daring one because of who she is, the black woman as sign simultaneously of gender, race and class oppression. Consequently the reception of Claude's creativity, its life chances in the wider world promises to be an oppositional one facing the prospect of a difficult passage even as it is natural to the black woman's body, hips, sex and heart. In Condé's metafiction, writing is viewed as the means of remaking Claude's world.

In the fictional world of *Green Cane and Juicy Flotsam*, a range of women of diverse ethnicity, class, race, sexual orientation and language are represented. The collection includes writers from Cuba, the Dominican Republic, Haiti, Puerto Rico, Martinique/France and Surinam. Unmistakably within the last two decades the voices of African and Asian women have begun to emerge from within the Caribbean. Before then, publication pattern across the region reflected the power structure of the region with white men first in print, followed by white women, followed by black males and later by black females. The literary production of this latest wave of Caribbean women, black women is, in part, the outcome of the "audacity" to write, borrowed from Maryse Condé's usage.

Three black women, Claude, Elinor and Vera, from different circumstances but with a similar compulsion to write, are foregrounded in Maryse Condé's 'Three Women in Manhattan'. The story reveals nuances of the difficult publication situation for black women writers: difficulties in the search for access to a published voice; in acquiring an audience; and in debating the material of their work. Even changing location from island home to metropolitan centre is not enough. Vera, eldest of the three and exiled from Haiti, though a prolific writer, remains unpublished.

The powerful, almost instinctual creative force is expressed most profoundly in Claude. Of the three women characters, Claude is neither schooled nor socially prepared to conceive of herself as a writer. She has hardly even begun to conceive of the notion of a 'room of her own'.[34] Yet, newcomer to the literary tradition, Claude comes to be stirred by the overpowering need to write.

The discourse concerning feminist metafiction refers to the text's relationship to the literary tradition. Black feminist criticism also shares similar questions of relatedness of texts to tradition. Whilst noting Hazel Carby's critical stance on this issue,[35] I want now to highlight the question of tradition in the context of Caribbean women's writing. As mentioned earlier, *Her True -True Name* marked the beginnings of a pattern of wider access to a regional literary tradition more inclusive of women. Two features of this process seem important, each stimulating the other. I refer to the increasing availability of critical writing and correspondingly, availability of the literature within an academic context, both indicative of the development of Caribbean women's writing.[36]

Directions

Critical readings offer valuable insight into recent directions in Caribbean women's literature. So does an appreciation of patterns of publication for Caribbean women and specifically for African Caribbean women, for within the literary history lies clues to the more recent directions taken.

During the last twenty years, a wave of anglophone Caribbean women writers were published by multinational publishers highly attuned to the education market within the region. From acceptance of manuscript to final marketing of texts, constraints operated which served to determine the range of genre made available. Reflecting on this period, Olive Senior stresses the positive promotion of work by the educational publishers despite the narrow focus on the education market. She points also to a bigger issue currently, namely, the continuing difficulty faced by Caribbean women writers in persuading multinational commercial publishers to accept work for publication.[37] In one sense, it is suggested, the struggle for publication remains, particularly for those women writers interested to explore the Creole voice.

Within the anglophone context in the 1990s, the dominance of multinational publishers interested mainly in an education market has been broken. Examination of patterns of publication reveals a gradual movement away from publication by monopoly mainstream presses with an education interest to a broader range of smaller publishing houses.[38] Feminist publishing houses have played a key role in making available a wider range of Caribbean women's voices and among them a good many black voices. Examples are Jean Buffong, Merle Collins, Joan Riley, Vernelle Fuller and Velma Pollard, to select a few.[39] Yet the demand for publication has been such that when publishing houses, from feminist to mainstream, have been slow to publish works and project an uncertainty of the market for that work, Caribbean women writers have become involved in the publishing and marketing process. The work of black women's presses such as Sister Vision in Canada is indicative of this movement in the mid 1990s.[40]

An outcome of publication processes just beginning to be appreciated is the generic range of writing indicated in this volume. Quantitative and qualitative output within the main generic divisions of poetry, drama, short story and novel writing are being published. Concern about the marketing of publications and therefore the availability of these works remain, however, issues in the debate.[41] Similarly concerns remain about access to mainstream publishing. Olive Senior maintains that still at the end of the 1990s 'access to mainstream publishing by visible minorities ... that is the debate; that is the great debate...'[42]

It was noted above that feminist metafiction, a genre described by Gayle Green as interested in the powerful signs of reading and writing[43] is of particular interest to this discussion. There is another tradition, however, apart from that which equates literary with scribal, to which some African Caribbean women's texts speak. I refer to those texts which also engage 'self consciously' with the oral word, the primary word still powerful in African-Caribbean communities. This necessitates a shift into the problematic area equating orature and wider elements of oral culture with literature and a literary tradition.

The term orature refers to work 'mainly known through oral transmission'. In her paper, 'Reading African Writers', Pauline Dodgson attributes use of the term to Ugandan linguist Pio Zirimu.[44] Giving an explanation of differences in the way in which literature and orature function, Nigerian critic, Chinweizu, also cited by Pauline Dodgson, elaborates upon orature as follows:

> In contrast orature usually communicates in public contexts: in work places as work songs; as oratory at social or political gatherings; as plays acted or stories told before audiences; as dirges at funerals; as chants, hymns and invocations at religious ceremonies; as songs of praise or thanksgiving during celebrations of births, harvests, marriages and the like.[45]

Pauline Dodgson indicates also that while some forms of orature are preserved through memory, some of the oral tales and poems have been preserved through having been transcribed.[46]

Gay Wilentz's study of black women writers similarly highlights the orature element of particular literary works from the African diaspora. Referring to such texts as 'oraliterature'. Gay Wilentz notes:

> For much of the literature of Africa and the diaspora, the debt to the orature is so evident that I have neologised the two disparate terms to convey the process: 'oraliterature'. Oraliterature refers to written creative works which retain elements of the orature that informed them.[47]

Her concern in the study, with texts which privilege orality and 'active presentation of the oral tradition' within fictional works, to some extent parallels my concern with literary texts demonstrating a 'self conscious' intertextual link with the oral tradition.

Merle Collins's writing indicates ways in which the oral word contributes to a re-visioning of African Caribbean womanhood. Education, reading and writing are perceived in the literature as a potential source of empowerment. At the same time, the writing critiques negative images of self and the distorted meanings distilled by post-colonial education structured upon its prestigious precursor, colonial education. For specific texts, validation of the (African female) self relates directly to the oral word, the word not acknowledged as powerful but experienced as such. Gayle Greene refers to 're-visions of the tradition'.[48] I apply this notion in a 'doubled' sense as it relates to literary or oraliterary tradition - encompassing orature and literature - in the African-Caribbean context.

Rain Darling, by Merle Collins was published in 1990, the beginning of a decade witnessing wider publication of an increasing number of Caribbean women writers using the short story form. Critical to the development of publication of the genre was Olive Senior's *Summer Lightning* , winner of the 1987 Commonwealth Writers Award.[49] Since the ground breaking *Summer Lightning*, African-Caribbean writers gaining publication have included voices as varied as Opal Palmer Adisa *Guava and Other Bakeface Stories*,[50] Makeda Silvera *Remembering G and Other Stories*,[51] Lorna Goodison *Baby Mother And the King of Swords*,[52] Beryl Gilroy *Sunlight On Sweet Water*,[53] and Hazelle Palmer *Tales From The Gardens and Beyond*.[54] The writing mentioned, from a selection of Caribbean women writers of the short story form, also represents current movements in narrative writing by women of the region. One such movement privileges 'oraliterature' forms as described by Gay Wilentz. Furthermore, an examination of the 'oraliterary' collection *Rain Darling* suggests additional levels of 'audacity' in terms of syntax and vocabulary usage as well as the appropriation of a range of oral culture forms into the written text.

Through selected stories of *Rain Darling*, depictions of African-Caribbean womanhood also show how constructions of womanhood are handed down through generations of women. 'Generational and cultural continuity', to borrow from Gay Wilentz, functions so as to recreate the female self. Central to the process of recreation or construction is the role played by oral culture.[55] The title story of 'Rain Darling' focuses on Rain. It is primarily through the 'womantalk' of her visitors in hospital, that Rain's fatal story is revealed. The talk amongst the women, 'womantalk' and indeed between the adult characters in the story of Rain is such as is referred to by Beryl Gilroy in a recently published paper as *discourse*. The article 'The Oral Culture - Effects and Expression' has been invaluable to this exploration.[56]

Beryl Gilroy states:

> The grandparents and their ancestors participated in talk and called it 'discourse', which did not mean a treatise on an academic subject. It meant an interchange of views in a social setting. 'Hey gal me come fe discourse wid you', was understood to demand both exchange and receptivity.[57]

Discourse, in this sense, is of specific literary significance, for woman's talk is an important source of continuity in the construction of African-Caribbean womanhood. Through such *discourse* the narrative of 'Rain Darling', the story, unfolds. The young Rain adores her father but is disowned by him because he believes that he did not father her. The consequences of Andrew Darling's rejection prove fatal to his daughter. The plot allows ample opportunity for the exchange and 'receptivity' highlighted by Beryl Gilroy. Among the predominantly women characters involved, a degree of consensus obtains concerning Andrew Darling's treatment of his daughter. The 'receptivity' of the women and girls to the view that Rain has been wronged is such that meaning is made of her father's behaviour by reference to generalised understanding of male behaviour.

Rain derives knowledge and comfort through understandings passed to her by her friend:

> Tisane's mother always said, 'Don't wait on nobody to make you happy; especially not no man. Man them is the most mix up set of people the good Lord ever create! Dem does only think about they self.[58]

At the same time constructions of manhood and womanhood are handed down and reinforced by perceptions received by young Tisane and Rain:

> Tisane had said that you couldn't depend on fathers; that usually they weren't there and visited only to shout and beat sometimes; Tisane had warned that on the whole children were better off without them.[59]

'Womantalk', though vital to the development of women's identities is not confined to an audience of women and girls. For example, Andrew Darling, confronted by the elder woman, Aunt Myra, is told:

The problem was both of all you own...But woman doesn't beat man and go on like beast when trouble take them.[60]

To account for Andrew's actions, going 'on like beast', that is, inhumane behaviour is attributed to men generally and more readily understood within the ascribed gender frame. Women are defined in contrast to such male behaviour patterns, giving rise to (women) folk wisdom freely handed down. 'Man is the strangest nation'.[61]

The girls become, in consequence, crucial to a cyclical process defining and re-defining womanhood in relation to men's behaviour. At an earlier stage in the coalescing of their received views, self definitions are articulated amongst a circle of women before being passed to girls who reactivate the process, first as girls, and later, with more conviction, as women.

The 'audacity' of African Caribbean women writers is suggested not only in the act of writing but also in 'the social acts that they perform in their language patterns' as Susanne Mühleisen, in this volume, describes the use of Creole.[62] Creole, which Merle Hodge stresses as having 'stubbornly survived generations of disrespect' and which is held in 'utter contempt' by many of its Caribbean speakers is nonetheless a significant medium of literary writing for African Caribbean women.[63] Why is this a daring literary enterprise? African Caribbean women writers, beneficiaries of wider access to formal education which by and large continues to discredit Creole, turn to familiar oral sources - Creole - in order to develop as writers. In so doing, I would argue that they have both to 'unlearn' much that had previously been learnt about literary writing and to challenge their own understanding and that of publishers about language.

'Oraliterature'

Familiar oral sources represented on the page variously treat humorous as well as more serious 'discourse'. An example taken from Merle Collins's 'Madelene' illustrates a lighter tone which simultaneously draws upon the joke genre from oral culture whilst satirically attacking male partner's infidelity. Madelene recalls a conversation with her sister about her own husband's suspected infidelity:

'That one wasn't husband. Was waste-band'.
'The man disappear from my house and my bed for seven days and seven nights'.
'A biblical man'.
'Biblical? I don't know. Was forty days and forty nights Christ went for'.[64]

Jokes and, in contrast, serious discourse form part of the wider oral culture of which, the Bible, Afrocentric traditions and folk tales are key reference points. The encoding of oral culture within literature serves to alter, albeit slowly, the continuing low status of Creole into literary language or, perhaps more accurately, the language of literature. The orature of the region or oral genres become, through literary writing, intertextually linked to literature through collections such as *Rain Darling* so that short stories of this nature bear a relation to the tradition that is at once complex and deceptive. In the story of Madelene, therefore, Merle Collins writes within and against the doubled tradition referred to earlier.

The folktale retelling of Konpé Macucu's greed is at the heart of the story entitled 'Madelene' and Auntie Madelene is the storyteller whose tales her niece, Corinne, 'would have to unravel' in order to add to an essential store of knowledge about life itself. Of her aunt's folk tales, Corinne had already learnt much: 'Her stories were always like a test. Leaving you ravelling and unravelling.[65]

Storytelling language in a Creole voice, artful and hyperbolic in turn, threads the story of Madelene allowing the reader into the world of two friends, folk figures, Zaè and Tigre, disarmingly hunting for more food while their companion, hungry Macucu watches over the food they leave cooking at home. Above all, it is African Caribbean woman as griot who presents the story, who analyses her niece's situation as well as her sister's and offers back to the younger woman a life sustaining parallel to assist Corinne to grow and learn. When, in traditional storytelling fashion, the teller's exaggerated account seems implausible, the listener, Corinne, protests and the teller ritualistically and matter of factly explains: 'How I buy it, is so I sell it. I make no profit'.[66]

It is not only that the characters are introduced by a Creole speaking narrator. The dialogue is also framed in the idiom of speech. 'Macucu say, "Me, I well tired. I not going any place now".'[67] The 'Me, I' reduplication, by Maureen Warner-Lewis's account, points to West African syntax embedded in the English lexis of the two sentences.[68] The language of narration contains similar linguistic features illustrating how voice in the literature echoes the competing linguistic influences which persist in spoken language. Aunt Madelene, in her storytelling role, switches from Creole to Standard English at will with the effect that one language contains the other as the story shifts and the focus changes from narrator to teacher/philosopher. Griot like, Aunt Madelene tells her tale, which is functional, for the stories serve the purpose of philosophical reflection. As Beryl Gilroy notes:

> The story-tellers and talkers were not keepers of history. They were philosophers able to reflect the bland and the sparse against the shining curtain of wisdom. They talked about quest and change, the hazards of the personal centre, of the presence of the loved ones through absence by death...[69]

At the intersections of literary and oral traditions highlighted, the key to an understanding of the gendered space is *womantalk*, a vital source of the wisdom handed down to girls, which bears African Caribbean specificity. Womantalk relates directly to a revisioning and self-definition of African Caribbean womanhood, part of the outcome of the 'audacious' writing project central to this essay.

Location, Audacity and Outcome

A pattern which emerges in Caribbean women's writing is that publication is unlikely to follow without audacity translated into action on the part of the woman writer. Twinned with this audacity there is a search for location responsive to the writer's publication needs. The question of location and access to a published voice represents a dilemma, an advantage of which is an increasing awareness of a range of possible sites for publication. Carole Boyce Davies and Molara Ogundipe-Leslie's two volume publication perhaps illustrates this trend.[70] The collection, entitled *Moving Beyond Boundaries* places creative and critical writing side by side. It juxtaposes, also, writing from black women from four continents.

As Elinor, the 'successful' black woman writer in 'Three Women In Manhattan' appreciates, publication is not the final hurdle. For this reason, African Caribbean women writers are increasingly to be found actively promoting the literature. Whether through public readings or performances; through attendance at conferences or through active marketing of published work, there is growing awareness and corresponding involvement indicating an appreciation that to be published alone is not the goal.[71]

In addition, concerned readers and writers are seizing the initiatives to promote debate about the literature. In London, the first issue of *Mango Season*, the British based publication of the Caribbean Women Writers Alliance began to be circulated following the first Caribbean Women Writers' Conference held in the UK.[72] Subsequent issues brought requests for subscription as far afield as Australia, many from the Caribbean and, of course, locally within the UK. Since *Mango Season* aims also to be a creative outlet, it plays a role in allowing further access to publication, in promoting the audacity to write.

The outcome of the 'audacity' discussed, then is multi-facetted. It is a revisioning of the orature of the region, its history and language. It is an increasingly confident articulation of the self within an expanding domain, a self that is at once critical and subject to self-critique. It is also the on-going challenge to parameters restrictive of the African Caribbean woman's voice; to boundaries 'fixed' by geography, historiography, language, heritage and so on. To these the 'womanish' response continues to be a renewed determination to be heard, and correspondingly the creation of greater access to publication.

African Caribbean womanhood as portrayed by a new wave of Caribbean writers are mothers, wives, lovers, grandmothers and so on. They offer fictional representation of the gamut of ordinary and extraordinary black women's lives. The African Caribbean woman is also depicted as griot and writer, figurations inscribing a special relationship to the orature and literature traditions of the region. Feminist metafiction, a recent direction in Caribbean women's writing is a critical site addressing and re-visioning the subject histories of black womanhood. In portraying black women as writers, griots and other such figures, African Caribbean women writers are simultaneously challenging the literary tradition they have recently appropriated and which has been a source of distortions and misrepresentation of black women's identity.

Notes

1. Maryse Condé, 'Three Women In Manhattan' in Carmen C. Esteves and Lizabeth Paravisini-Gebert *Green Cane and Juicy Flotsam: Short Stories By Caribbean Women*, Rutgers University Press, New Jersey, 1991.
2. Ibid, p.59.
3. I refer specifically to publication of longer narrative fiction within the anglophone context.
4. Ibid, pp.57 and 65.
5. Ibid, p.60.
6. Ibid, p.59.
7. Carmen Esteves and Lizabeth Paravisini-Gebert, 1991, op. cit.
8. Merle Collins, *Rain Darling*, Women's Press, London, 1990.
9. See Merle Collins's essay in this volume p.6
10. Condé, 1991, op. cit., p.57.
11. Ibid, p.63
12. Deborah E. McDowell 'New Directions for Black Feminist Criticism' in Mary Eagleton (ed.), *Feminist Literary Theory*, Blackwell, Oxford, 1986, p.164.
13. See Merle Collins's essay in this volume.
14. Sylvia Wynter, *The Hills of Hebron*, Jonathan Cape, London, 1962. Mary Prince, *The History of Mary Prince, A West Indian Slave Related by Herself*, Pandora, London, 1987, was first published 1831. Mary Seacole, *Wonderful Adventures of Mary Seacole in Many Lands*, James Blackwood, London 1858. Whilst there is only some twenty years between two nineteenth century publications, there is a hundred and thirty one year gap between Mary Prince's and Sylvia Wynter's.
15. Gayle Greene, *Changing The Story: Feminist Fiction and the Tradition*, Indiana University Press, Bloomington & Indianapolis, 1991.
16. Ibid, p.24.
17. Merle Hodge, *Crick Crack Monkey* , Heinemann, London, 1970.

18. Ibid, p.20.
19. See Kenneth Ramchand's essay in this volume.
20. Mervyn Morris (ed.), *The Faber Book of Contemporary Caribbean Short Stories*, Faber & Faber, London, 1990.
21. See this volume p.225.
22. Betty Wilson and Pam Mordecai, *Her True -True Name*, Heinemann, London, 1989.
23. Janet H. Momsen, *Women and Change In The Caribbean*.
24. Merle Collins, *The Colour of Forgetting*, Virago, London, 1995.
25. Merle Collins, 'Interview', *Mango Season*, April, 1996.
26. Hazel Carby, *Reconstructing Womanhood*, Oxford University Press, New York, 1987, p.17.
27. Ibid, p.18.
28. See Daryl Cumber Dance, *Fifty Caribbean Writers*, Greenwood Press, Connecticut, 1986.
29. Jean Rhys, The Day They Burned The Books in Carmen C. Esteves and Lizabeth Paravisini-Gebert , 1991, op.cit.
30. Ibid, p.25.
31. Carmen C. Esteves and Lizabeth Paravisini-Gebert, 1991, op.cit., p.66.
32. Alice Walker, *Everyday Use*, Rutgers University Press, New Brunswick, NJ, 1994, cited in Valerie Lee, 'Testifying Theory; Womanist Intellectual Thought', in *Women: A Cultural Review*, 6(2), Autumn, 1995, p.205.
33. Kristeva's view is cited in Margaret Dickie's 'The Maternal Gaze: Women Modernists and Poetic Authority' in Linda Marie Brooks (ed.) *Alternative Identities*, Garland Publishing, New York and London, 1995, p.224.
34. Refers to Virginia Woolf, *A Room of Her Own*, and the notion of space and independence for the woman writer.
35. Hazel Carby, op. cit., 1987, p.16.
36. See, for example, introduction to this volume.
37. See *Mango Season*, Summer, 1996.
38. In the UK small presses such as Bogle L'Ouverture, Peepal Tree and New Beacon are key publication outlets.
39. Examples are all taken from Women's Press, London publications.
40. Similar patterns are to be found in various metropolitan areas.
41. Merle Collins echoes these concerns in interview, *Mango Season*, April, 1996.
42. See Olive Senior, 'Interview', *Mango Season*, Summer, 1996.
43. Gayle Greene, 1991, op. cit., p.9.
44. Pauline Dodgson, *Reading African Writers*, Working Paper 3, University of Sussex, 1990.
45. Onwuchekwa Chinweizu, 'Cries For Freedom', *The Times Higher Education Supplement,* 17 February, 1989, p13.
46. Pauline Dodgson, 1990, op. cit.

47. Gay Wilentz, *Binding Cultures*, Indiana University Press, Bloomington and Indianapolis, 1992. p.xvii.
48. Gayle Greene, 1991, op. cit., p.8.
49. Olive Senior, *Summer Lightning*, Longman, Essex, 1986.
50. Opal Palmer, *Adisa Guava and Other Bakeface Stories*, Kelsey Street Press.
51. Makeda Silvera, *Remembering G and Other Stories*, Sister Vision, Ontario, 1991.
52. Lorna Goodison, *Baby Mother And the King of Swords*, Longman, Essex, 1990.
53. Beryl Gilroy, *Sunlight On Sweet Water,* Peepal Tree Press, Leeds, 1994.
54. Hazelle Palmer, *Tales From The Gardens and Beyond,* Sister Vision Press, Ontario, 1995.
55. Gay Wilentz, op. cit., 1992, p.xiv.
56. Beryl Gilroy, 'The Oral Culture - Effects and Expression', *Wasafiri*, Autumn 1995, p.64.
57. Ibid, p.64.
58. Merle Collins, 1990, op. cit., p.25.
59. Ibid, p.16.
60. Ibid, p.30.
61. Ibid, p.35.
62. See p.171 of this volume.
63. Merle Hodge, 'Challenges of The Struggle for Sovereignty' in S. Cudjoe *Caribbean Women Writers*, Calaloux, Massachusetts, 1990, p.204.
64. Merle Collins, op. cit., 1990, p.79.
65. Ibid, p.72.
66. Ibid, p.75.
67. Ibid, p.72.
68. Maureen Warner-Lewis, *Guinea's Other Suns: The African Dynamic in Trinidad Culture*, Majority Press, Mass. 1991.
69. Beryl Gilroy, op. cit., p.65.
70. Carole Boyce Davies and Molara Ogundipe-Leslie, *Moving Beyond Boundaries*, Pluto Press, 1995.
71. Merle Collins, for example refers to marketing and Maryse Conde's *Elinor* refers to the trials of promoting her books.
72. *Mango Season* is the publication of the London based Caribbean Women Writers' Alliance.

Note: Some of the ideas have been developed from an earlier paper, 'Woman Centred Narratives - Short Stories of Merle Collins', Angers University Press (forthcoming).

Coming Out of Repression: Lakshmi Persaud's *Butterfly in the Wind*

Kenneth Ramchand

Women in the English-speaking West Indies have been writing poems and short stories for most of the twentieth century, but the publication of Olive Senior's *Summer Lightning* in 1986,[1] marked the beginning of a deluge. The most exciting new voices in West Indian literature in the last ten years, and the dominant figures, have been women. Lakshmi Persaud's *Butterfly in the Wind*[2] is part of this upsurge, but it has special standing as the first full-length work by a woman of Indian origin.

People of Indian origin first came to the islands as indentured labourers about one hundred and fifty years ago, and there was a steady stream until the indenture system was terminated in 1917. Today, the descendants of indentured Indians make up over half the population in Guyana and Trinidad, the territories that had the largest intake. This ethnic group has made a crucial contribution in agriculture; it has thrown up major artists in literature, painting, and music; and, in the modern period, its members operate visibly and significantly in business and industry. In spite of certain tensions generated by entrenched interests who feel threatened, descendents of Indians have begun to take up their equal social and political place in relation to the other ethnic groups in their societies. But there is an anomaly within the group. The silence, including the literary and artistic silence, of Indian women, and their subdued position in the social and cultural life of Guyana and Trinidad have only just begun to be addressed. *Butterfly in the Wind* makes a telling contribution to this necessary process, and may well be the first sign of an upsurge within the literary upsurge referred to above.

Lakshmi Persaud's book is referred to in the publisher's blurb as 'fictionalised autobiography'. As a matter of fact, it was first written as an account of Lakshmi Persaud's own growing up, and only subsequently converted into fiction. The connection between the experiences of the main character Kamla and the author Lakshmi Persaud is therefore direct and strong. Like Lakshmi Persaud, Kamla was born in Pasea village; she enjoys the same family connections and domestic arrangements; and she follows the same educational route as the author. But it is a much more mature author who is writing about the young girl Kamla, and for that reason alone it would be unwise to identify author and protagonist. Since the book takes the form of a novel, it might be helpful to accept it as a novel and maintain a distinction between Kamla the fictional character and the author. So *Butterfly in the Wind* is a novel about growing up and the influences that shaped the growing up of a Hindu girl in an Indian community in Trinidad in the 1940s and 1950s. The school introduces Kamla to Western influence, the home and the village supply her with images of India. Straddling the two worlds is the cinema which provides African jungles, Tarzan, Robin Hood and the 'lazy glamorous American way of life', and which is also the place where Kamla sees Indian religious films in which snakes are used by gods and devils to test the faith of saints, and where gods take the form of stray dogs and beggars so that one has to cultivate reverence in real life just in case.

This novel is not complicated in structure or plot. It is divided into five parts arranged in chronological order. It begins with 'Simple Joys' covering the early protected years with its regulating institutions (grandmother, temple, and school), familiar sights and sounds, and stabilising agencies like parents and other members of the household including Renee the washerwoman and Daya the cook. The second part, 'And Darkness Falls', comprehends primary school days and the cinema, the cinema being important as the only form of entertainment outside the family and the group permitted to Hindu girls in those days. In this section, Kamla is exposed to bullying and extortion at the hands of schoolgirls Inez, Millicent and Monica, the unmotivated cruelty of friends who lead her into a nest of large stinging ants or bachacs, and the comically rendered self-indulgence of her cinema-loving aunt. Next comes 'Awakening' in which the young teenager becomes aware of the adult world and the society around her, and in which the sustainment of family affection, village life and traditional culture and religion are described. The fourth part is called 'Forms of Imperfection', and in it Kamla goes to secondary school, first the Roman Catholic Fatima Girls High School where her Hinduism is tested by the wealth, order and authoritarianism of Roman Catholicism, then to the new High School for Presbyterian Girls at St Augustine, and finally to the Convent in Port of Spain where she takes the exams that allow her to seek entry to an overseas university. In the final Part Five, 'Standing On The Other Side', Kamla becomes a teacher and makes preparations for University overseas.

The shape-shifting background and context of Kamla's process is Streatham Lodge (now called Pasea) and the surrounding villages near Tunapuna in Trinidad:

> Some may think that because the Pasea villagers were East Indians there was amongst them a uniformity of colour and culture. What we had, in reality, was a mosaic of peoples: Moslems who would not eat pork but would eat beef and who distrusted Hindus, and we Hindus who ate neither and distrusted the Moslems. There were also short dark Madrassis and the ivory-coloured Brahmins from Northern India...[3]

It sometimes needs to be pointed out, even to people in the Caribbean, that there has never been an Indian community as such in Trinidad though the various Indian communities had and have many things in common, and look back to a common origin which the early settlers sought to re-create in their new context:

> At dusk it was easy to believe you were in India: shadows and sounds of bullock carts, the aroma of *roties* on *chulhas*; fresh water in buckets and cut grass in bales; off-white houses with thatched roofs and glowing wood fires in the yards; the soft gentle sound of Hindi in the night carried by warm winds along red earth tracks. Even as late as the 1930s it was easy to believe.[4]

For the older generation, it was impossible not to believe.

By the 1940s, however, 'this gigantic glacier of tradition and conservatism had begun to thaw', this vulnerable world was collapsing in upon itself, yielding to pressures from within as well as to incursions from the non-Indian world without. The consequences are so visible that Kamla's mother is commended for bringing Kamla to the temple:

> It is a good thing, Maharajin, to bring the children. You have to introduce the young to their own tradition. You have to start young for by the time they reach fourteen fifteen it is too late.[5]

The comedy in Seepersad Naipaul's *Guredeva and Other Indian Tales*[6] and his later stories, written in the thick of the process, captures the confusions and contradictions engendered by this traumatic moment. But there is a problem with the novel, *Butterfly in the Wind*. Its nostalgic tone, its innocent ambivalence, and its non-punitive irony take some of the shock off the changes that are occurring, and they make less stressful some of the tensions brewing beneath the accommodating surface of what the writer still wants to project as a coherent world. When the milkman Baboo abandons his wife and elopes to the small island of Tobago with his young lover, the novel wants us to think of the couple as persons who have cut themselves off from a sustaining community:

> As the years went by, I sometimes thought of him: living on a small, thinly populated island with his son, growing greyer amongst strangers, outside his

> own East India village community. What would the few black fishermen there know of him? What could he tell them? In my mind's eye I used to see him walking on the seashore, a lonely man, with a son who would not understand his father's melancholy.
>
> And the young woman, what became of her? Where would she find that uniquely comforting friendship of the village women with its string of reassuring maternal and sisterly advice, its warmth of shared experiences, that therapy of female understanding and care?[7]

But it is the burden of Lakshmi Persaud's book that this sustaining world, including the community of women, is undergoing changes at every level. The author's awareness of this contradiction (the condition of the younger Lakshmi or the fictional Kamla) is to be seen in the bestowing upon Kamla of an inner voice speaking for a contrary and inquiring mind, a voice that is a burden and a danger (as it had been to Joan of Arc) because it sometimes wants to speak of things that are not safe. Kamla's inner voice plants disturbed and disturbing signals, making the character much less intact than she thinks she is, and the book much more of a critical and feminist text than suggested by the author's conscious perspectives.

This story of the development of a Hindu girl in a multi-cultural society during the colonial period is a story with religious, gender, cultural, and political cross-currents. Here, inter-culturation is partial and its implications only partly understood. Colonialism is condemned but many of its provisions are consumed by those who criticise it. The Hindu world is losing its solidity but the religion and the way of life remain whole in the minds of many of its members. Female liberation is espoused, but the institution of marriage remains inviolable. The book is ripe for deconstruction and misconstruction since it could not possibly escape the confusion of overlapping realms and the familiar enough phenomenon of a lack of synchronisation between experience, emotion and ideology.

The trouble with Kamla's inner voice is that it does not develop into an analytic instrument or an agency promoting greater social, political and cultural awareness. During a history lesson, the inner voice actually speaks out to challenge the teacher's 'objective' account of the slave trade as something that made Britannia and her colonies rich. Mr Brathwaite, a Eurocentric mimic man, punishes his insolent pupil for disrespecting her betters. From this moment Kamla decides to smother the inner voice, sublimating it into a gentle friend coming at night and at other moments of aloneness to whisper to her difficult things she could not answer.

It is significant that this suppression is provoked by an incident at school, for one of the catalysts of social, cultural and political change in the novel, and therefore one of the sources of inner and outer conflicts, is education or the school. The book's recognition of education as an instrument of control by the colonial authorities and its critique of the way in which the education supplied from abroad took little account of the cultures, life-styles, and values of subject peoples link it with novels like George Lamming's *In the Castle of My Skin,*[8] and Austin Clarke's *Growing Up Stupid Under the Union Jack.*[9] It differs from them in that it looks at the effects of this education on a girl, and on Hinduism as a religion and a way of life. In addition, and significantly, as we shall see below, it includes under the heading of education, the traditional shaping to which a young girl is subjected through Hindu texts and Hindu custom and practice.

The education provided in the schools is a sound colonising education aimed at establishing authority, and suppressing the ability to think. School was 'a time for learning by rote'.[10] It was a time when 'reasons for things were not given', a time for the imposition of 'ideas, concepts, formulae' so that 'we could neither assess nor give meaning to things'. The operations of Kamla's inner voice and its repression and silencing allow us to read *Butterfly in the Wind* as a critique not only of the imposed system of education, but also of the traditional education handed down through the elders, the institutions, the festivals, the rituals and the ruling values within the Hindu community. It is part of the book's implicit critique that it sees little difference in effect and intention between a colonial education and the traditional shaping to which the Hindu female especially is subject. It shows the reduction of the will to protest to a helpless and private irony. It has already been hinted that it is this irony that paradoxically grants licence to the reader to notice the feminist perspective in the book.

When the news comes that a secondary school for girls, to be called Fatima Girls High School, is to be opened in Curepe, Kamla's mother makes uniforms and distributes application forms to other Hindu families but she gets a poor response. According to Kamla's uncle, a girl does not need to be as educated as her husband, and may not need to be educated at all. For she will be married in the long run, and then 'her Latin and French and Algebra would be of no help'. Lakshmi Persaud explores the attitude of Hindu parents to the education of girls along the lines projected comically in Naipaul's A *House for Mr Biswas*[11] where the prospective in-laws hasten to assure the protagonist that there is nothing to worry about, for his child-bride will rapidly forget the little bit of education she has taken in. The firmness and the studied diplomacy with which Kamla's mother argues against her brother-in-law's male chauvinism, and the terms in her argument suggest not only that there is a suppressed mother behind the dutiful mother, but that Lakshmi Persaud herself wants to make a larger and more direct statement than she actually does about the behaviour of the Indian male from which education might be an escape:

> If heaven forbid, she should not be blessed in marriage, it would be better for her to leave her husband's home and find a job. That would be preferable to *a life of humiliation, cruelty and suffering*[12] (my italics).

In another episode, Kamla's mother responds in gnomic fashion to her daughter's question about why people want to chew pan, a mild drug, all day: 'When life is painful, Who knows? I don't know the answer. I have had to bear pain without *pan*'. Less reticent female voices in the 1990s have been more explicit about what is being hinted at in *Butterfly in the Wind* - repression and the different kinds of violence practised by male upon female in Indo-Caribbean communities.

But Mrs Persaud's book also records change. By the mid 1950s, a quiet revolution was taking place among descendents of Indians. Education had become more acceptable. The Hindu Mahasabha began building their own schools for Hindu and other Indian children in the 1950s and the Presbyterian mission was expanding its provisions and even thinking about providing the same kinds of opportunity for girls that it had been providing for boys. From all over Northern Trinidad, girls of East Indian descent came 'pouring into St Augustine Girls High School as if it were a colossal magnet'. Many other mothers were now either taking the stance held by Kamla's mother or simply following the trend:

> Many of the students came from homes where parents had not had a primary school education, homes with traditional Hindu mothers, conservative women, whose own marriages had been arranged, but who were now giving their daughters a freedom undreamt of in their own childhood.[13]

Kamla notices that there were many casualties of this new freedom: some were unable to see themselves in new roles; some were unable to combine roles; and many formed unsuitable connections too early.[14] It might be argued that the celebration of the new freedom for women is compromised by an underlying conventional norm implicit in the account of the casualties. But the emphasis is really elsewhere: is it a comment on the relative lack of interest of the male, and an indication of a level of late rebellion in the female that in Lakshmi Persaud's account it is the mothers who seem to be the moving force in the education of their daughters?

In her critique of the educational provision and attitudes to it, Lakshmi Persaud enters territory which suggests that however conservative her instincts, she is indeed concerned with the larger question of female liberation and especially with the troubled question of female sexuality:

> Their own experiences and observations had left Hindu parents distrustful of the warm energy and daring of youth, and the pitfalls of teen-age infatuations, particularly in the environment of a city far away from home. They kept these fears to themselves and their daughters at home.[15]

In the version of Hinduism that the writer seems to adhere to, the passions tend to be regarded as things that everybody ought to be on the alert to control:

> Men are like gods...They can bridle so many things, even the roaring thunderous water that falls from great heights can be harnessed; why then can't he harness himself?[16]

But this attitude seems to be more strictly applied to the female of the species. The protection of the female comes over as a repression of the female, and the watchers over female sexuality,[17] come close to making female sexuality an evil influence from the Devil, something in the female flesh that must be played down or denied.

Kamla herself is a victim of this male propaganda. Saying goodbye to the young man Surin who had shown interest in her, Kamla feels a desire to embrace him and be embraced in turn. She ignores this feeling, however, and seems to accept that feelings ought to be bridled neither should tender feelings be allowed to cloud one's reason:

> As I walked down the steps a feeling of sadness came over me, and I was aware that there were deep feelings within me that had not been fully bridled by my culture or my upbringing. How did it come about? Had I not been fasting during feast days since the age of four and so knew what restraint was? Had I not been told numerous stories about self-discipline and self-denial by my mother? For the first time I saw how easy it was to drift into falling in love. I told myself that I must be on my guard lest my tender feelings overcame my reason.[18]

Passages like this make it essential to recognise that Kamla is not Lakshmi Persaud, and that the author may be trying to show that the character is a victim of the situation she is being used to describe. Although she leaves the reader to do too much of the work, the author's focus on mothers, grandmothers, daughters, and serving women highlights female oppression. A gender interest makes for the description of the sufferings of women of lesser means and greater desperations than Kamla. The fatalistic washerwoman Renee, a person of African origin, turns to cigarettes and the bottle as the only available relief in an unhappy life. The cook Daya is shown trying to make something of her marriage to a ne'er-do-well husband. It is she who is responsible for their acquiring a decent house. She rises at 5.00am to prepare her husband's meals for the day, and then turns up for a long stint in the kitchen of Kamla's mother. Her husband hands in his pay-packet on 'good Fridays', but on 'bad Fridays' she has to catch him in the rum shop before he spends it all. The advice of seven year old Kamla is: 'Daya, you should leave your husband. He is no good'.[19]

But here once again, the writer's position seems ambivalent. Daya opts to hold on to the marriage, and then, as if satisfied with having expressed the feminist response of her inner voice, Kamla falls back into a position consistent with the traditional indoctrination:

> From that day on Daya went up in my estimation. I felt here was a woman struggling so hard to build a home and a relationship with someone not appreciative of her. But she held on, and orphan as she was, appreciated more than I could ever have understood then, the importance of having at least one human being, however imperfect, as a close companion.[20]

In this last respect, Daya appears to Kamla to be better off than the single woman Renee who is abandoned by the father of her children, 'her short life harnessed to a cartload of burdens as she trudged on alone'.[21]

This attitude might seem conservative or traditional and might suggest that the author's upbringing still makes it hard for her to reject wifely submissiveness and male privilege and dominance, a dilemma that informs Kamla's pronouncements on marriages, arranged marriages and parental wisdom.[22] Yet, in discussing the sacred Hindu texts with her mother, Kamla is allowed to argue explicitly against male privilege and the indoctrination of the female.

The narrating Kamla reports that in the village, adultery and pre-marital pregnancy meant at least social death for the female. And if, 'youthful passion overleapt cultural barriers', the father would lay the blame on the mother. In this system, Kamla notices, the mother is obliged to be an agent of patriarchy: 'She was ultimately held responsible for what was perceived as the imperfections in her daughter's upbringing and character'.[23] In this context, Kamla recalls a story that is used to validate chastity among Hindu females. It is the story of how the courtier Dur-yodhana fails in his attempt to violate Draupadi:

> Her soft silk sari glided through his arrogant fingers as he pulled and pulled - and the more his desire grew, the more he pulled - and as he pulled, yards and yards of silk passed through his now moist fingers.[24]

When he falls exhausted to the ground a high mountain of the softest strongest silk lies behind him, and a still unravished Draupadi before.

Kamla doesn't criticise this story in particular. But she questions in general the use made of stories from the Ramayana and from the Mahabharata to control women, and she does so as an incipient feminist:

> Such stories affected me greatly and brought my mother and I closer together. But as the years rolled on I couldn't help thinking that such tales had little effect on men. This may have been because adultery committed by men had a lot going for it, since it was seen as the way of men, one of the crosses wives had to bear with stoic calmness. That I felt was unfair and unjust and I saw women's acceptance of this, not a result of their having a greater capacity to absorb pain or to forgive, as older women believed, but because of their helpless dependence upon their husbands. I was overcome by a deep sorrow for my sex in bondage, and for the real and terrifying predicament biology and custom had placed them in.[25]

Kamla goes on to question the necessity for Lord Rama to establish publicly through the ordeal by fire that all through the years of captivity Sita has been faithful to him in thought and in deed. And when her mother justifies the process by affirming that Sita's purity needed to be established beyond even unreasonable doubt since, as Queen and wife she held a position of trust, the traditional daughter shows respect for the mother by dropping the subject though not without putting a leading question for the reader's consideration (and for the mother's, if she dares to question what she has been taught to accept): 'Do Husbands hold position of trust?'

This gives a special kind of interest to Kamla's encounter with the nuns and the Roman Catholic religion. Kamla is disturbed by the absolute, excluding and comforting power of the Roman Catholic religion. At home, in the garden she draws pictures of limbo, purgatory and hell, and invents tableaux in which pundits and nuns are arranged in opposed attitudes.[26] The Roman Catholicism to which she is being exposed at the Fatima school is modern, urban, wealthy and sophisticated, is part of the system of power on earth, and has access to the heavenly powers also: 'The high altar, the confidence, the power: it all seemed closer to an omnipotent being than the simple rural ways of the Hinduism I knew'.[27] It is possible, although Lakshmi Persaud does not seek to make the point, that Kamla's intimidation by Roman Catholicism, her respect for its worldly power and spiritual confidence, and her wavering in its direction during the early years at school is an indirect reflection of the need of the Hindu female to escape from what is without a doubt a strict and repressive background.

Moving between two worlds, however, the Hindu female is constantly opposing one form of determination by another. The most drastic expression of what looks like a general sense of being manipulated comes out in

Kamla's account of a dance to take place at her school in Port of Spain. Kamla describes[28] the degrees of Westernisation reflected in the dresses of the girls who come to the dance, and in their attitudes to the arrival of the music. She represents herself as being 'never at ease with modern Western dance' since it entailed 'aspects of physical contact' contrary to her upbringing, and besides *'I did not desire to be jostled, to be guided or to be led - with or without the aid of music'*.[29] When the dancing starts, she realises it is time for her to go, a displaced person whose displacement is accentuated by the circumstance of being female:

> I walked down Pembroke Street, a displaced person between two worlds whose rules of etiquette were foreign to one another. Here in this urban setting, having a boyfriend and being able to dance in the manner I have described were assets. In the place I was walking towards, my home, my village, such behaviour would be regarded as uncouth, unladylike, sullied and sullying. When I reached Frederick Street, the city's smells of oranges, open drains, urine, car exhausts, beggars, syrup, shoe boxes, bales of cloth and parched nuts, awakened me from my reverie; I quickened my steps to the bus terminus in Henry Street.[30]

Just as revealing of Kamla's need for space and love and enlightenment are the terms in which she describes Christmas, with light 'penetrating into the furthest corner, unimpeded by the day to day accumulation of trivia and clutter', and 'with the feeling of space around everything'. For once, it seems, wherever the eye roamed, 'one was met by beauty and affection, and by signs of human care'. It would be irresponsible to make too much of this, but I am trying to suggest that the book is an account of a girl's growing up and out of a Hindu community that is sustaining but repressive and lacking in shows of affection; a series of takes of a life growing at the confusing meeting point of cultures and peoples, a life whose emergence is accompanied by contradictory feelings of excitement and fear, all the more so because it is female and has for so long been sheltered and repressed. Kamla recognises the general movement, but she is too close to the conflicting emotions engendered by it to be as whole as her summary of it might suggest:

> I saw ten year olds move easily from one culture to another, from rolling out roties in the morning, cooked on a chulha with wood from the forest, to making carefully written observations through a microscope an hour later. It convinced me that the human mind had the capacity to move from rural to urban; from swimming near the seashore to exploring the ocean's deep canyons - and the galaxies above, all in one generation.[31]

For all that, it is not at all surprising that like so many West Indian novels, *Butterfly in the Wind* ends with a departure. A motorcade has brought an extended Indian family to Piarco Airport to see off Kamla, a young Hindu woman who is leaving the island to go and study at an Irish University. At the house, before the party leaves for the airport, her father's oldest sister speaks to Kamla about the departure from India, at an earlier time, of Kamla's ancestors whose success in spite of indenture and the stigma of indenture, made possible this new journey into the unknown:

> Who would have thought of a day like this when our grandmothers and great grandmothers left India not knowing where they were going? All they were told was there would be work. They came in good faith; they placed themselves in God's hands. And look at this now, look at this success story'. She was smiling. 'Your father can today finance not only his son but also a daughter. What do you call that?' And she beamed with so much pride and so much happiness, I felt humble and so inadequate. She continued: 'Do you know what my grandmother said? She was a little girl at the time, of course. She said there was nothing, nothing at all to see only water; turn this way, turn that way, nothing else but water for six slow months. And how do you think they were treated? What do you think they were given to eat? She was frightened you know, but she trusted in God and she kept all those doubts to herself. But all that is behind us now, we are healthy and God has blessed us and He has also blessed our children. Thank God.[32]

The reader may detect a tinge of irony in Kamla's reporting of her aunt's satisfaction, but the life and struggles of Indian toilers as the foundation for the modern generations is an important motif in *Butterfly in the Wind.* Although Lakshmi Persaud's novel celebrates the achievements of those who made something out of the horrors of that historical departure, her construction of the closing scene insinuates a double perspectives on a success story that clearly is not enough for Kamla. Kamla is going to an unknown place, she has no clue as to what awaits her, and the pain of knowing that she will not see her parents for three years gushes out. But she is determined to go. On the other hand, she knows that the journey she is about to make cannot be across any blacker waters than her ancestors had crossed, and its outcome cannot be less successful. The solid achievements of the indentures, and Kamla's assurance that the place they have earned is a place to which she can return sustain the departing character, a comfort not available to the indentures making the original journey.

A different attitude to family, friends and familiar place emerges in Lakshmi Persaud's second novel, *Sastra*[33] which also ends in departure and with a resolute return to a strange place. In this novel, change and movement are accepted as laws of the universe, and the writer turns the Hinduism of the first novel into an inner resource that allows the individual to face up to the trauma of flight and fragmentation, the dissolution of old ties, in a transchanged modern world. After a brief visit to the island of her birth, Sastra returns to Toronto feeling that in spite of 'the rich pleasure of being with her family, seeing old friends and dear places', the old life 'was now behind her, all that was of the past'. From her apartment window in the Canadian city, she looks out into a possible future:

> Across the city, other communities from all parts of the world were establishing and making lives for themselves: Chinese, Jamaicans, Trinidadians, Italians, Greeks, Indians from the sub-continent, and Indians like herself from the Caribbean. For all there were choices; they could be part of communities or they could be whom they pleased. Each choice carried its own cost; now she could not envisage being without the choice. Maybe they were all becoming Canadians.[34]

Sastra, the dislodged or isolated individual is aware of the new formations that are theoretically possible, although she has not yet selected any of the options. She will not return to the island, but she does not feel 'sad or lonely or lost as she once had', and the novel closes with her sensing 'a peace and a strength growing within her'. What we see at the end of Sastra is the logic of a process that is present in the first book......

I want to turn finally then to what lies just beneath the gentle ironies, the reasonable compromises and nostalgic recall in this pleasing book. Briefly, it is a set of unspoken tensions and unresolved dilemmas manifesting themselves in certain recurrent figures all of which indicate Kamla's sense of female oppression, and her longing to escape both her traditional world and the new world.

We have already noticed Kamla's cultivation of an inner voice which serves as an outlet for all the awkward questions that tradition and family do not permit her to ask, and which she cannot even articulate out loud to herself. Then there are two dreams that she keeps having in her childhood, one of being chased by a bull, and one of going under the house looking for eggs and finding the house falling down and pinning her to earth.[35] In addition, there is a whole series of images of entrapment and longing for escape. The primary school is an open prison, and when she gets out it is as if an iron cage that had been clasping her brain and her chest has suddenly let her go. Then too there are the haunting figures of Baboo and Renee, casualties of the quest for another life whom Kamla cannot stop thinking about. Especially Renee who, wrapped up and with the fire of Vat 19 rum in her throat, and pulling at the warm nicotine, seemed, if only for moment 'to have opened the closed casement and allowed her spirit to soar out into the air, the trees, the clouds and the fragrance of flowers'.[36]

To attend to these images, symbols and emblems is to understand the full force of Lakshmi Persaud's sense of female oppression and entrapment, and the fragile hope of escape from swaddling cerements. In the opening scene, a young girl is looking for the chance to go out and play in the rain. 'Our big yard was surrounded by tall brick walls', and 'concrete drains surrounded our house channelling the water that gushed from the spouts', but 'Whenever it rained I would stand and stare at the moving, dancing energy outside, and wish I was part of it'. Kamla goes out into the flooded yard and is transported:

'There were bubbles sailing away like domed ships in a vast ocean. Everywhere there were circles, ever widening, ever moving outwards, newly formed revolving circles'.[37] The reverie is roughly interrupted by a peremptory order from the mother to come out at once, and the straying 'own way' child is towelled dry and placed under flannelette sheets.

In this opening movement, then, the novel gives comprehensive expression to the dilemma of the young girl, surrounded by protecting institutions and persons, but longing to be part of the dancing energy outside. In the sub-section entitled 'The Conductor And The Butterfly',[38] the butterfly being stalked by Kamla is fascinating because although she looked so delicate she was 'throbbing with the magic of life' and she was enjoying 'the sunbeams and the nectar of all that was around her'. Once again the loud voice of authority shatters the dream world and the butterfly too is disturbed:

> Over the tops of the pigeon peas she rose, struggling against the wind, tumbling awkwardly this way and that, higher and higher still until she climbed our brick walls, rising eighteen feet high, to escape the fortified yard.[39]

This image of the butterfly - fragile, beautiful, vulnerable, enjoying where it is but needing to escape seems to me to be the most effective image of Kamla's participation in a world that is in the process of composing itself, an image of the fragile and beautiful human spirit that is of this place and this earth, but cannot help dreaming of rising above and beyond.

Butterfly in the Wind is a restrained and understated novel about female repression. To some extent it is symptomatic of the condition it is trying to describe for it often makes its case by indirection and by working subliminally through a series of more or less unconscious images and symbols.

Notes

1. Olive Senior, *Summer Lightning*, Longman, Essex, 1986.
2. Lakshmi Persaud, *Butterfly in the Wind*, Peepal Tree Press, Leeds, 1990.
3. Ibid, pp.92-93.
4. Ibid, p.83.
5. Ibid, pp.43.
6. Seepersad Naipaul, *Guredeva and Other Indian Tales*, 1942.
7. Lakshmi Persaud, 1990, op. cit., pp.126-27.
8. George Lamming, *In the Castle of My Skin*, Michael Joseph, London, 1953.
9. See Austin Clark, *Growing Up Stupid Under the Union Jack*, Casas de las Americas, Havana, 1980, pp.50-71; McClelland and Stewart, Toronto, 1980.
10. Lakshmi Persaud, 1990, op. cit., p.52.
11. V.S. Naipaul, *A House for Mr Biswas*, Andre Deutsch, London, 1961.
12. Lakshmi Persaud, 1990, op. cit., p.136.
13. Ibid, p.161.
14. Ibid, p.162.
15. Ibid, p.136.
16. Ibid, p.127.
17. See Savitri's case, Ibid, p.107.
18. Ibid, p.188.
19. Ibid, p.40.
20. Ibid, p.40.
21. Ibid, p.33.
22. Ibid, pp.188-89.
23. Ibid, p.102.
24. Ibid, p.103.
25. Ibid, p.103.
26. Ibid, pp.143.
27. Ibid, p.144.
28. Ibid, p.174.
29. My italics, Ibid, pp.174-75.
30. Ibid, pp.175-76.
31. Ibid, p.162.
32. Ibid, p.200-201.
33. Lakshmi Persaud, *Sastra*, Peepal Tree Press, Leeds, 1993.
34. Lakshmi Persaud, 1993, op. cit., p.272.
35. See 'Chased and Trapped', Lakshmi Persaud, 1990, op. cit., pp.176-79.
36. Ibid, p.33.
37. Ibid, p.8.
38. Ibid, pp.25-28.
39. Ibid, p.27.

Notes on Contributors

Joan Anim-Addo was born in Grenada. She is a writer/teacher currently based at the Caribbean Centre, Goldsmiths College, University of London where she teaches Caribbean women's writing. She is founder editor of *Mango Season*, the publication of the Caribbean Women Writers' Alliance and author of *Longest Journey: A History of Black Lewisham*.

Petronella Breinburg was born in Surinam. Petronella is probably best known for her *Sean* picture books currently translated into five languages. Her short stories have been anthologised in *The Plot Against Mary* and *And a Happy New Year* (Women's Press) as well as in a number of folk tale collections such as *Under The Storyteller's Spell*. Petronella's writing regularly appears in Dutch as well as English. Petronella Breinburg has a PhD from Keele University and heads the Caribbean Centre, Goldsmiths College, University of London.

Jane Bryce was born in Tanzania, and subsequently worked and studied for five years in Nigeria. She received her PhD on Nigerian Women's Writing from Obafemi Awolowo University. The switch to the Caribbean came in 1991, when she was appointed to the Cave Hill Department of English, University of the West Indies as their African Literature Specialist. The experience of living and teaching in the Caribbean has stimulated her to extend some of her African research interests, notably in popular culture and romance fiction. Jane Bryce has published widely on African writing.

Jean Buffong left Grenada her birth home many many years ago. She started writing seriously about ten years ago. Since then Jean has juggled being a full time civil servant, an active member of various organisations for the advancement of black people, and a successful writer. Jean's novels include *Jump Up and Kiss Me*, *Under the Silk Cotton Tree* and *Snowflakes in the Sun*. Jean's work can also be found in *The Women's Press Book of Myths and Magic* and *Hearsay*. Jean is co-editor of the anthology *Just a Breath Away*. Jean lives in London, visiting Grenada whenever possible for revitalisation.

Merle Collins is from Grenada. A writer and scholar, Merle Collins's major publications include *Watchers and Seekers*, *Angel*, *Rain Darling*, *Rotten Pomerack* and *The Colour of Forgetting*. Merle Collins taught at the University of North London before moving to the University of Maryland, USA, where she is currently an Associate Professor teaching Creative Writing and leading writing workshops.

Mary Condé lectures in English in the School of English and Drama, Queen Mary and Westfield College, University of London. She has published on American literature and new literatures in English. She is co-editing a book on Caribbean women's writing forthcoming from Macmillan 1997.

Giovanna Covi has a PhD in English from the State University of New York, Binghamton and is a researcher in English language and literature at the University of Trento, Italy. Her work is inspired by feminist theory and by an interest to isolate the various aspects of a discourse on subjectivity which is situated beyond the sex-gender binarism. Giovanna's writing on Caribbean women writers is widely published.

Morgan Dalphinis was born in St Lucia in 1950. He studied in England and gained his PhD in 1981. Morgan worked as a teacher, Lecturer, Inspector, Senior Inspector and Chief Inspector. He published a number of articles and two books, *For Those Who Will Come After* (poetry) and *Caribbean and African Languages*. Morgan Dalphinis is currently working on *Caribbean and African Languages,* volume II. He is Senior Lecturer/Caribbean Coordinator at Handsworth College, Birmingham.

Catherine Davies is Professor, in the Department of Spanish and Portuguese, Manchester University. She is author of *Rosalia de Castro no seu tempo* (Vigo, Galaxia, 1987). *Rosalia de Castro e Folias Novas* (Vigo, Galaxia, 1990), and *Contemporary Feminist Fiction in Spain, Montserrat Roig and Rosa Montero* (Berg, Oxford, 1994) and editor of *Women Writers in Spain and Spanish American* (Mellen Press, Lewiston, 1993). She has published numerous essays on Spanish and Spanish American literature and is currently co-editing a book on feminist readings of the work of Latin American women writers. She is also completing a book on women writers in Cuba with Verity Smith. Catherine Davies is a member of the editorial board of the *Journal of Hispanic Studies*.

Alison Donnell lecturers in post-colonial literatures at Nottingham Trent University. Her doctoral thesis examined Jamaican women's poetry 1900-1945, and she is currently co-editing a Reader in Anglophone Caribbean Literature aimed at bringing the region's early writings to critical attention.

Beryl Gilroy was born in Guyana and has been teaching and writing since the 1950s. Beryl's major publications include *Black Teacher, Frangipani House, Boy Sandwich, Stedman and Joanna, Sunlight on Sweet Water, In Praise of Love and Children, Gather The Faces* and *Inkle and Yarico.* Beryl Gilroy is a qualified psychologist and gained her PhD in ethno-psychology. In 1995 Beryl Gilroy received an honorary doctorate from the University of North London and the following year received the Caribbean Woman Writer's award at Florida International University (1996).

Conrad James was born in Jamaica. He is a Lecturer in the Department of Spanish and Italian, University of Durham and is currently researching at Cambridge University.

Thorunn Lonsdale is currently researching at Queen Mary and Westfield College, University of London, and is co-editing a book on Caribbean women writers (Macmillan, forthcoming).

David Marriott teaches literary and cultural studies at Queen Mary and Westfield College, University of London, He has published on black masculinities and Frantz Fanon. His poetry has been widely anthologised and he is currently completing a manuscript, 'Names of The Fathers', as well as working on a study of 'Black male fantasies'.

Susanne Mühleisen studied at the FU Berlin and the University of the West Indies, St Augustine, completing her studies with an MA thesis on 'Attitudes Towards Language Varieties in Trinidad' in 1993. Having specialised in sociolinguistics and Creole languages, she now teaches linguistics at the Department of English, University of Hanover, Germany.

Thelma Perkins is a teacher from South East London. She is co-author of *In Search of Mr MacKenzie* (Women's Press) and author of *Wishing On A Wooden Spoon* (Mantra). Thelma is a founder member of the Caribbean Women Writer's Alliance.

Kenneth Ramchand is author of *The West Indian Novel and Its Background* and *An Introduction To The Study of West Indian Literature.* He is Professor of West Indian Literature at the University of the West Indies, St Augustine, and Professor of English, Colgate University, New York. He is currently at work on two books to be published by Macmillan on the West Indian short story and the West Indian novel since 1970.

Elaine Savory used to write as Elaine Savory Fido. She co-edited *Out of the Kumbla: Women and Caribbean Literature* with Carole Boyce Davies (1990) and her first volume of poetry, *Flame Tree Time* was published in 1993. Elaine Savory has written extensively on Caribbean, African and Indian women writers. She teaches now at the New School for Social Research, New York City.

Susanna Steele holds a Senior Lecturer post at the University of Greenwich. She is also a writer and professional storyteller. Susanna has edited the anthologies *Inky Pinky Ponky* (Collins Picture Lions) and *Mother Gave a Shout*. Susanna is currently preparing an anthology of her poems for publication.

Selected Bibliography

Acosta, Rodríguez *La vida manda*, 1929.

Agosin, M. and Franzen, C. (eds.). *The Renewal of the Vision. Voices of Latin American Women Poets 1940-1980*, Spectacular Diseases, London, 1987.

Alcoff, Linda, 'Cultural Feminism vs Post-Structuralism: the Identity Crisis in Feminist Theory', *Signs,* 13(3), 1988.

Ali, Lyn-Anne, *Hand in Hand*, Heinemann, London, 1993.

Allfrey, Phyllis Shand, *The Orchid House*, Constable, London, 1953.

Ammon, U. and Hellinger, M. (eds.), *Status Change of Languages,* Mouton de Gruyter, Berlin, 1991.

Anderson, Benedict, *Imagined Communities: Reflections on the Origins and Spread of Nationalism*, Verso, London, 1992, 1983.

Andrés, Cira, *Plural* [Mexico], July, 1991.

Andrés, Cira, *Sobre el brocado de los ojos* (On the Brocade of Eyes, plaquette), 1991.

Anthony, P.A.B., 'The Literature in the Flower Festivals of St Lucia', *Bulletin of the Folk Research Centre*, 1(1), Castries, St Lucia, 1974.

Antrobus, P., 'Crisis, Challenge and the Experiences of Caribbean Women', *Caribbean Quarterly* , 35 (1 and 2), 1989.

Arbor, Jane, *One Brief Sweet Hour*, Mills & Boon, 1980.

Ashcroft, Bill, Griffiths, Gareth and Tiffin, Helen, *The Empire Writes Back. Theory and Practice in Post-Colonial Literatures*, Routledge, London, 1989.

Atwan, Robert, 'Foreword' in Sontag, Susan (ed.). *Best American Essays*, Ticknor and Fields, New York, 1992.

Atwood, Thomas, *The History of the Island of Dominica*, Frank Cass, London, 1971 (first published 1791).

Bailey, Beryl. L., *Jamaican Creole Syntax*, Cambridge University Press, Cambridge, 1966.

Barthes, Roland, 'The Death of the Author' in Heath, Stephen (ed.), *Image, Music, Text*, Fontana, London, 1977.

Basnett, S. (ed.), *Knives and Angels*, Zed Books, 1990.

Beck, E. *Caribbean Quarterly*, 29(1), March, 1983.

Bejel, Emilio, *Escribir en Cuba,* Universidad de Puerto Rico, Río Piedras, 1991.

Belgrave, Valerie, *Ti Marie*, Heinemann, UK, 1988.

Belgrave, Valerie, 'On Combining Batik Art and Novel Writing' in Cudjoe, Selwyn, (ed.) *Caribbean Women Writers*, Mass, Calaloux Publications, 1990.

Belgrave, Valerie, 'Thoughts on the Choice of Theme and Approach in Writing *Ti Marie*' in Cudjoe, Selwyn, (ed.) *Caribbean Women Writers*, Mass, Calaloux Publications, 1990.

Belgrave, Valerie, *Sun Valley Romance,* Heinemann, London, 1993.

Bennett, Louise, *Dialect Verses,* Herald, Kingston, 1942.

Bennett, Louise, *Jamaican Humour in Dialect*, Jamaican Press Association, Kingston, 1943.

Bennett, Louise, *Jamaica Labrish*, Sangster's Book Stores, Kingston, 1966.

Berrian, Brenda, *Bibliography of Women Writers from the Caribbean (1831-1988)*, Three Continents Press, Washington, 1985.

Bhabha, Homi K. (ed.), *Nation and Narration,* Routledge, London, 1991, 1990.
Bloom, Valerie, *Duppy Jamboree*, Cambridge.
Lyn Joseph's, *Coconut Kind of Day*, Picture Puffins, Middlesex, 1992.
Boyce-Davies, Carole and Savory Fido, Elaine (eds.), *Out of the Kumbla*, Africa World Press, Trenton, NJ, 1990.
Brathwaite, Edward Kamau, *Contradictory Omens & Cultural Diversity and Integration in the Caribbean,* Savacou, Mona, Kingston, Jamaica, 1974.
Brathwaite, Edward Kamau, *A History of the Voice; the Development of Nation Language in Anglophone Caribbean Poetry,* New Beacon, London, 1984.
Breinburg, Petronella, *Legends of Surinam*, New Beacon, London, 1971.
Breinburg, Petronella, 'Some Creation' in Charles, Faustin, (ed.), *Under the Storytellers Spell*, Viking Kestrel, London, 1989.
Brodber, Erna, *Jane and Louisa Will Soon Come Home*, New Beacon, London, 1980.
Brooks, Linda Marie (ed.) *Alternative Identities*, Garland Publishing, New York and London, 1995.
Brown, Lloyd W. *West Indian Poetry*, Heinemann, London, 1978.
Bryce, Jane and Dako, Kari, 'Textual Deviancy and Cultural Syncretism: Romantic Fiction as a Subversive Strain in Black Women's Writing', *Wasafiri,* 17, Spring, 1993.
Buffong, Jean, *Under The Silk Cotton Tree,* Women's Press, London, 1989.
Burnett, Paula (ed.), *The Penguin Book of Caribbean Verse in English,* Penguin, Harmondsworth, 1986.
Busby, M. (ed.), *Daughters of Africa*, Jonathan Cape, London, 1992.
Bush, Barbara, *Slave Women in Caribbean Society 1650-1838,* James Currey, London, 1990.
Cambridge, Joan, *Clarise Cumberbatch Want To Go Home*, Women's Press, London, 1987.
Campbell, Hazel D., *Tilly Bummie*, Kingston Publishers, Kingston.
Captain-Hidalgo, Yvonne, *Nancy Morejón*, 1944.
Carascoe, Beryl, 'Women's Participation ion Non-Formal Educational Activities' in Ellis, P. *Women of the Caribbean*, 1986, Zed Books, London and New Jersey.
Carby, Hazel, *Reconstructing Womanhood: The Emergence of the African-American Woman Novelist*, OUP, New York, 1987.
Carter, Angela, 'Notes from the Frontline' in Wandor, Michelene (ed.), *On Gender and Writing*, Pandora, London, 1983.
Cassidy, Frederic G. and LePage, Robert B., *Dictionary of Jamaican English*, 1967, Cambridge University Press, Cambridge.
Chamberlain, Mary (ed.), *Conversations*, Virago, London, 1988.
Charles, Annette, *Love in Hiding*, Heinemann, London, 1993.
Chinweizu, Onwuchekwa, 'Cries For Freedom', *The Times Higher Education Supplement,* 17 February, 1989.
Cixous, Helen and Clément, C., *The Newly Born Woman*, Manchester University Press, Manchester, 1986.
Clark, Austin, *Growing Up Stupid Under the Union Jack*, Casas de las Americas, Havana, 1980.
Claro, Elsa, *Agua y fuego*, 1980.
Cobham, Rhonda and Collins, Merle (eds.), *Watchers and Seekers*, The Women's Press, London, 1987.
Cohan, Steven, and Shires, Linda M., *Telling Stories: A Theoretical Analysis of Narrative Fiction*, Routledge, London, 1988.

Colleton, Lucille, *Merchant of Dreams*, Heinemann, London, 1993.

Collins, Merle, *Angel*, Women's Press, London, 1987.

Collins, Merle, *Rain Darling*, Women's Press, London, 1990

Collins, Merle, *Rotten Pomerack*, Virago, London, 1992.

Collins, Merle, *The Colour of Forgetting*, Virago, London, 1995.

Collins, Merle, 'Interview', *Mango Season*, April, 1996.

Collins, Patricia Hill, *Black Feminist Thought*, Routledge, 1990.

Condé, L. and Hart, S.M. (eds.), *Feminist Readings on Spanish and Latin American Literature*, Edwin Mellen Press, Lewiston, 1991.

Condé, Maryse, 'Three Women In Manhattan' in Esteves, Carmen C. and Paravisini-Gebert, Lizabeth *Green Cane and Juicy Flotsam: Short Stories By Caribbean Women*, Rutgers University Press, New Jersey, 1991.

Cooper, Carolyn, 'Loosely Talking Theory: Oral/Sexual Discourse in Jamaican Popular Culture', paper given at the Society for Caribbean Studies Conference, Oxford, 1993.

Cooper, Carolyn, *Noises in the Blood*, Macmillan, London, 1993.

Coulon, Virginia, 'Onitsha Goes National: Nigerian Writing in Macmillan's Pacesetter Series', *Research in African Literatures*, 18(3), Fall, 1987.

Coulthard, George R., *Race and Colour in Caribbean Literature,* OUP, Oxford, 1962.

Covi, Giovanna, 'Jamaica Kincaid's Political Place: A Review Essay', *Caribana*, 1, 1990.

Cowley, D.J. 'Song and Dance in Saint Lucia', *Ethnomusicology*, 9, 1957.

Crow, M. (ed.) *Woman Who Has Sprouted Wings: Poems by Contemporary Latin American Women Poets*, Latin American Literary Review Press, Pittsburg, 1984.

Cruz, Maria Elena, '¿Legado?', *Letras cubanas*, 1(4), abril-junio, 1987.

Cudjoe, Selwyn, (ed.) *Caribbean Women Writers*, Calaloux Publications, Massachusetts, 1990.

d'Allan, Deidre, *Fantasy of Love* , Heinemann, London, 1993.

Dabydeen, David, *Slave Song*, Dangaroo, Oxford, 1984.

Dalphinis, Morgan, *African Language Influences in Creoles Lexically Based on Portuguese, English and French*, PhD Thesis, School of Oriental and African Studies, University of London, 1981, University Microfilms Intl, 1986.

Dalphinis, Morgan, *Caribbean and African Languages,* Karia Press, London, 1985.

Dance, Daryl Cumber, *Fifty Caribbean Writers*, Greenwood Press, Connecticut, 1986.

Davies, Carole Boyce and Ogundipe-Leslie, Molara, *Moving Beyond Boundaries*, Pluto Press, 1995.

Davies, Carole Boyce and Savory Fido, Elaine (eds.), *Out of the Kumbla*, Africa World Press, Trenton, NJ, 1990.

Davies, Catherine, 'Beastly Women and Underdogs. The Short Fiction of Dora Alonso' in *Women Writers in Twentieth-Century Spain and Spanish America*, Edwin Mellen Press, Lewiston, 1992.

Davies, Catherine, 'Writing the African Subject: The Work Of Two Cuban Women Poets', *Women, A Cultural Review*, 4(1), Spring, 1993.

Davies, Catherine, 'Women Writers in Cuba 1975-1994. A Bibliographical Note', *Bulletin of Latin American Research,* 14(2).

de Abruna, Laura Niesen, 'Family Connections: Mother and Mother Country in the Fiction of Jean Rhys and Jamaica Kincaid' in Susheila, Nasts, (ed.), *Motherlands: Black Women's Writing from Africa, the Caribbean and South Asia*, The Women's Press, London, 1991.

de Avellaneda, Gertrudis Gómez, *Sab and Autobiography*, translated by Nina M. Scott, University of Texas Press, Austin, 1993.

de Feria, Lina, *A mansalva de los años*, 1990.
Dhingra, Leena ' Breaking Out of the Labels' in Cobham, Rhonda and Collins, Merle (eds.), *Watchers and Seekers*, The Women's Press, London, 1987.
Dickie, Margaret, The Maternal Gaze: Women Modernists and Poetic Authority' in Brooks, Linda Marie (ed.) *Alternative Identities*, Garland Publishing, New York and London, 1995.
Diocaretz, Miriam Díaz, 'I Will Be a Scandal in Your Boat': Women Poets And The Tradition' in Basnett, S. (ed.), *Knives and Angels*, Zed Books, 1990.
Dodgson, Pauline, *Reading African Writers*, Working Paper 3, University of Sussex, 1990.
Döring, Tobias, 'Dub and Beyond', Interview with Jean 'Binta' Breeze at the Berlin Festival, June, 1995, unpublished.
Douglass, F., *Narrative of the Life of Frederick Douglass An American Slave, Written by Himself*, Signet, New York, 1987.
Eagleton, Mary (ed.), *Feminist Literary Theory*, Blackwell, Oxford, 1986.
Ellis, P. *Women of the Caribbean*, 1986, Zed Books, London and New Jersey.
Espinet, Ramabai, *Creation Fire*, Sister Vision Press, Canada, 1990.
Esteves, Carmen C. and Paravisini-Gebert, Lizabeth *Green Cane and Juicy Flotsam: Short Stories By Caribbean Women*, Rutgers University Press, New Jersey, 1991.
Felski, Rita, Beyond *Feminist Aesthetics*, Hutchinson Radius, London, 1989.
Ferguson, Moira, *Subject to Others; British Women Writers and Colonial Slavery, 1670-1834,* Routledge, London, 1991.
Ferguson, Moira, *Jamaica Kincaid, Where the Land Meets the Body*, University Press of Virginia, Charlottesville, 1994.
Foster, Cecil, *No Man in the House*, Ballantine Books, New York.
Fuller, Vernella, *Going Back Home*, Women's Press, London, 1992.
Gaines, Nora (ed.), *Jean Rhys Review*, 6(2).
Gaines, Nora, 'Etcetera' in Gaines, Nora (ed.), *Jean Rhys Review*, 6(2).
Garfield, Evelyn Picon *Poder y sexualidad en la obra de Gertrudis Gómez de Avellaneda*, Barcelona, 1994.
Garis, Leslie, 'Through West Indian Eyes', *New York Times Magazine,* 7 October, 1990.
Gates, Henry Louis Jr, 'Criticism in the Jungle' in Gates, Henry Louis (ed.), *Black Literature and Literary Theory*, Routledge, London, 1984.
Gates, Henry Louis Jr., *The Signifying Monkey*, Oxford University Press, New York, 1988.
Gilroy, Beryl, *Boy Sandwich*, Longman, Harlow, 1985.
Gilroy, Beryl, *Frangipani House*, Heinemann, London, 1986.
Gilroy, Beryl, *Sunlight On Sweet Water,* Peepal Tree Press, Leeds, 1994.
Gilroy, Beryl, 'The Oral Culture - Effects and Expression', *Wasafiri*, Autumn 1995.
Giovanni, Nikki (ed.), *Grand Mothers: Poems, Reminiscences and Short Stories About the Keepers of Our Traditions*, Henry Holt, NY, 1994.
Glissant, E., *Poétique de la Relation*, Gallimard, Paris, 1990.
Goodison, Lorna, *I Am Becoming My Mother*, New Beacon, London, 1986.
Goodison, Lorna, *Baby Mother And the King of Swords*, Longman, Essex, 1990.
Görlach, M. and Holms, J. (eds.) *Focus on the Caribbean*, John Benjamin, Amsterdam, 1986.
Green-Williams, Claudette Rose, 'Rewriting the History of the Afro-Cuban Woman: Nancy Morejón's 'Mujer negra', *Afro-Hispanic Review,* VIII(5), September, 1989.
Greene, Gayle, *Changing The Story: Feminist Fiction and the Tradition*, Indiana University Press, Bloomington & Indianapolis, 1991.

Griswold, Wendy and Bastian, Misty, 'Continuities and Reconstructions in Cross Cultural Literary Transmission: The Case of the Nigerian Romance Novel', *Poetics*, (16), 1987.

Guerra, Soledad Cruz, *Documentos de la otra* (Documents of the Other), 1991.

Hall, Stuart, 'Cultural Identity and Diaspora' in Williams, Patrick and Chrisman, Laura (eds.), *Colonial Discourse and Postcolonial Theory; A Reader,* Harvester Wheatsheaf, Hemel Hempstead, 1993.

Harney, Steve, 'Men Goh Respect All O' We: Valerie Belgrave's *Ti Marie* and the Invention of Trinidad', *World Literature Written in English*, 30(2), Autumn, 1990.

Harris, Wilson, 'The Fabric of Imagination', *Third World Quarterly*, 12(1), January.

Harter, Hugh A., *Gertrudis Gómez de Avellaneda*, Twayne, Boston, 1981.

Hellinger, Marlis, 'On Writing English-Related Creoles in the Caribbean' in Görlach, M. and Holms, J. (eds.) *Focus on the Caribbean*, John Benjamin, Amsterdam, 1986.

Hellinger, Marlis, 'Function and Status Change of Pidgin and Creole Languages' in Ammon, U. and Hellinger, M. (eds.), *Status Change of Languages,* Mouton de Gruyter, Berlin, 1991.

Henfrey, June, *Coming Home and Other Stories*, Peepal Tree Press, Leeds, 1994.

Hodge, Merle, 'Challenges of The Struggle for Sovereignty' in Cudjoe, Selwyn, *Caribbean Women Writers*, Calaloux, Massachusetts, 1990.

Hodge, Merle, *Crick Crack Monkey* , Heinemann, London, 1970.

Hollar, Constance, *Songs of Empire*, Gleaner, Kingston, 1932.

hooks, bell, *Yearning: Race, Gender and Cultural Politics,* Turnaround Press, London and Boston, Mass, 1991.

Hopkinson, A. (ed.), *Lovers and Comrades. Women's Resistance Poetry from Central America*, The Women's Press, London, 1989.

Howells, Coral Ann, , *Jean Rhys,* Harvester Wheatsheaf, Hemel Hempstead, Hertfordshire, 1991.

Hulme, Peter, 'The Locked Heart: The Creole Family Romance of Wide Sargasso Sea - An Historical and Biographical Analysis' in Gaines, Nora (ed.), *Jean Rhys Review*, 6(1).

Hutcheon, Linda, 'Circling the Downspout of Empire', *Ariel,* 22, 4 October, 1989.

Hutton, Albinia Catherine, 'The Empire's Flag' in *Hill Songs and Wayside Verses*, Gleaner, Kingston, 1932.

Irigaray, L., *This Sex Which Is Not One*, Ithaca, Cornell University Press, New York, 1981.

Johnson, Amryl, *Sequins for a Ragged Hem*, Virago, London, 1988.

Jolley, Elizabeth, *Mr Scobie's Riddle*, Penguin, Harmondsworth, 1983.

Jolly, Dorothy, *Heartaches and Roses.* Heinemann, 1993.

Kempen, Michiel van, *Sirito: 50 Surinaamse Vertellingen*, Kennedy Stichting, Paramaribo, 1993.

Kennedy, Louise, 'A Writer Retraces Her Steps', *Boston Globe*, 7 November, 1990.

Kincaid, Jamaica, 'On Seeing England for the First Time', *Translations*, 51, 1991.

Kincaid, Jamaica, *Annie John,* Farrar, Straus & Giroux, 1983.

Kincaid, Jamaica, *At the Bottom of the River*, Farrar, New York, 1983 and Vintage-Random, New York, 1985.

Kincaid, Jamaica, *A Small Place*, Farrar, New York, 1988, Virago, London, 1988.

Kincaid, Jamaica, *Lucy*, Farrar, New York, 1990, Picador, London, 1990.

King-Aribisala, Karen, *Our Wife and Other Stories*, Malthouse Press Ltd., Lagos, 1990.

Kingston, Maxine Hong, *The Woman Warrior,* Vintage, New York, 1976.

Kirkpatrick, Susan, *Las Romanticas. Women Writers and Subjectivity in Spain 1833-1850* , University of California Press, Berkely and London, 1989.

Kristeva, J., 'Woman Can Never Be Defined' in Marks, E. and de Courtivron, I. (eds.), *New French Feminisms: An Anthology,* University of Massachusetts Press, Amherst, 1981.
Kristeva, J., *Powers of Horror. An Essay in Abjection*, Columbia University Press, New York, 1982.
Kristeva, J., in Moi, T. (ed.), *The Kristeva Reader,* Basil Blackwell, Oxford, 1986.
Labra, Carilda Oliver, *Antología poetica*, 1992.
Lamming, George, *In the Castle of My Skin*, Michael Joseph, 1953.
Le Page, R.B. 'Dialect in West Indian Literature', *Journal of Commonwealth Literature*, 7, 1969.
Lebeau, V., *Lost Angels: Psychoanalysis and Cinema*, Routledge, London, 1995.
Lee, Valerie, 'Testifying Theory; Womanist Intellectual Thought', *Women: A Cultural Review*, 6(2), Autumn, 1995.
Leech, Geoffrey N. and Short, Michael H., *Style in Fiction. A Linguistic Introduction to English Fictional Prose*, Longman, London, 1981.
Lewin, Olive, *Caribbean Quarterly*, 29(1), March, 1983.
Lima, Chely, *Terriblemente iluminados* (Terribly Illuminated), 1988.
Lima, Chely, 'Enunciation', *Rock sucio* (Dirty Rock), 1992.
Lorde, Audre, *Zami: A New Spelling of My Name*, Trumansburg, NY, 1982.
Lorde, Audre, *Sister Outsider*, Crossing, Trumansburg, NY, 1984.
Mango Season, Caribbean Women Writers Alliance, London.
Marks, E. and de Courtivron, I. (eds.), *New French Feminisms: An Anthology,* University of Massachusetts Press, Amherst, 1981.
Marruz, Fina García, *Visitaciones*, 1970.
Martínez-Echazábal, Lourdes, 'Oposiciones Binarias en *Octubre impresinible* y *Cuaderno de Granada*', *Cimarrón*, 1(3), Spring, 1988.
Marting, D. (ed.), *Spanish-American Women Writers. A Bio-Bibliographical Source Book*, Greenwood Press, Westport, 1990.
Marting, Diane, 'The Representation of Female Sexuality in Nancy Morejón's 'Amor. cuidad atribuida', *Afro-Hispanic Review*, 7(1-3), 1988.
Martini, Jurgen, 'Sex, Class and Power: The Emergence of a Capitalist Youth Culture in Nigeria', *Journal of African Children's Literature*, 1, 1987.
McDowell, Deborah E., 'New Directions for Black Feminist Criticism' in Eagleton, Mary (ed.), *Feminist Literary Theory*, Blackwell, Oxford, 1986.
McGowan, John, *Postmodernism and Its Critics*, Ithaca, Cornell UP, 1991.
McKenzie-Mavinga, Isha and Perkins, Thelma, *In Search of Mr McKenzie*, Women's Press, London, 1991.
Menéndez, Nina R. *No Woman Is An Island: Cuban Women's Fiction in the 1920s and 1930s*, PhD dissertation, Stanford University, 1993.
Menton, Seymour, *Prose Fiction of the Cuban Revolution*, Texas UP, Austin, 1975.
Mes douze premières années, Paris, 1831.
Milanés, María Luisa, *La poesía moderna*, 1926.
Minh-ha, Trinh T., *Woman, Native, Other*, Indiana University Press, Bloomington and Indiana, 1989.
Minh-ha, Trinh T., *When the Moon Waxes Red: Representation, Gender and Cultural Politics*, Routledge, New York, 1991.
Modleski, *Tania, Loving With A Vengeance*, Routledge, London, 1990.
Mohammed, Abdul Jan, 'The Economy of the Manichean Allegory: The Function of Racial Difference in Colonialist Literature' in *'Race' Writing and Difference*, Chicago University Press, Chicago, 1986.

Mohanty, C., 'Under Western Eyes: Feminist Scholarship and Colonial Discourses', *Feminist Review*, 30, 1988.
Moi, T. (ed.), *The Kristeva Reader*, Basil Blackwell, Oxford, 1986.
Molloy, Sylvia, *At Face Value: Autobiographical Writing in Spanish America*, CUP, 1991.
Momsen, Janet H., *Women and Change In The Caribbean*.
Mordecai, Pamela, 'A Crystal of Ambiguities: Metaphors for Creativity and the Art of Writing' in Walcott, Derek (ed.). Another Life: West Indian Poetry', Jackson and Allis, College of the Virgin Islands, St Thomas, 1986.
Mordecai, Pamela, *Journey Poem*, Gandberry Press, Kingston, 1989.
Mordecai, Pamela and Wilson, Betty, *Her True - True Name*, Heinemann, Oxford, 1989.
Morejón, Nancy, *Recopilación de textos sobre Nicolás Guillén*, Ediciones Unión, La Habana, 1974.
Morejón, Nancy, 'Mujer negra/Black Woman'; 'La cena/Dinner'; 'Para escapar herido/To escape wounded' in Pereira, J.R. (ed.), *Poems from Cuba*, The University of the West Indies, Mona, Jamaica, 1977.
Morejón, Nancy, 'Poesía del Caribe', *Revolución y cultura 82*, June, 1979.
Morejón, Nancy, *Nación y mestizaje en Nicolás Guillén*, Ediciones Unión, La Habana, 1982.
Morejón, Nancy, 'A un muchacho/To a boy'; 'Hay el calor/There is the warmth'; 'Masacre/Massacre' in Crow, M. (ed.) *Woman Who Has Sprouted Wings: Poems by Contemporary Latin American Women Poets*, Latin American Literary Review Press, Pittsburg, 1984.
Morejón, Nancy, *Piedra Pulida* (On Polished Stone), Letras Cubanas, La Habana, 1986.
Morejón, Nancy, 'Black Woman'; 'Barely Hero'; 'A Rose'; 'Impressions'; 'Farewell'; 'The Ocujal mine' in Agosin, M. and Franzen, C. (eds.). *The Renewal of the Vision. Voices of Latin American Women Poets 1940-1980*, Spectacular Diseases, London, 1987.
Morejón, Nancy, *Fundación de la imagen,* Letras Cubanas, La Habana, 1988.
Morejón, Nancy, 'Black Woman'; 'Confession' in Hopkinson, A. (ed.), *Lovers and Comrades. Women's Resistance Poetry from Central America*, The Women's Press, London, 1989.
Morris, Mervyn (ed.), *The Faber Book of Contemporary Caribbean Short Stories,* Faber & Faber, London, 1990.
Morrison, Toni, *Beloved*, Picador, London, 1988.
Morrison, Sir William Kt, 'Foreword' in Hollar, Constance, *Songs of Empire*, Gleaner, Kingston, 1932.
Naipaul, V.S., *A House for Mr Biswas*, Andre Deutsch, London, 1961.
Nardi, Rafaela Chacón, *Del silencio y las voces*, 1978.
Nettleford, Rex, 'Introduction' in Bennett, Louise, *Jamaica Labrish*, Sangster's Book Stores, Kingston, 1966.
Nichols, Grace, *Fat Black Woman's Poems,* Virago, 1984.
O'Callaghan, Evelyn, *Woman Version*, Macmillan, London, 1993.
Oliver, K. (ed.), *Ethics, Politics, and Difference in Julia Kristeva's Writing,* Routledge, London and New York, 1993.
Ong, Walter J., 'Orality, Literacy and Medieval Textualization', *New Literary History*, 16, 1984.
Palmer, Hazelle, *Tales From The Gardens and Beyond,* Sister Vision Press, Ontario, 1995.
Palmer, Opal, *Adisa Guava and Other Bakeface Stories*, Kelsey Street Press.
Patterson, O., *Slavery and Social Death*, Harvard University Press, Harvard, 1982.
Pereira, Joe, *Ours the Earth: Poems from Cuba.*

Pereira, J.R. (ed.), *Poems from Cuba*, The University of the West Indies, Mona, Jamaica, 1977.

Pereira, J.R. (ed.), *Ours the Earth: Poems by Nancy Morejón*, Institute of Caribbean Studies, University of the West Indies, Mona, 1990.

Perkins, Thelma, *Wishing on a Wooden Spoon*, Mantra, London, 1992.

Persaud, Lakshmi, *Butterfly in the Wind*, Peepal Tree Press, Leeds, 1990.

Persaud, Lakshmi, *Sastra*, Peepal Tree Press, Leeds, 1993.

Philip, M. Nourbese, *She Tries her Tongue, Her Silence Softly Breaks,* Ragweed Press, Charlottetown, 1989.

Philip, M. Nourbese, *She Tries Her Tongue, Her Silence Softly Breaks*, Women's Press, 1993.

Philip, Marlene Nourbese, *Looking For Livingstone: An Odyssey of Silence*, The Mercury Press, Stratford, Ontario, 1991.

Philip, Marlene Nourbese, 'The Habit of: Poetry, Rats, and Cats' in Spahr, J. and Wallace, M., et al. (eds.), *A Poetics of Criticism*, Leave Books, New York, 1994.

Pollard, Velma, *Considering Woman,* Women's Press, London, 1989.

Pollard, Velma, *Homestretch*, Longman, Harlow, 1994.

Powell, Patricia, *A Small Gathering of Bones*, Heinemann, Oxford, 1994.

Prince, Mary, *The History of Mary Prince, A West Indian Slave, Related by Herself,* edited with 'Introduction' by Moira Ferguson and 'Preface' by Ziggi Alexander, Pandora, London, 1987, (first published 1831).

Pynchon, *Thomas, Gravity's Rainbow*, Viking, New York, 1973.

Ramchand, Kenneth, *The West Indian Novel and Its Background*, Faber, London, 1970.

Ramchand, Kenneth, 'West Indian Literary History: Literariness, Orality and Periodization, *Callaloo*, 11(1), Winter, 1988.

Randall, Margaret, *Breaking The Silences Twentieth Century Poetry by Cuban Women,* Pulp Press, Vancouver, 1982.

Renan, Ernest, 'What Is a Nation?' in Bhabha, Homi K. (ed.), *Nation and Narration,* Routledge, London, 1991, 1990.

Rhys, Jean, *Wide Sargasso Sea*, Andre Deutsch Limited, London, 1966.

Rhys, Jean, *Good Morning, Midnight*, Penguin, Harmondsworth, 1969 (first published Constable, 1939).

Rhys, Jean, *The Collected Short Stories*, W.W. Norton and Company, London, 1987.

Rhys, Jean, *Voyage in the Dark*, Penguin, Harmondsworth, 1987 (first published by Constable, 1934).

Rhys, Jean, *After Leaving Mr. Mackenzie*, Penguin, Harmondsworth, 1987, 1971 (first published Jonathan Cape, 1930).

Rhys, Jean, *Quartet,* Penguin, Harmondsworth, 1988, 1977 (first published Chatto and Windus, 1928).

Rhys, Jean, 'The Day They Burned The Books' in Esteves, Carmen C. and Paravisini-Gebert, Lizabeth *Green Cane and Juicy Flotsam: Short Stories By Caribbean Women*, Rutgers University Press, New Jersey, 1991.

Riley, Joan, *Romance*, Women's Press, 1988.

Ríos, Soleida *Entre mundo y juguete* (Between World and Toy), 1987.

Rodriguez, Maria Christina, 'Women Writers of the Spanish-Speaking Caribbean: An Overview' in Cudjoe, Selwyn, *Caribbean Women Writers,* Calaloux, Mass, 1990.

Rodríguez, Reina María, *En la arena de padua*, 1992.

Rojas, Niurka Pérez, *Características sociodemográficas de la familia cubana 1953-1970,* Editorial de Ciencias Sociales, 1979.

Rose, J., 'Julia Kristeva: Take Two' in Oliver, K. (ed.), *Ethics, Politics, and Difference in Julia Kristeva's Writing,* Routledge, London and New York, 1993.

Ross et al. (eds.), *Nationalism and Sexualities*, Routledge, New York, 1991.

Rowell, Charles H., 'An Interview with Olive Senior', *Callaloo*, 11, 1988.

Said, Edward, *The World, The Text and The Critic*, Harvard University Press, Cambridge, Mass.

Said, Edward, 'Figures, Configurations, Transfigurations' in *From Commonwealth to Post Colonial*, Dangaroo Press, Coventry, 1992.

Saldaña, Excilia, *Monólogo de la esposa* (Monologue of the Wife), Casa de las Americas, 1985.

Saldaña, Excilia, *Mi nombre. Antilegia familiar* (My name. Antielegy for the Family), 1991.

Savory Fido, Elaine, 'A Womanist Vision of the Caribbean' in Boyce-Davies, Carole and Fido, Elaine (eds.), *Out of the Kumbla*, Africa World Press, Trenton, NJ, 1990.

Scott, J.D., *Domination and the Arts of Resistance. Hidden Transcripts*, Yale University Press, New Haven and London, 1990.

Seacole, Mary *Wonderful Adventures of Mary Seacole in Many Lands*, James Blackwood, London, 1858.

Selvon, Samuel, *The Lonely Londoners*, Longman, London, 1972.

Senior, Olive, *Summer Lightning and Other Stories*, Longman, Harlow, 1986.

Senior, Olive, *Arrival of the Snake Woman*, Longman, Essex, 1989.

Shelton, Marie Denise *Women Writers of the French Speaking Caribbean* in Cudjoe, Selwyn, *Caribbean Women Writers,* Calaloux Publications, Mass, 1990.

Shepherd, Verene, et al. (eds.), *Engendering History: Caribbean Women in Historical Perspective*, James Curry, London, 1995.

Silvera, Makeda, *Remembering G and Other Stories*, Sister Vision, Ontario, 1991.

Smith, Sidonie, *A Poetics of Women's Autobiography: Marginality and the Fictions of Self-Representation,* Indiana University Press, Bloomington, 1987.

Sontag, Susan (ed.). *Best American Essays*, Ticknor and Fields, New York, 1992.

Spahr, J. and Wallace, M., et al. (eds.), *A Poetics of Criticism*, Leave Books, New York, 1994.

Spillers, H.J., 'Mama's Baby, Papa's Maybe: An American Grammar Book', *Diacritics*, 1987.

Spivak, Gayatra C., 'French Feminism in an International Frame', *Yale French Studies*, 61, 1981.

Spivak, Gayatra C., 'Woman in Difference: Mahasweta Devi's Douloti the Bountiful' in Ross et al. (eds.), *Nationalism and Sexualities*, Routledge, New York, 1991.

Stewart, Pauline, 'Goodbye Granny' in *Singing Down the Breadfruit*, Bodley Head Poetry, London, 1993.

Stoner, K. Lynn, *From The House To The Streets. The Cuban Woman's Movement For Legal Reform 1898-1940* , Duke UP, 1991.

Surinaams Nieuws, Amsterdam, 1993.

Susheila, Nasts, (ed.), *Motherlands: Black Women's Writing from Africa, the Caribbean and South Asia*, The Women's Press, London, 1991.

Thomas, Elean, *The Last Room*, Virago, London, 1991.

Tiffin, Helen, 'Decolonization and Audience: Erna Brodber's *Myal* and Jamaica Kincaid's *A Small Place*, *SPAN*, 30, 1990.

Todorov, Tzvetan, *The Conquest of America: The Question of the Other,* translated Richard Howard, Harper and Row, New York, 1982.

Valdés, Zoe, *Travesía. Journal of Latin American Cultural Studies*, 2, Kings College London, 1992.
Vega, Ana Lydia 'Cloud Cover Caribbean' in Mordecai, Pamela and Wilson, Betty, *Her True - True Name*, Heinemann, Oxford, 1989.
Smith, Verity, 'Dwarfed By Snow White: Feminist Revisions of Fairy Tale Discourse In the Narrative Of María Luisa Bombal And Dulce María Loynaz' in Condé, L. and Hart, S.M. (eds.), *Feminist Readings on Spanish and Latin American Literature*, Edwin Mellen Press, Lewiston, 1991.
Voorhoeve, Jan and Litchveld, *Ursy, Creole Drum*, trans. Vernie A. February, Yale University Press, New Haven, 1975.
Walcott, Derek, *The Castaway*, Jonathan Cape, London, 1965.
Walcott, Derek, *Sea Grapes*, Jonathan Cape, 1976.
Walcott, Derek, *Collected Poems: 1948-1984*, The Noonday Press, Farrar, Straus and Giroux, New York, 1962, 1986.
Walcott, Derek (ed.). Another Life: West Indian Poetry', Jackson and Allis, College of the Virgin Islands, St Thomas, 1986.
Walker, Alice, *In Search of Our Mother's Gardens,* Women's Press, London, 1984.
Walker, Alice, *Everyday Use*, Rutgers University Press, New Brunswick, NJ, 1994.
Walmsley, Anne, *The Sun's Eye,* Longman, Harlow, 1968.
Walmsley, Anne, 'From 'Nature' to 'Roots': School Anthologies and a Caribbean Canon', *Wasafiri*, 11, 1990.
Wandor, Michelene (ed.), *On Gender and Writing*, Pandora, London, 1983.
Warner-Lewis, Maureen, *Guinea's Other Suns: The African Dynamic in Trinidad Culture*, Majority Press, Mass. 1991.
Weaver, K. (ed.), *The Island Sleeps Like a Wing. Selected Poetry of Nancy Morejón*, Black Scholar Press, San Francisco, 1985.
Wilcox, Christina, *The Nights Belong to the Novelist*, documentary video, 1987.
Wilentz, Gay, *Binding Cultures*, Indiana University Press, Bloomington and Indianapolis, 1992.
Williams, Cheryl, 'The Role of Women in Caribbean Culture' in Ellis, P. *Women of the Caribbean*, 1986, Zed Books, London and New Jersey.
Williams, Eric, *From Colombus to Castro*, André Deutsch, 1970.
Williams, Patrick and Chrisman, Laura (eds.), *Colonial Discourse and Postcolonial Theory; A Reader,* Harvester Wheatsheaf, Hemel Hempstead, 1993.
Willis, Miriam de Costa, 'The Caribbean as Idea and Image in the Poetry of Nancy Morejón', *Journal of Caribbean Studies*, 7(2-3), 1990.
Wilson, Betty and Mordecai, Pam, *Her True -True Name*, Heinemann, London, 1989.
Wynter, Sylvia, *The Hills of Hebron*, Jonathan Cape, London, 1962.
Xenes, Nieves, *Arpas cubanas*, 1904.
Yotanka, Tatanka, *Dorothea's Ambition,* Caribbean OPC Consultants, Barbados, 1989.
Zamora, Margarita, 'Abreast of Colombus: Gender and Discovery', *Cultural Critique,* Winter, 1990-91.

Index